D1297729

Leader Dogs for The Blind®

"For Whither Thou Goest"

By Margaret Gibbs

Denlinger's Publishers, Ltd.
Box 76, Fairfax, Virginia 22030

Library of Congress Cataloging in Publication Data

Gibbs, Margaret.
    Leader dogs for the blind.

    Bibliography: p.
    Includes index.
    1. Leader Dogs for the Blind (Training school)
I. Title.
HV1780.S4G5   1982   362.4'183   82-4612
ISBN 0-87714-095-2
ISBN 0-87714-094-4 (pbk.)

International standard book number: 0-87714-095-2 hardbound.

International st̶ ̶ber: 0-87714-094-4 softbound.

Library of Congress catalog number: 82-7427

ISBN 0-87714-095-2
ISBN 0-87714-094-4

dedicated to dog guides

their trainers

and their owners

Acknowledgments

I should like to thank the following people for their generous time and help: Donald Schuur; Harold and Maryan Pocklington; the entire office and training staff of Leader Dogs for the Blind, especially Jim Henderson, Ed Lange, Harold Smith, Mickey Loesser, Steve Solwold, Larry Heflin and Randy Horn; the student graduating class of August 31, 1979; Dr. John Paul Scott, Regents Professor of Psychology Emeritus, Bowling Green State University, Bowling Green, Ohio, for his continual help and encouragement; Robert Self, co-editor of *Front & Finish*; Mary Francis and Maria Betlinski, who know the devious ways of commas; Dave Terrill, A.K.C. obedience judge and enthusiastic Lions Club member who introduced me to the late Evan "Red" Carrison, who gave so much to Lions, Leader Dogs, and the formation of this book; Joe and Mary Nessinger, fellow Leader Dog lecturers and friends who taught me a great deal about life with Leader Dog, Lady; the Lapeer County, Michigan, 4-H members and especially leaders Pat Brauer and Nan Nellenbach; Benny Larsen, executive director of Guide Dogs for the Blind, Inc., who updated school policies in relationship to the puppy program; Stuart Grout, executive vice president, The Seeing Eye, Inc., for special research concerning the early years of the dog guide movement; the sources listed below for use of photographs and other materials from various books and publications; and my husband, Andy, for his help with photographs.

Front & Finish for permission to use material from Margaret Gibbs, "They Also Serve—An Analysis of Dog Guide Training," February–August, 1975.

Leader Dogs for the Blind for permission to reprint the lyrics to "Proud Leader Dog," words and music by Janine Jamison for movie *Leader Dog Tour*.

John Wiley & Sons, Inc. for permission to reprint the chart "Time Relationships of Certain Developmental Organizational Processes in the Dog" by J. P. Scott, John M. Stewart, Victor J. De Ghett, *Developmental Psychobiology*, "Critical Periods in the Organization of Systems," 7 (6): p. 495. Copyright 1974 by John Wiley & Sons, Inc. All rights reserved.

Pure-Bred Dogs—American Kennel Gazette for permission to use material from Margaret Gibbs, "Kennel Dog to House Pet: Looking at Kennel Dog Syndrome," January 1978, pp. 23-33. Copyright 1978 by American Kennel Club. All rights reserved.

Dr. John Paul Scott, Regents Professor of Psychology Emeritus, Bowling Green State University, Bowling Green, Ohio for permission to quote from a personal letter dated June 4, 1980.

The University of Chicago Press for permission to reprint several photographs from John P. Scott, John L. Fuller *Genetics and the Social Behavior of the Dog*, Copyright 1965 by the University of Chicago. All rights reserved.

Donald Schuur, The Seeing Eye, Inc., and Guide Dogs for the Blind, Inc., for use of photographs.

––––––––

Other photographs by Andrew and Margaret Gibbs, and through the courtesy of Leader Dogs for the Blind.

Harold "Poc" Pocklington, Excecutive Director of Leader Dogs.

Foreword

Marge Gibbs is a lady with the special gift of combining effective practical knowledge of dogs with an appreciation of the value of basic research. The results of her untiring efforts are evident in this description of the formation of a leading dog guide school.

Marge Gibbs spent untold hours researching the early history of dog guides and brought the story down to the "on-the-street trials and tribulations" of teaching an ordinary pet to be a miracle worker. This meant undergoing preliminary training herself, suffering the same embarrassing moments as a newly blinded person, then progressing to a degree of independent mobility.

In this story the writer tells of the beginning when a few determined men had four hundred dollars and a hatful of ideas. She tells of the many years of collaboration and frustration as a new, unique, project took shape, a project not defined by written direction or word.

I highly recommend this book as being factually accurate as Marge Gibbs writes about man's best friend as it relates to making the path of blind people much easier to travel.

Harold L. Pocklington
Executive Director & Vice President
LEADER DOGS FOR THE BLIND

Preface

This is a book about people who are sightless, the dogs that lead them, and a school in Rochester, Michigan, that trains them both to work together—Leader Dogs for the Blind, the largest producing dog guide school in the world.

Over the years, dogs that lead the blind have come to be looked upon as the epitome of dogdom. In spite of this, very few people understand how these animals are selected or taught to perform their tasks. Even individuals who are actively involved in training dogs often have unusual ideas as to what dog guides can and cannot do. As a result, the public has created an image of animals trained to computerized precision, possessing reasoning powers that defy explanation.

A few years ago, I was asked by Robert Self, co-editor of a dog training magazine entitled *Front & Finish* to write a series of articles on the selection and training of dog guides. As practical dog trainers we felt far too little was known about these animals. We thought a definitive training series would be educational and interesting to everyone involved in breeding, training, or showing dogs.

Although there are excellent books and articles on the history of guide work and a wealth of information on initial behavioral research which resulted in an increased ability to breed and select puppies that show potential to be future guides, we could find very little written on the detailed selection process of adult dogs at dog guide schools or their training. Although there are excellent autobiographies of several people who own dog guides and material on a few individual dogs, we could find little on groups of animals with comparisons between working styles and characters or on the process of matching these dogs to people who themselves have individual characters and abilities. We wanted to fill these informational gaps and contacted Leader Dogs for the Blind in Rochester, Michigan, whose staff agreed with the worth of our project.

I was invited to work at Leader Dogs in order to analyze the school's testing and training procedures and to compare these to the standard methods utilized in obedience classes for household pets and American Kennel Club obedience competition dogs. The articles were fascinating to research and write and earned a "Best Series of the Year" award from the Dog Writers' Association of America. "Maybe someday you'll write a book on our program and your experiences here," the school's staff said.

Dogs—their behavioral patterns, breed characteristics, individual temperaments, and working abilities—have been a large portion of my life, but I know very little about blindness or the mechanics of living in a world where sight plays no part. If I were to write a book on a dog guide program, I would have to research and include material on the people who ultimately received these animals. I decided to do this and soon realized that the general public has several inaccurate concepts concerning blindness and its implications on the lives it touches.

Returning to Leader Dogs, I shared the working days of blind students as they learned to handle their trained dogs. These students, ranging in age from sixteen to seventy-four, came from all walks of life and educational backgrounds. Some were returning for a second, a third and, in one case, a seventh dog! Others had never owned a dog of any kind. Some had been blind from birth. Others had only recently lost their vision. Each willingly discussed and compared the world one sees with eyes to the world one "sees" in different ways. Several students asked, "When you write your book, are you going to include some facts on how we envision the world around us?" I've tried to do so.

Not all sightless individuals want or can utilize dog guides. The students at Leader Dogs had given their decisions a great deal of thought and were anticipating increased freedom of mobility as a result. However, with the exception of those students who were returning for replacement dogs, all were more or less unprepared for the individual canine personalities they encountered and the necessity of proper handling in order to secure a response to commands. "I was forewarned," one student stated, "but I thought to myself, 'In just a couple of minutes I'll have that dog wrapped around my little finger.' I now have the feeling the dog was thinking the same thing."

Needing constant reassurance from the instructing staff, each person repeatedly asked, "When the training is over, will I honestly be able to go home alone?" "Will I truly be able to go where I want, when I want by myself?" They would do these things and do them well, and each would discover, in due time, how wrong he was in initially referring to future actions as solitary endeavors. What begins as a hesitant, frustrating, often humorous experience in learning to live with a strange animal and develop its trust and loyalty will ultimately develop into an inseparable relationship between man and dog which few, if any, of us with vision will ever experience.

A dog guide is the culmination of all that is finest in man's best friend.

Contents

Donald Schuur, the founder of Leader Dogs for the Blind. Schuur still serves on the school's Board of Trustees.

Chapter 1

Bit of History

If anyone had told Donald Schuur and the Uptown Detroit Lions
ub members that their ideas would result in the formation of the
rgest producing dog guide school in the world, they would have shaken
eir heads in disbelief. That was not what they had in mind on an early
mmer's day in 1938, as they met to discuss the future of Dr. Glenn
heeler, who was blind. All they wanted was to secure a dog guide for a
ry deserving man, known personally to nearly all of them.

It had seemed like a simple club project. As a chartered member of the
ternational Association of Lions Clubs, the Uptown Detroit Lions
ub was dedicated to general community welfare and especially
terested in projects involving the visually handicapped. Dr. Wheeler,
osteopath, had expressed an interest in having a dog guide, and the
ptown Detroit Lions Club stood ready to help him. Donald Schuur
d phoned The Seeing Eye in Morristown, New Jersey, stating that the
ub would like to pay all expenses throughout the training of both dog
d Dr. Wheeler. The school informed him that applicants could not be
onsored by any organization or individual and that all contributions
ere used where needed. The club's offer had been turned down, and it
as a shocking set-back. Members could understand The Seeing Eye's
olicy, but the disappointment was bitter.

Donald Schuur, who was then president of the Uptown Detroit Lions
ub, explained these policies to the members. Should Dr. Wheeler's
pplication be accepted by The Seeing Eye, the funds collected for this
an would be used in a variety of ways. He then asked for ideas and
ggestions from the membership. Would members want to encourage
r. Wheeler to apply to The Seeing Eye anyway, offering the school a
ntribution covering the supposed training costs of this man and dog
am?

"Can't we try somewhere else?" someone asked as the discussion went
. "Is The Seeing Eye the only such school?"

Donald Schuur shook his head to the first question and slowly
dded to the second. There seemed nowhere else to go. In 1938, The
eing Eye was the only organized, non-profit school devoted to the
aining and placement of dog guides within North America.

The concept of using specially trained dogs to lead the blind h originated during World War I in Germany (Humphrey and Warn 1934). Prior to that time, individuals who were visually handicapp either relied on the help of family and friends or hired someone accompany them. In either case they were dependent on the availabil and whims of other human beings. Once in a great while, resourcef blind individuals had utilized their own dogs in some capacity, these were rare exceptions, creating a great deal of astonished comm from the public, but little else.

White canes for the blind were introduced in France shortly af World War I (Putnam, 1979), and their use gradually spre throughout Europe and eventually to North America. These canes w not expected to be any real aid to the blind, but rather a visual aid to sighted, a warning for vehicular and pedestrian traffic alike.

It wasn't until World War II that any program of mobility train utilizing canes was thoroughly developed. During this time, Dr. Rich E. Hoover (Putnam, 1979) designed an aluminum cane which was lc enough to pinpoint obstructions or changes in footing by being sw from side to side in front of the user. Quite literally, therefore, until Germans experimented with the practicality of using dogs dur World War I, blind individuals managed as best they could. For most part, they managed poorly.

Centuries of acquired attitudes did not help the situation. Blindn was considered such a terrible handicap that individuals so afflic could not be expected to cope in the sighted world. They were shelter protected, pitied, and often shunned. They were "different," and hum nature being human nature, anyone "different" easily became thou of, if erroneously, as "abnormal."

The history of medicine in the western world indicates an extrem slow advancement where practical knowledge is concerned. For ce turies theories were preferred over research of any kind. During t sixteenth century, physicians knew little more about the inner mechan and functions of the human body than their predecessors of fourte hundred years earlier. Eye disorders of all kinds were often attributed toxic stomach "vapors" rising into the eyes. A popular Flem treatment (Foote, 1968) involved blowing into the afflicted eyes w breath sweetened by cloves or fennel.

By the mid-eighteenth century the practice of medicine had begun assume the scientific character we know today, and much more w known about blindness and its causes. Theories, however, of a different sort abounded. Denis Diderot (1713–1784) (Monbeck, 1973), for example, an eminent French philosopher of the time, theorized that those who were blind lived by a distorted moral code. Since they were unable to see the pain, misery, sorrow, and joy in the faces of humanity, they were supposedly unable to share the feelings of those around them. Diderot reasoned that since they were unable to experience a sense of communion with the rest of mankind, their very thought processes became warped. This type of thinking was shared by many, and the residual effects of theories such as these were carried over into the nineteenth and early twentieth centuries.

As the twentieth century dawned, attitudes towards blindness were beginning to change, but change came slowly. Schools for blind youngsters existed, but they were segregated from the mainstream of life, and the public usually referred to them as "asylums." Within the United States instructors familiar with one of the numerous raised alphabets were available to teach blind individuals in their homes, but this was a frustrating, if not hopeless, task. Although Louis Braille (Keller, 1929) had invented his system of raised print in 1829, it took nearly a century for his technique to become standardized. In 1916, there were five separate systems of raised print and few books published in any of them. It was easier to hire a reader or to wait for the convenience of family or friends.

Job opportunities for the blind were scarce. Organized agencies for the visually handicapped were coming into existence, but they rarely offered employment. Workshops were scattered here and there, but the few lucky enough to be accepted found themselves in a sheltered environment, relegated to making brooms or pot holders at a meager salary with no hope of advancement. Numerous others, not so lucky, often resorted to begging in order to earn some sort of living. "Blind beggar" was a phrase known in every household.

Helen Keller (1880–1968), the world famous blind and deaf humanitarian, had more than a passing acquaintance with the lifestyle expected of the visually handicapped. Although she considered deafness the more difficult handicap of the two, she and her teacher, Anne Sullivan, devoted their lives to educating the general public as to the needs of the visually handicapped. Miss Keller (1929), as do most blind individuals, found her constant reliance on others to be the most aggravating aspect of her handicap. At home she strung ropes around her garden, and visitors often found her walking alone or helping the gardener, deftly feeling each plant with her sensitive fingers, pulling weeds almost as soon as they sprouted. She treasured self-sufficiency and felt this should be the ultimate goal for all visually handicapped individuals. Through her books, lectures and other public appearances she tirelessly fought against attitudes which tended to keep the blind dependent, isolated, and protected.

People such as Helen Keller could only influence receptive individuals. War, however, for all its horrors, has a way of jolting entire nations into new ways of thinking. During World War I Germany was forced to reevaluate current attitudes towards the visually handicapped. Increasing numbers of blinded veterans were discharged into communities where human help simply was nonexistent. Families, friends and paid guides were all busy with the war effort.

In 1916, a program was started at Oldenburg to see if German Shepherd Dogs could be trained to take the place of human guides in helping the blind. The Germans had been singularly successful in training dogs for various types of service work and had introduced them with great success into the military service. Under the direction of Capt. Konrad Most (1954), an estimated forty-eight thousand dogs were serving along the front at the close of World War I. They were used as patrol, draft, liaison, and search and rescue dogs. They had proved so capable and trustworthy that it seemed a logical next step to devise some sort of program that would enable them to help blinded veterans.

At Oldenburg, selected dogs were trained to avoid traffic; to stop at obstructions, curbs, and stairs; and to move rapidly, often alerting sighted pedestrians to move aside by barking. The dogs learned quickly and the program proved successful, with the result that a second school was opened at Württemberg. As soon as the war was over, the program was expanded to include the civilian blind, with additional schools organized at Potsdam and Munich.

The Germans were excited about dog guide training and the results they were seeing in their own country. The people utilizing these dogs were experiencing a freedom of movement they had never dreamed possible, and the psychological benefits were enormous. The rest of the world, however, did not initially seem overly impressed. Most nations were skeptical of using dogs for other than time-honored tasks centering on herding or droving livestock, hunting, and protecting hearth and home. It's also probably safe to say that initial skepticism was increased due to national prejudices resulting from the war. Whatever the reasons, most people could not accept the seemingly outlandish idea of using dogs for such a serious task as leading the blind.

Dorothy Harrison Eustis (Humphrey and Warner, 1934), an American by birth, did not find the idea outlandish at all. Mrs. Eustis was intensely interested in every facet of training dogs and deeply loved the working characteristics of the German Shepherd Dog. In 1923, accompanied by her husband, George, and her German Shepherd Dog, Hans, she founded the Fortunate Fields research, breeding, and training center for German Shepherd Dogs on Mount Pelerin, above Vevey, in Switzerland.

Dorothy Harrison Eustis and two of her German Shepherd Dogs.

While the rest of Europe and North America were swept into the post World War I frenzy that came to be called "The Roaring Twenties," Mrs. Eustis and her training staff, headed by Elliott "Jack" Humphrey, another American, devoted themselves to a scientific breeding and training program that quickly began producing army and police dogs of the highest caliber. They often visited and studied at the German dog training centers where Mrs. Eustis became highly interested in the newly organized dog guide programs, marveling at the abilities these dogs possessed.

The *Saturday Evening Post* eventually asked Mrs. Eustis to write something for the American public about her successful programs at Fortunate Fields, but the article she contributed, published in November 1927, avoided all mention of her own work. She chose to write about the dogs being trained in Germany to lead the blind. Her article, entitled, "The Seeing Eye" broke through the barriers of skepticism surrounding German dog guides and brought her an avalanche of mail, including a letter from a blind teenager named Morris Frank in Nashville, Tennessee, who wanted one of these dogs. He explained to Mrs. Eustis that he was incapable of acquiescing to the prevailing, depressing public attitudes toward his handicap. He wanted the freedom of movement he knew such a dog would bring. He was certain other blind individuals in the United States felt as he did. If she would somehow help him, he would foster a dog guide movement within the United States.

The American Foundation for the Blind had been contacted about sponsoring a dog guide program within the United States but had refused. Mrs. Eustis wanted to help Morris Frank and ultimately offered to pay his way to the Fortunate Fields center in Switzerland where a dog guide would be placed with him. She intended to purchase this dog from the German school at Potsdam, but her request was denied. Since Jack Humphrey and George Eustis had both spent considerable time at the German schools learning the rudiments of dog guide training, it was decided to select and train a Fortunate Fields dog for young Mr. Frank. This female German Shepherd Dog, named Buddy, became the first Seeing Eye dog.

Morris Frank returned to the United States with Buddy in June 1928, and, true to his word, devoted as much time as possible to The Seeing Eye until his death at the age of seventy-two, on November 22, 1980. (Mr. Frank worked for The Seeing Eye until 1956, at which time he

Morris Frank and Buddy #2. Frank fostered the dog guide movement within the United States and worked for The Seeing Eye until 1956. He died in 1980 at the age of 72.

established an insurance agency in Morristown. He was still active in this business at the time of his death.) In January 1929, The Seeing Eye was incorporated (Putnam, 1979), and soon graduated its first class of two students under the training direction of Jack Humphrey, on loan from Fortunate Fields; Willi Ebeling, a well-known breeder of German Shepherd Dogs who offered to learn dog guide training techniques; and Adelaide Clifford, a young woman who had helped around the kennels while on vacation in Switzerland, discovering, in the process, that she was a natural dog trainer.

Buddy #1, the first Seeing Eye dog, bred and trained at Fortunate Fields, Vevey, Switzerland, and placed with Morris Frank of Nashville, Tennessee, in June 1928.

The growth of The Seeing Eye was slow but steady. Classes gradually increased in size, with each graduate going back to his or her community as proof that the sightless need not be dependent on others. The dogs made friends for the program wherever they went as they calmly and quietly performed their duties. Service organizations for the blind gradually began to pledge support, while a nationwide network of Seeing Eye volunteers helped educate the public. Enthusiasm and interest more than offset the trials of the depression years.

In 1934, Mrs. Eustis closed The Seeing Eye division in Switzerland (called by the French equivalent, *l'Oeil qui Voit*), deciding to concentrate on the American school. Then, in 1938, with Europe poised on the brink of World War II, she closed the Fortunate Fields breeding, research, and training center altogether, returning permanently to the United States. By this time, the same year that Donald Schuur met with his Uptown Lions Club to discuss Dr. Wheeler, The Seeing Eye was graduating over one hundred students a year.

Although The Seeing Eye was the only organized, non-profit school for dog guides in North America, Donald Schuur was informed that several independent dog trainers appeared qualified as dog guide instructors, often having worked with the German Army dog programs during World War I before emigrating to the United States. These trainers sold such dogs on an individual basis. One of the Uptown Lions Club members happened to know a breeder and trainer of Doberman Pinschers who seemed to be equally qualified. His name was Glen Staines, and it was decided to contact him to see if he could help.

As discussions were held with Mr. Staines, the membership felt he possessed the necessary training background and decided to hire him. Now the thought occurred to them that perhaps other blind individuals in the area might be interested, especially since Mr. Staines offered to train initially as many as four of his dogs.

An agreement between the Uptown Detroit Lions Club and Glen Staines was signed on October 6, 1938. Mr. Staines agreed to provide four Doberman Pinschers, suitably trained for guide work, at a cost of eight hundred dollars. If students could not be located for the dogs the agreement would be terminated, with the Uptown Lions Club retaining two of the dogs.

As the project moved forward, Mr. Staines began training his selected dogs, and the Uptown Lions Club immediately interested three more blind individuals in addition to Dr. Wheeler: Earl Morrey from Detroit;

21

Donald Schuur works with one of the first trained dogs on a Detroit street in late 1938.

Edward Martin of the Uptown Detroit Lions Club handles one of the first trained dogs. Martin gave great support to the Leader Dog project.

The first graduating class at Leader Dogs in February 1939. From left, William Joyce, Earl Morrey, Dr. Glenn Wheeler, Paul Brown.

a young law student named William Joyce; and Paul Brown, a musician from Toledo, Ohio, who happened to be the brother of movie actor Joe E. Brown. The management of the Park Avenue Hotel in downtown Detroit heard about the program and offered accommodations without charge for the period of time in which the students would learn to handle their dogs.

The club members found excitement mounting. They had a trainer, dogs-in-training, a waiting class and accommodations for their students. What had initially been a disappointing experience was turning into one of the most exciting projects in which they had ever been involved. It was time to tell all Lions Clubs.

A four-page report was sent to every member club of Lions International. This report not only described the project but requested that clubs submit a suitable name for it. To the astonishment of the Uptown Lions Club, over 500 names or phrases were submitted by Lions Clubs from Panama to British Columbia, California to Maine. The selected name, as reported in newspapers on December 14, 1938, was "Lions Leader" submitted by the Lions Club of Coulterville, Illinois.

Wayne University Law School honor student, William Joyce, center, receives dog guide in 1939. Dean of Students Joseph P. Selden and Donald P. Schuur, President, Uptown Detroit Lions Club, look on. Joyce was employed as an Assistant Prosecuting Attorney for Wayne County, Michigan, after law school. He died in 1978.

During this time, Mr. Staines continued to train his dogs, and in February 1939, four Doberman Pinschers were teamed with Paul Brown, William Joyce, Earl Morrey, and Dr. Glenn Wheeler. Club members also discovered that their project might well grow beyond the scope of a single Lions Club. They were being inundated with requests and weren't quite sure how to proceed.

Once again Donald Schuur found himself presiding over a club meeting, seeking ideas from the membership. Everyone agreed that a project with so much outside interest should not be allowed to end, although the Uptown Lions Club alone was not in a position to handle something of this scope. A permanent organization was envisioned, one in which all interested people could play a part. Accordingly, on April 4, 1939, "Lion's Leader Dog Foundation" was incorporated.

Figure 1—Dates, Events and People

October 6, 1938	Uptown Detroit Lions Club, Donald P. Schuur, president, Harold D. Davenport, secretary, sign written training agreement with Glen S. Staines, Ponchartrain Kennels
December 14, 1938	Project named "Lions Leader" in contest involving all member clubs of Lions International. Winning entry submitted by Lions Club of Coulterville, Illinois
February 1939	First class was graduated: William Joyce, law student, Wayne University; Paul Brown, musician, Toledo, Ohio; Dr. Glenn Wheeler, Detroit, Michigan; Earl Morrey, Detroit, Michigan
April 4, 1939	Corporation formed—"Lion's Leader Dog Foundation" Incorporators: Edward U. Martin (Uptown Lions Club), Donald P. Schuur (Uptown Lions Club), Harold Davenport (Uptown Lions Club)
	Board of Directors: Frank D. Beadle (St. Clair Lions Club), Harold Davenport, Donald P. Schuur, Edward U. Martin, Paul Brown, Wilbur E. Darling (Downtown Lions Club), H. Irvine Wiley (Lions Club of Windsor. Ontario), L. H. Evans (Toledo Lions Club), Charles Nutting (East Side Detroit Lions Club), S. A. Dodge (Northwest Detroit Lions Club)
May 18, 1939	Training agreement terminated with Glen S. Staines
May 19, 1939	Chalmers R. Donaldson approved as training director
June 1, 1939	Property rented at Rochester and Avon Roads, Rochester, Michigan, from Leonard Martell for fifty dollars per month
June 1, 1939 June 1, 1940	Eighteen dogs and handlers graduate
June 15, 1940	Name changed to "Leader Dog League for the Blind"

Other People Instrumental in Formative Years

William E. ("Major") Bartram who served as executive secretary

Harold Warman who served as executive secretary as well as a public speaker with his Leader Dog

Elizabeth McCormick, executive secretary of the Detroit League for the Handicapped, who assisted with her knowledge of social workers and handicapped people

Dr. James E. Patterson, veterinarian who assisted in the establishment of admittance procedures for dogs and general medical care

Dr. Albert Reudemann, noted ophthalmologist who assisted in the establishment of procedures to determine the qualifications of the blind

25

A Detroit News photo announcing the forming of Lions Leader Dog Foundation in April 1939. From left, Charles Nutting, Donald Schuur, S. A. Dodge.

Almost immediately, Dick Fowler was sent on a two-day study visit to The Seeing Eye. Mr. Fowler had joined the newly formed corporation on a full-time basis, even though it had been explained to him that any sort of salary was unthinkable at the moment. His study visit on April 10 and 11, 1939, was a most productive one. The Seeing Eye did not resent the formation of a rival school but was very concerned about the quality of training any such school would supply. The visit ended cordially. A few weeks later, one of The Seeing Eye's instructors, Chalmers Donaldson, joined the staff at Lion's Leader Dog Foundation and the agreement with Glen Staines was terminated. From that day forward only trainers who had served an apprenticeship in dog guide work would be used as instructors.

Since both the German schools and The Seeing Eye had found the German Shepherd Dog to be ideally suited for guide work, Lion's Leader Dog Foundation immediately contacted German Shepherd Dog breeders for donation animals, although other breeds were considered and used. The public was also alerted to the new school's needs and asked to bring suitable dogs to the school for possible donation, a policy continued to this day.

Bringing dogs to the school proved to be an initial problem, as the school had no home. Donald Schuur was using his law office as a mailing address, but a place was needed where dogs, students, and staff could be comfortably housed at one location. The new school did not want to repeat the early history of The Seeing Eye, whose trainers and dogs initially moved from city to city in order to accommodate students, while office personnel remained far removed from day-to-day problems and crises.

In their spare time, Donald Schuur and his family toured the area in search of available property. Eventually they located a small farm at the corner of Rochester and Avon Roads just outside the rural community of Rochester, Michigan. There was a house, barn and small garage on the property, and the owner, Leonard Martell, agreed to let the school lease the entire premises for fifty dollars a month. As quickly as

Farmhouse at Rochester and Avon Roads, Rochester, Michigan, rented for $50 per month in June 1939. Today, the Leader Dog student dormitory connects to this building with the main floor serving as the school's dining room.

27

possible, Dick Fowler and his wife, Beulah, moved into the house, and Chalmers Donaldson was approved as the first instructor.

By 1940, the foundation's board of directors was devoting its time to making contacts with the outside world. Lions International, however, decided there were too many legal risks to be formally associated with the tiny corporation. At a state convention in Benton Harbor, Michigan, it was voted to drop the word "Lion's" from the corporation name. Accordingly, on June 15, 1940, "Lion's Leader Dog Foundation" was formally changed to "Leader Dog League for the Blind." Board members had originally hoped for the complete support of Lions International, but they quickly realized that such support might keep other interested organizations and individuals from pledging assistance. Perhaps the decision of Lions International was a blessing in disguise, as it would force the foundation to sink or swim on its own efforts.

Donald Schuur recalls the first year of the school's existence:

"We constantly had three avenues of problems and perhaps these even exist today to some degree. We had always the problem of either money (a shortage of it), dogs (a shortage of them) or blind students (a shortage of them). Whenever we had money on hand, we had no dogs.

Barn which served as the original Leader Dog kennel. In the early days, many dogs died from distemper and other causes.

Whenever we had dogs, we had no money. When we had students, we had no dogs and so forth. We always had difficulty in one of those three departments and never could attain a proper balance. Of course, needless to say, during our first months in carrying on the work at the Rochester-Avon Road location, we lost several dogs due to distemper and other causes, inasmuch as the dogs were housed during the cold winter months in the old barn which had only small oil heaters to dispense the cold. This was really a trying period."

In spite of the hardships, the school placed eighteen dogs with blind masters during the first year. Chalmers Donaldson, who was initially the only trainer, found his responsibilities almost too much to handle. The fledgling staff had to cope with cramped, drafty quarters, buildings in need of constant repair, and, always, insufficient funds.

At regular intervals Dick Fowler suggested to the board that perhaps the project should be terminated while there were still a few hundred dollars in the bank to pay outstanding debts. His suggestion was always turned down. When things seemed bleakest, the school managed to remain solvent. More often than not, employees offered to put their salaries on the books rather than in their pockets. Donations, too, began to dribble in—ten dollars from an individual here, one hundred dollars from a dog club there. The Uptown Detroit Lions Club quietly continued to underwrite many expenses. Donation campaigns were attempted, and, "ultimately and slowly," Donald Schuur says today with satisfaction, "we did get the message across and funds began to flow in our direction."

Ultimately and slowly also, Leader Dogs began to grow. Just as World War I had done, World War II was forcing further reevaluations in attitudes towards the visually handicapped. Blinded veterans were returning in large numbers to North America, unwilling to be dependent on society. Many companies, short of personnel, were hiring individuals who were blind, discovering that they could perform numerous tasks once thought only the sighted could perform. Many of these blind individuals wanted dog guides.

The dog's place as an active participant in service programs was now assured and had been for several years. Servicemen, returning home after World War I, had helped inform the public as to the phenomenal success of the numerous German service dog programs. A German Shepherd Dog by the name of Rin-Tin-Tin showed the average citizen some of these skills as he performed almost unbelievable training feats

Four members of the Uptown Detroit Lions Club, above, with the four initial Doberman Pinschers trained for the future Leader Dogs, October 1938. Left to right, Edward U. Martin, First Vice-President; Charles Stanley, Committeeman; Donald P. Schuur, President; Hy M. Steed, Past President. Below, the student lounge in 1942. From left, Donald Schuur; Harold Warman, Executive Director with his Leader Dog; student; Fred Maynard, Director of Training; and student.

Sonja Henie, figure skater and actress, Winthrop Gardiner, and Fred Maynard, Director of Training (pointing) inspect improved Leader Dog kennels. The school emerged after World War II as one of the foremost dog guide schools in the world.

Above, Fred Maynard, trainer, works a German Shepherd Dog on the Leader Dog premises in 1940. Below, exercise pen for early Leader Dogs, a far cry from housing conditions today.

"Lions Leader" is the winning name. Over 500 names were submitted by Lions Clubs in a contest to name the Uptown Detroit Lions Club project. Left to right, Hal G. Trump, Mrs. Arthur H. Buhl, Jr., and Donald P. Schuur.

and acts of courage for the benefit of movie cameras. The German schools and Fortunate Fields had been placing dogs into army programs, police departments and federal offices in numerous countries where their presence and working abilities were completely accepted. Similar programs were being organized around the world. During World War II dogs were extensively used by Allied and Axis powers alike, serving as patrol dogs, line runners, draft dogs, message carriers, bomb detectors, search, rescue, and avalanche dogs, with the United States especially contributing to the training of dogs that could be used effectively in jungle warfare.

As the demand by veterans for dog guides grew during World War II, the government of the United States eventually promised federal funds for dog guide programs. At this news dog guide "schools" and "trainers" sprouted up like mushrooms around the country. By 1942, there were twenty-seven such enterprises (Putnam, 1979), most of which disappeared as quickly as they started. When World War II ended, The Seeing Eye, Leader Dogs for the Blind, and Guide Dogs for the Blind (located in San Rafael, California, and organized in 1942) emerged intact with untarnished reputations for training excellence. Although

Figure 2—Major Dog Guide Schools Within Continental United States

Leader Dogs for the Blind
1039 Rochester Road
Rochester, Michigan 48063

Second Sight
109-19 Seventy Second Avenue
Forest Hills
Long Island, New York 11375

The Seeing Eye, Inc.
Morristown, New Jersey 07960

Guiding Eyes for the Blind, Inc.
106 East 41st Street
New York, New York 10017

Guide Dogs for the Blind, Inc.
PO Box 1200
San Rafael, California 94902

International Guiding Eye Corporation
5431 Denny Avenue
Hollywood, California 91601

Pilot Dogs, Inc.
625 West Town Street
Columbus, Ohio 43215

Guide Dogs of the Desert
PO Box 1692
Palm Springs, California 92262

A dog guide is traditionally called by the name of the graduating school. If one does not know the graduating school, it is proper to refer to the animal as a "dog guide."

other excellent schools joined their ranks, these three would remain the foremost dog guide schools within the United States.

During the formative years of Leader Dogs, Donald Schuur, considered today to be the school's founder, served as president. Charles Nutting assumed the presidency for one year, gratefully turning the role back to Schuur when he found the work too demanding.

Donald Schuur still serves on the school's board of trustees, pleased that the decision within the Uptown Detroit Lions Club to help a blind individual in 1939 was acted upon. Today, the school Schuur and his club members founded is graduating well over three hundred teams of dogs and handlers per year and is one of the major dog guide schools in the world.

Leader Dog supporters listen to a lecture at the home of Mrs. Arthur Buhl, Jr., in September 1948.

Aerial view of Leader Dogs today.

Chapter 2

Leader Dogs Today

The close affiliation with Lions that began with Donald Schuur and the Uptown Detroit Lions Club has remained and intensified through the years. Each year, Lions Clubs have increased their contributions. In 1981, they contributed almost $1,500,000 to the school, nearly the entire year's operating budget. These donations come from clubs around the world, and the school's debt of gratitude is a very deep one.

The International Association of Lions Clubs is the world's largest service club organization, with a membership of over 33,000 clubs and 1,200,000 individuals (Lions Clubs International, 1980). It was founded in Chicago, Illinois, in 1917, by Melvin Jones (1879-1961), who felt the then-popular businessmen's luncheon clubs should be expanded and altered with members dedicated to community welfare. His fellow businessmen agreed, and the growth of the new association was phenomenal.

In a broad sense Lions Clubs are involved with all aspects of health, education, community, national, and international welfare and services. However, since 1925, when Helen Keller addressed the Association's International Convention and asked the participants to help her in her "crusade against darkness," Lions Clubs have become almost synonymous with services for the visually impaired. They establish glaucoma screening centers, eye banks, and rehabilitation institutes. they provide scholarships for blind students and funds for workshops and research into sight conservation. They provide mobility aids such as canes and, best known of all, dog guides.

Leader Dogs relies heavily on contributions from Lions Clubs and, as a non-profit organization, depends completely on public donations to accomplish its work. The school, however, has a policy of never openly soliciting funds, even when needed. "We're just too proud to do that," one of the staff said.

Thousands of visitors have signed the school's guest register, and tours are arranged if the staff is notified in advance. A day rarely goes by without several groups or individual visitors who want to learn something about what is accomplished at a dog guide school.

Student buses outside the main office building. The lion at the office entrance is a reminder of the school's close affiliation with the International Association of Lions Clubs.

The visitor's first stop is the main office where personnel records are kept, and accounting, kennel and student-related paper work are performed, together with public relations on a global basis. Meetings and film presentations are arranged throughout North America and beyond; personal thank-you letters are sent for each donation received; student applications are checked; field follow-up is arranged; files on previous students are kept current; travel arrangements are made for all incoming and graduating students who are treated as "family."

Overseeing the general operation of the school is Harold L. Pocklington, who has been serving Leader Dogs as executive director since 1951. "Poc," as he is affectionately called by colleagues and former students, is helped by his wife, Maryan, who serves as his assistant.

By the time he was twenty-nine years old, Poc was deeply involved in Lions, organizing the Algonac Lions Club, in Algonac, Michigan, during the same year (1939) that Donald Schuur was incorporating Leader Dogs. Over the span of the next few decades, Poc organized forty-six Lions Clubs, eventually serving on the international board of directors. He has since lectured for Lions throughout the United States, Canada, Europe, and Africa, and, as a life member, has earned nearly every possible award from this organization.

In 1948, Poc was elected to the Leader Dog board of trustees, and he was immediately asked to look over and comment on the school's operation. He undertook this task as a part-time volunteer, discovering that the school was desperately in need of firm financial management. His volunteer hours began to stretch into full working days, until, in 1950, he decided to take a year's leave of absence from his regular position as sales manager for Warner Brothers Foundry and Electro Lunch Company in order to devote himself completely to Leader Dogs. He never went back to his waiting job.

Poc does not think of himself as a catalyst in the growth of the school. If anyone mentions his enormous contributions of time, energy, and management expertise, he is apt to shrug and say that he just happened to be available to do what needed to be done. Poc's basic love of people and his friendships within Lions and the communications media as a result of his prior position with Warner Brothers all served to help lift Leader Dogs from its first decade of financial doldrums.

The Leader Dog complex is still located on the outskirts of Rochester, twenty-five miles north of Detroit, the farm having been purchased in early 1940. The landscaped grounds of approximately

Paved paths meander over the school grounds. The apple trees, part of the original farm's orchard, still bear fruit.

Newly constructed 1.5 million dollar kennel addition. The new complex holds up to 184 dogs.

fifteen acres were once part of the apple orchard and the gnarled trees still bear fruit. The original farmhouse still stands and is attached directly to the dormitory. Today, the main floor serves as the school's dining room, and the upstairs is used for storage. Although the building has been completely renovated, memories of the early years are still vivid and stories are passed down from employee to employee.

Dick Fowler and his wife, Beulah, who moved into the house as soon as the farm was rented, coped with the drafty rooms as best they could. The upstairs bedrooms accommodated six students and one instructor, and everyone had to share one bathroom. "The bathroom situation was bad enough," comments Ed Lange, who serves as coordinator of the Leader Dog Puppy Program as well as part of the school's public relations team, "especially in the morning when everyone was trying to get dressed and get the dogs out. Then they had to go up and down those narrow, creaky stairs, and that was worse than the bathroom! The instructor used to watch the handlers and dogs on those stairs and mouth silent prayers every step of the way, marveling that no one was ever seriously hurt in the process. One anxious dog, one misstep, one failure to halt at the proper moment and we would have had a catastrophe. We knew a dormitory was only a matter of time, and you can see how the school began to grow out from the old house as additions were built."

The school really did "grow out." Today, the major buildings— general offices, garages, and kennels—flank the parking area. The students' dormitory, extending outwards from the original farmhouse, is set slightly off to one side and is closed off by a gate. Fifty-eight people are employed by the school including twenty trainers, and the kennels currently house three hundred dogs.

The dormitory has room for thirty-two students. The twin-bedded rooms, each with private bath, are comfortable and spacious. Meals are eaten family style in the large dining room. There is a gameroom where students can play board games, such as *Monopoly*, in Braille editions, although the favorite gathering spot is the wood paneled main lounge where a natural brick fireplace extends along an entire wall. The piano and guitar are in constant use. There are typewriters, television sets, a library of Braille books, magazines, and talking books, Braille cards and dominoes. Snack machines are located in the students' laundry room, and a live-in housemother cares for the needs of those, such as diabetics, requiring a special diet at odd hours. Besides the housemother at least two instructors are always on the premises during the month the students learn to handle their trained dogs. The atmosphere is relaxed and happy.

Meals are homemade, from dinner rolls to desserts, and as one meal ends the next is started. The women who manage the kitchen are adept at handling meetings in the lower level conference room for as many as five hundred people and are always well-prepared for last-minute guests.

Off to one side of the dormitory is a covered exercise area where students walk their dogs at intervals throughout the day. One section is composed of grass and gravel, while another is a simulated section of city street, sidewalk and curb for the benefit of urban dwellers. There is also a narrow, fenced area where students can unsnap leads, remove harnesses and individually play with their dogs without fear of "losing"

The conference room seats up to 500 people comfortably.

The dormitory with paved "practice" court for students.

them. Paved pathways meander through the apple orchard off the dormitory patio, and there is a practice court for students to use as they familiarize themselves with dog guide commands and maneuvers.

Living conditions for the canine students at Leader Dogs also have changed since the early days when small oil heaters were used to ward off the bitter Michigan winters. Today the kennels boast radiant heat, the finest disinfectant apparatus, and a construction pattern that makes maximum use of daylight and sunlight. The ventilation system changes air three times per minute. Each dog is housed in a single, large stall with glazed tile walls and an automatic watering device that turns on when the nozzle is lapped. Each row of stalls faces the back of the next row. Since dogs cannot see each other, barking is kept to a minimum. Each row is closed off by an iron gate which opens at the other end to a huge exercise yard. The dogs are exercised in rows and not individually.

Recently constructed training headquarters in downtown Rochester serves as a base for training days in town.

Dr. J.W. "Gus" Eastman, Leader Dogs' full-time veterinarian checks over trainees. The school has fully equipped surgery, laboratory and x-ray facility.

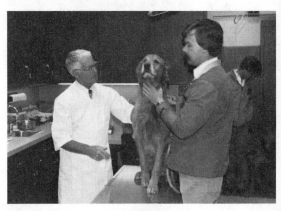

Employees all manage to visit puppies whenever they're at the school. These Labrador and Golden Retriever puppies are part of the school's foster puppy program.

Overhead heaters in the exercise areas ensure that snow and ice are never problems for dogs or kennel staff.

At intervals all dogs in training are allowed to play together in a special fenced-in area used for just that purpose. This, as the trainers admit, "is fun—but bedlam, especially when we want them to come in!"

Visitors to Leader Dogs are nearly always disappointed when informed they cannot go into the training kennels and personally meet the dogs. They can, however, view the inside of the kennels through glass windows from the corridors. A quiet atmosphere is important to the working progress and well-being of the animals, and their routine is disrupted as little as possible.

Dogs accepted for training are housed initially in a quarantine section where they are watched for approximately ten to fourteen days while extensive physical tests are made. Leader Dogs has a full-time veterinarian on the staff, Dr. J. W. "Gus" Eastman, and there is a completely equipped surgery, laboratory, and x-ray facility on the premises. The quarantine section consists of several large, indoor stalls with its own separate outdoor exercise yard. When dogs pass quarantine, they are moved into the Beginner's Kennel and then into the Advanced Training Kennel until completion of their program and final placement.

Inside the new kennel addition dogs enjoy radiant heat, individual water fountains, and a superior air exchange system.

45

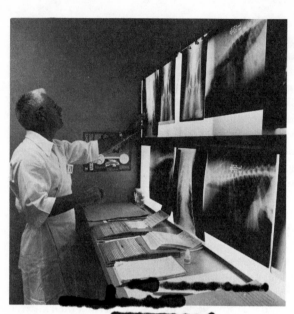

Dr. Eastman studies x-rays.

Outside the kennel office is one of the favorite spots of the school's staff, the fenced yard for future foster puppies. These puppies, specially bred for the school, are brought for testing during their sixth week of life and subsequently placed with foster families. Usually they spend a day or two on the premises.

During a typical working day, the atmosphere at Leader Dogs is quiet. Visitors are always surprised at the general lack of commotion. "Where are the blind students?" they usually ask, or, "Where are all the dogs?" The dormitory is still except for the isolated sounds and voices coming from the kitchen. Half the stalls in the training kennel are empty. The training program of this and all dog guide schools is conducted off the premises. The vans, filled with dogs, pull out at approximately half-past eight in the morning, returning for lunch, then out again, returning between four and half-past four in the afternoon. Except for a few preliminary lessons at the school, the routine for blind students is similar. By nine o'clock in the morning, the training buses have left the premises. Students return for lunch and to exercise their dogs, and then they are off again for the afternoon assignment.

Visitors hoping to see dogs working should plan on driving into downtown Rochester where a recently constructed building serves as a base for training days in town. The downtown training center has an indoor garage large enough to house the school's entire fleet of vans as well as the student buses. The lounge can accommodate the entire class of blind students as they wait to work with their instructors. Should weather conditions be too severe for outdoor training, there is enough room inside to accomplish a few exercises such as the mechanics of entering and leaving passenger cars with dogs.

From this location blind students begin learning to handle their trained dogs as instructors map out routings. From here, also, the dogs receive their first lessons, moving along the streets of Rochester and learning the basic tasks necessary to enable them to safely lead unsighted human beings.

Visitors who do take time to watch trainers, students, and dogs, however, usually find the essence of what they have come to see eluding them. What they observe is not likely to be what they envisioned, and the experience can be unsettling. One of the school's trainers commented on this phenomenon: "You'd be surprised at the ideas people have when they come to the school. Even people actively involved in breeding or

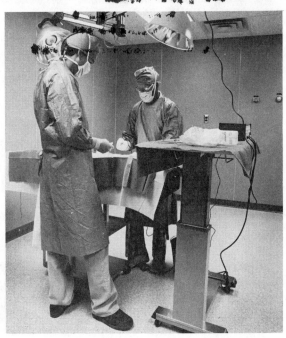

All animals are neutered in advanced training. These operations are performed in the school's surgery.

The kennel kitchen is a busy place.

Students wait their turn for training in the lounge of the Rochester training headquarters.

training dogs have very definite preconceived ideas as to what we do and how we do it. Dog trainers, for example, expect to see the same flashy, stylish performances that are associated with obedience trials, and that just isn't the way a dog guide works. People with no background in dogs assume we teach animals to do impossible things, such as read traffic lights and follow verbal instructions to locate places in a strange environment. I think everybody expects to see blind students who gratefully relinquish all responsibility for their safety and well-being to their dogs, and this isn't what occurs."

What does occur? What makes this work and these dogs so special? What goes on at a dog guide school that isn't discernible during a brief tour or a few hours in town observing some of the training? How are these dogs selected and trained? How do they differ from the average house pet? What qualifies the trainers for their profession? What types of people receive these animals and how do they feel about their handicap? Will dog guides change their lives or perform "miracles"? In a much broader sense, what can we learn at a dog guide school about blindness and our attitudes toward the visually handicapped? What can we learn that will enable us to select and raise better puppies or adult dogs as pets, breeding stock, working or competition dogs?

Questions such as these are asked at the school every day, but answering them in a few simple sentences is not possible. The same trainer who commented on the expectations of visitors went on to say, "You can't explain this work in a short period of time. You have to experience it."

A dog guide school is more than history, buildings, budgets, donations, public relations, and business management, although no one denies that these are extremely important. It is a place where man and animal form a unique and unusual relationship, one in which trainers, visually handicapped individuals, and dogs equally contribute to the success of what is ultimately accomplished.

"A trainer always enjoys developing the abilities of a good dog and placing him in the hands of someone who will use and appreciate him," one trainer said, "but it's not only training dogs that makes this work special. We see all kinds of people come in here and watch them leave with a new outlook on life. I guess you could say both dogs and people are transformed here but there is no way anyone can absorb this in an hour's visit."

It was my privilege to experience this transformation.

49

Left, this beginning dog has become distracted as it nears a curb and the trainer will make a correction.

Right, Leader Dog trainers check information on upcoming students. Trainers live at the school during the month blind students learn to handle their dogs.

Left, in the apprentice program, which lasts three years, team captains work with new trainers. An apprentice follows Harold "Smitty" Smith as he works.

Chapter 3

The Training Staff

It was a bright, sunny Saturday in early spring when I arrived at Leader Dogs for the first time. Mr. Pocklington had arranged an interview with Jim Henderson, who has been a dog guide trainer for twenty-six years. Poc, as I later came to know him, mentioned that my plans to analyze dog guide testing and training procedures had to meet the trainers' approval. "We have reporters and writers here all the time," he had said over the phone. "Everyone likes human interest stories, and there are plenty of those at a dog guide school. However, your plans are different. As far as I know, no one has ever written in depth about dog guide training procedures. You'll have to discuss your idea directly with the training staff."

As a dog trainer, I wanted to compare dog guide training methods to the techniques with which I was familiar for teaching household pets and American Kennel Club obedience competition dogs. As a writer, I wanted to share this information with the readership of a dog trainer's magazine entitled *Front and Finish*. The co-editor of the magazine, Robert Self, and I felt that if more dog trainers had access to the procedures used to test and train dog guides, they would be better able to set similar standards of excellence for themselves, helping to ensure that the best possible dogs are selected by families, regardless of breed or selling age.

The kennel office, where I was to meet Jim Henderson, seemed to be filled with people who were coming and going in all directions. Employees were busy with kennel tasks which know no weekends or holidays. Two trainers brushed past me on their way to the parking lot to test several dogs for possible donation. A tour group of ladies came noisily through the door, and their guide was forced to raise his voice to explain the purpose of the area they were entering.

Jim seemed oblivious to all this as he greeted me. "Poc tells me you have some interesting ideas," he said as he introduced himself. "Let's hear what you'd like to do, and then we'll see what might be possible.

As Jim listened to my proposed plans, he immediately agreed that most people, including those actively involved in training dogs, do not understand what dog guides do. He said that even those who observe a portion of the training often leave with a very inaccurate analysis of what occurred. They assume dog guides never make mistakes, never need corrections, and work through a superior mental process that defies explanation. The general public consistently underestimates the intelligence and common sense of dogs in general, marveling, for example, at the dog guide's ability to safely lead his master through heavy traffic or construction areas. In other ways, the public can be extremely naive, assuming all dogs on earth possess equal abilities and expecting trained dogs to react like robots rather than individual animals with distinct personalities and needs.

As our dialogue continued, Jim offered to show me some of the dogs already in training. As we moved into the kennel, his conversation touched on canine behavior, various types of training methods and the history of service work. As we paused at the various stalls, he pointed out subtle temperament differences in the dogs. When he opened the kennel stalls and "his" dogs bounded out to cover him with slurping laps, there was no doubt as to the mutual feelings he and the dogs shared.

As we walked back to the kennel office, Jim commented that it would be impossible to analyze the school's training and testing program in a short visit. "Why don't you come back for an extended period of time?" he asked. "We'll put you into a sort of 'accelerated apprenticeship,' and you'll learn exactly how our dogs are selected and trained." I had hoped the school would allow me to observe the program for a few days, but to be asked to join the training staff was more than I had expected, and I could hardly wait to begin!

Before I left the school on this visit, however, I wanted to know more about my upcoming "apprenticeship." Had I been someone actually hired as a trainer, how would I have been selected and what could I expect?

Jim explained that the current instructing staff is composed of eighteen men and two women. All have undergone or are completing the mandatory three-year apprenticeship before assuming full responsibility for training dogs or instructing blind students. In selecting applicants, who must be twenty-one years of age or older, the school initially looks for good scholastic and previous work records as well as outstanding character references. Experience in training dogs is not mandatory. Applicants must be in excellent physical condition, able to work and walk outdoors for long hours everyday without fatigue under all weather conditions. All instructors fall within a certain weight range and body build, and seem to be naturally athletic. When weekends come, they enjoy scuba-diving, skiing, golfing, back-packing, tennis, and many are active members of local baseball and football teams. Friendly, outgoing personalities are imperative. Not only do the trainers meet and cope with the general public every day while working, but they also hold the responsibility of instructing blind students from all walks of life who are initially very nervous. They must be well-spoken, soft-spoken, tactful, patient, and even-tempered. Their own personalities and egos must always take second place to those of their students, both canine and human.

All instructors share a basic love and "feel" for dogs, although their experience with them varies. A few have trained dogs with the Army and Air Force K-9 programs and have developed an interest in service dog work that has led them into this field. Others come into the program with no dog training background. A few own hunting dogs they have trained for personal use. Others own house dogs and have had no formal training whatsoever.

The prerequisites of superb dog trainers, however, are immediately apparent in each instructor: patience, calmness, super-fast reflexes, split-second timing, smooth movements, vocal control, ability to treat each animal as an individual and partner in the learning process, and ability to instantly analyze every canine action or anticipated action and react accordingly. Although the school's apprenticeship lasts three years, the trainers deny learning these things on the job. They are surprised these points are even raised. They view themselves as simply "having a way" with dogs, and the natural abilities of great dog trainers have luckily found expression in this work.

Many applicants are disappointed when informed that the apprenticeship begins with a period working in the kennels. Ed Lange, who works closely with apprentices, later told me the usual newcomer's reaction. "Some of them feel insulted. They want to train dogs, not hose down runs. It's ego-deflating, but dog training is not all glamour. It's necessary to learn about health, sanitation, grooming, and diet. The apprentice learns about canine character while working in the kennels and later participates in the selection process.

"During this period the apprentice also learns how to handle himself around people. There's a lot of public relations work involved, such as escorting visitors around the premises."

If the necessary stint in the kennels discourages many applicants, the following list of the profession's working requirements causes others to reevaluate their desires to become dog guide trainers:

1. The trainer must remain in top physical condition. If he allows himself to become overweight or out of condition, he will find reflex actions and movements slowing down. Back, foot, and leg problems, however, may develop and are occupational hazards.

2. Although classes for blind students may be altered due to weather conditions, dogs are trained in rain and snow.

3. The trainer is on call seven days a week. If there is a sick dog within the string he is training, he assumes responsibility with the help of the kennel staff and veterinarian—weekends, holidays, and around the clock if need be.

4. The training period for dogs lasts four months, and then the trainer moves into the school for the study session with blind students who will be placed with the animals he has trained. During this month he is on the premises twenty-four hours a day, although he will rotate nights off with two other instructors after the first three days.

5. Because of the continual training programs and waiting list for dogs, there are few holidays, and vacations are apt to be sporadic, usually long weekends or week-long breaks between classes. One trainer later told me, "Once a class starts, we hate to miss a single day, even for illness. The dogs can't wait a week or so while we recuperate."

6. Work days are long ones. Trainers are on the premises at approximately half-past seven in the morning and rarely leave before half-past four or five in the afternoon.

7. Additional study is expected of trainers on their personal time. They must keep abreast of the latest dog training techniques, behavioral studies and medical research. Classes in psychology and animal behavior are continually encouraged.

8. The work is mentally exhausting due to the very nature and responsibilities of the program. Trainers must be constantly alert and aware of every detail in their immediate environments. One slight error or one moment's loss of concentration can create serious problems for dogs or blind students alike. The mental pressure can take its toll.

9. Pay is minimal.

Once a commitment is made, however, an apprentice becomes dedicated to his profession. After the initial working period in the kennels, he is transferred to a team composed of three instructors and a team captain who usually has seniority of about five years. The team captain serves as the apprentice's instructor.

Once the apprentice begins work with a team, he progresses at his own speed. Initially the captain holds a harness and literally takes the place of a dog. During this period, called "Juno" by the school, the apprentice learns which commands are necessary and how to enforce them. Later he works alongside the captain who explains maneuvers while actually training dogs. The captain calls attention to differences in canine response, variables in the environment, and other factors which might alter training procedures. Later, the apprentice critiques the captain's work, keeping up a running commentary on each dog including what should be done, why, and how. The captain points out any overlooked factors.

The team captain decides when the apprentice is ready to handle dogs. Now the roles reverse and the captain works alongside the apprentice, pointing out errors in trainer and dog alike. Throughout the apprenticeship, the novice trainer eases into work with blind students. Once again, he is taught and later asked to comment on the work he is observing, instructing only when his captain feels he is qualified to do so.

Team captain Harold Smith, with whom I later worked, has instructed several apprentices and feels the hardest aspect of this job is to teach someone who has trained dogs in some capacity. "Those who worked with the Army or Air Force programs are used to tougher dogs and have to readjust methods and utilize techniques suitable to the softer dogs with which we work. Practical dog trainers often have a reflex action that must be changed or their dogs will be corrected too soon, something a blind person would never be able to imitate. This timing breaks down canine initiative. It's difficult to change techniques, so it's often easier to work with apprentices who have never trained dogs before. We can see soon enough if they have the natural abilities we want."

As would be expected, training procedures vary from school to school. Each dog guide school reevaluates its program in light of the latest discoveries in medical and behavioral research and will introduce variations in the training program if changes are deemed worthwhile.

For many years dog guide schools did not seriously consider women for apprenticeships, in spite of the fact that one of the first trainers, Adelaide Clifford, was a woman. It was felt that women were a poor employment risk for a three-year apprenticeship program, as the young, single women who applied were apt to leave the work force to marry and raise a family. Some schools also argued that women would be unable to cope with the continual mental and physical pressures of the work.

Today, most dog guide schools have women instructors. Not only can they manage the pressures, but, in today's society they also tend to keep working after marriage. Leader Dogs feels the entire program benefits from utilizing male and female trainers, and women applicants are always given full consideration.

The three-year apprenticeship is standard at all dog guide schools and, in this respect, has changed little from the original programs in Germany and Switzerland. Today's trainer, however, has the advantage of drawing on the results of outstanding scientific and practical research where dogs are concerned as well as the accumulated knowledge resulting from several decades of dog guide training.

The first trainers had to mold role models from the dogs they trained. Methods and goals had to be developed, and minor errors were made and corrected in the process. The early German dogs, for example, were trained to move at an extremely fast pace until it was realized that not all blind individuals could move that quickly. As the program gained in popularity, it was noted that subtle character differences were desirable in the dogs so that they could be better matched with people who had varying personalities, lifestyles, and interests. The importance of extensive early exposure to people, places, and things became apparent when trained dogs were suddenly expected to cope in new environments and situations for which they had not been prepared.

As the program developed, dog guide trainers were constantly on the alert for suitable dogs. At Fortunate Fields (Humphrey and Warner, 1934) research was conducted in order to pinpoint physical and behavioral traits which appeared advantageous for various types of service work. As a result, the staff was eventually able to select untrained adult dogs exhibiting attributes for guide work based on basic physical makeups and characters. Today, as a result of this and subsequent research, dog guide schools select adult dogs with high potential through a brief series of observational tests.

When the Fortunate Fields program drew to a close in the years prior to World War II, the staff members voiced a plea and hope for future generations of researchers to build on their work. They dreamed of the day when it would be possible for very young puppies to be tested in similar fashion. Wouldn't it be wonderful, they asked, if puppies could be analyzed almost from birth as to their adult characters and abilities? Time and effort could then be devoted to those showing most potential.

Less than a decade later this dream became reality. In 1945, some of the foremost scientists in the United States began a research project at the Roscoe B. Jackson Memorial Laboratory in Bar Harbor, Maine (Scott and Fuller, 1965). The purpose was to learn more about human behavior in relationship to heredity and the effects of environment. These scientists could not use human beings for the controlled environment tests which would last throughout the maturing process, so the dog was selected as the study animal. Data would be compared to the behavior of human babies, children, adolescents, and adults.

The dog was an ideal study choice. It not only is closely associated with man but also shares basic human behavioral traits and hereditary diseases. Different breeds or types of dogs can be chosen that have characters very similar to human character types. The dog matures quickly, so that a complete generation can be studied in a year's time, and it breeds at a young age, usually producing several puppies for comparison study. This research project not only paved the way for new and exciting theories involving human behavior but also gave the world its most complete body of research to date involving the formation of canine behavioral patterns.

As a direct result of this specific research project and its utilization on a practical basis at Guide Dogs for the Blind in California (Pfaffenberger, 1963, and Pfaffenberger et al., 1976), it is now possible to breed animals that are apt to possess dog guide attributes and to test puppies as young as six weeks of age to ascertain if they possess the basic character traits adult guides must possess. The dog guide trainer today knows that the preselected animals waiting to be trained are literally the best of the best.

Scott Heywood begins testing.

Notes dog's reaction to leash.

Dog is not wary of glass.

Curious but not aggressive.

Dog walks close to highway.

He shows no fear.

Chapter 4

Choosing the Potential Guide

The quarantine section of Leader Dogs is a quiet place in spite of its proximity to the regular kennels. The three dogs currently in residence looked up quizzically as Jim Henderson and I entered the area on one of my first working days at the school. Each of these animals had been accepted during the previous week, having passed the school's basic requirements which include a brief series of tests completed while the donors wait. Over half the dogs taking these tests are rejected. Of those accepted, another percentage is rejected in quarantine or during training. Over seven out of ten dogs tested never become guides.

Similar high rejection percentages are common at all dog guide schools, causing many of them to rely on their own breeding programs in hopes of reducing rejection percentages. The Seeing Eye and Guide Dogs for the Blind have had breeding programs since their inceptions, yet in recent years have found themselves supplementing their own stock through donations. The demand for dog guides has grown beyond supply in every instance.

Leader Dogs did not initiate its own puppy program until 1973, relying instead on donated animals. This meant that blind individuals often had a long wait before acceptance into classes due to the high canine rejection percentage. After experimenting with a puppy-raising program, the school felt a breeding program would be worthwhile. Leader Dogs now averages 62 percent acceptance at adulthood with its own stock, and the percentage is increasing every year.

"Do you foresee the day when the school will rely only on its own breeding stock?" I asked Jim.

He shook his head. "We are constantly looking for good dogs," he said. "If a good dog walks through the door, we want him, whether he is our stock or not. I think every dog guide school feels the same way."

He turned to the kennel stalls and said, "These are nice dogs, and they were all donated."

We approached the stalls and each dog reacted in its own way. A quiet, heavyset, female Golden Retriever lacked the usual zest of her breed. In fact, she appeared extremely lethargic. She bent her head under my fingers and gazed up with sad eyes. Jim moved over and rubbed her ears. "She's not sure why she's here or what's happening to her," he said. "We're spending time with her now, getting to know her, play with her, and so forth."

We moved to the next stall. An alert, composed, male German Shepherd Dog cocked his head and looked up in a confident, gentle manner. He was friendly but not exuberant, typical of good German Shepherd temperament.

In the last stall was a lop-eared, male German Shepherd Dog-mix. He was bouncy, happy, and jumped up eagerly to have his ears scratched.

These were the "winners" as accepted dogs are called by the school. Within the next several days, every other animal coming in for testing was to be rejected.

Dogs scheduled for testing are prescreened by the office. All dog guide schools have general requirements encompassing the age of the dog, size, breed, and the donation process itself. These requirements vary from school to school. If the animal sounds suitable, an appointment is made to bring the dog in for testing.

Leader Dogs does not purchase animals; they are all donated. Neither are dogs tested anywhere but on the school grounds.

Both males and females are accepted, but they must be between one and two years of age. An animal over the age of two has already lost valuable working time. Since the school hopes for a working life of approximately eight years and the training process costs six thousand dollars, it would be unfair to all concerned to accept an older dog, knowing it will have to be replaced in a shorter period of time.

The school does not ordinarily evaluate puppies for possible future donation unless they are part of the school's breeding program. Even these latter puppies, discussed in the following chapters, are retested in the usual fashion when brought back at adulthood.

The size of the animal is important. The dog must measure between twenty-two and twenty-six inches at the shoulder. A dog any smaller will lack the necessary feel in harness. One any larger will be too much dog for the average blind person to handle comfortably.

Most commonly used are German Shepherd Dogs, Golden Retrievers, Labrador Retrievers, crosses of these breeds, and German Shepherd-Collie crosses. The school has experimented with numerous breeds and mixes and will accept isolated specimens of many breeds.

A relatively short coat is preferred for ease in grooming, although animals have been accepted with long coats if other attributes are outstanding. Recently the school placed a Belgian Tervuren as well as a Samoyed-mix, both with long coats. Since the school stresses the importance of daily grooming, longer coats have not been a problem.

The animal must be able to adapt to temperature changes and various weather conditions. Some dogs with short coats are incapable of functioning outdoors without extreme discomfort in cold, wet weather. Others with short coats, such as Labrador Retrievers, do not mind inclement weather or sub-freezing temperatures.

Breed characteristics are always taken into account before acceptance, whether it is adaptability to weather or other traits not directly related to the work itself. At least two breeds are no longer used because of tendencies to be aggressive towards other dogs. A few breeds, noted for household chewing, are accepted only when the training staff is convinced an individual animal does not have this bad habit.

"We want good-looking dogs that are intelligent, friendly, and physically sound," Jim explained as he continued to rub the ears of the sad-eyed Golden Retriever. "It's also interesting that we will accept some purebred dogs that might be disqualified from American Kennel Club shows due to breed faults." He pointed out that white German Shepherd Dogs often make excellent guides although this color is an automatic disqualification in the AKC conformation show ring. He also noted that the school had recently placed a Rhodesian Ridgeback that had been born without the distinctive ridge of fur along the back that characterizes the breed. "Don't misunderstand," he added quickly, "we want superior breed specimens in this work, but we overlook a few cosmetic faults such as eye color, coat color, or some such minor thing. Our number one priority is working ability."

Some dog guide schools do not utilize mixed-breed dogs, but Leader Dogs often accepts them, preferring crosses of the most commonly used breeds. "The advantage of using a purebred dog is that we are always fairly certain of breed characteristics and abilities," Jim explained. "Mixed breeds, however, often result in the combined, best character traits of each breed. In selecting our mixed-breeds we look for this kind of genetic background. Sometimes, we secure a dog that contributes some excellent characteristics from a breed not associated with guide work. For example, we just placed a German Shepherd-Saint Bernard mix. This was a nice dog to train, combining German Shepherd intelligence, willingness and initiative with Saint Bernard composure, patience and gentleness. It's hard to beat a combination like that!

"One other thing we verify before a dog is brought in for testing is the animal's previous lifestyle," Jim further explained. "A dog guide not only will work but will share the complete life of the person with whom it is placed. A dog that has matured in a kennel or that has been an 'outside' dog will lack the background preparation for this type of life. We can't use dogs raised like that. We want housedogs."

As we discussed the school's requirements, we noticed a van parked near the kennel entrance. A young couple was trying unsuccessfully to entice a large Alaskan Malamute to come out. Dick Dodd, the kennel master, was watching from a little distance, trying to make the embarrassing moment as comfortable as possible. Jim turned to me. "That dog is already rejected," he said flatly. "He's exhibiting uncertainty in a new environment and is hesitant to leave the security of his van. He might react the same way with a blind person. We can't afford to take that kind of chance."

With Jim's comments I realized that dog guide selection is based initially on the tester's observations of a dog's natural behavior and emotional reactions to quite commonplace situations. The requirements are so stringent that even this Malamute's initial hesitancy was cause for immediate rejection.

Test 1. Reaction to Immediate Environment
When a dog arrives at the school, the donor usually parks and seeks out the kennel office. The assigned staff member, usually Dick Dodd, then approaches the car. The testing has begun, although the donor is unaware of the fact. The dog's every action is being observed and analyzed. Is it placidly sitting on the car seat, looking about with interest, or is it nervously darting back and forth? Is it whining or panting heavily? Does it appear frightened, nervous, or overly excited? Dog guides must be relaxed and at ease wherever they go. The dog that appears nervous, anxious, overly excited, or frightened in this situation will most likely exhibit the same characteristics elsewhere. The ideal dog appears composed and in complete control, ready to deal with its surroundings in a sensible, confident manner. It should be watching what is going on with docile interest.

Test 2. Reaction to Stranger Approaching

As he approaches the car, the tester carefully observes the dog. When does the animal become alert to a stranger's presence, and what occurs at that moment? A normal amount of protective instinct is expected, but an openly aggressive dog will be rejected. It should not, for example, lunge against the windows in a frenzy of aggressive barking. The dog should appear watchful, interested, and calm.

The tester then stands back while the donor takes the dog from the car. The animal's every move is continually analyzed. Does the dog now appear aggressive, perhaps growling or barking with hackles raised? Does it appear rigid, tense, or sullen? Does it repeatedly attempt to get back in the car? Does it put its tail between its legs and attempt to dart or hide behind the donor's back? Does it seem highly nervous or overly excited? Is it panting, whining, or attempting to run in circles? All these are negative signs and cause for rejection. The dog should be relaxed, confident, and friendly as it is removed from the car to meet the tester. It should not exhibit any sign of aggressiveness, shyness, fear, distrust, nervousness, tenseness, or sullenness.

Test 3. Reaction to Stranger Touch

At this point, the tester approaches to pet the dog. Now how does the dog react? Does it accept this greeting in a friendly fashion? It should willingly and confidently accept the tester's touch and exhibit no sign of fear, nervousness, shyness, aggressiveness, uncertainty, or distrust. Its whole attitude must indicate that it likes people and has an outstanding background in being around strangers.

Test 4. Reaction to Stranger Taking Leash—Leash Restraint

A good number of dogs have failed by this time, although only a few minutes have elapsed and donors are usually unaware any testing has occurred. Those dogs that haven't failed are now taken on leash for a short walk across the parking lot and along the neighboring highway shoulder for perhaps five minutes.

The dog's reactions are noted as soon as the tester takes the lead. Does it resent or fear being taken from the donor, perhaps swiveling on leash, violently pulling, whining, barking, or attempting to nip or mouth the tester's hands or legs in an effort to get away? Does it exhibit any other signs of resentment, aggressiveness, panic, fear, or nervousness not seen before? Such dogs must be rejected. They are too dependent on existing family members, unable to instantly adjust in a controlled fashion to a new and confusing situation. Ideally, the dog will exhibit interest and some uncertainty at being turned over to a complete stranger, but it should not react in any of the negative ways listed above.

As the walk begins, the tester notes the dog's reactions to the leash itself. Does the dog resent this restraint or fear it in some fashion? Dogs that resent being on leash often are not leash-broken, indicating a lack of background socialization as well as learning experiences around people, animals, and in strange places or they may be exhibiting an independent nature that will also resent training efforts. Whatever the reason, these dogs are rejected.

Dogs that fear being on leash are equally difficult to teach. Sometimes this fear stems from an extremely sensitive nature that would result in an inability to adjust to the demands and complexities of the training program. At other times this fear develops as a result of overly harsh training techniques or use of the leash as a means of punishment. Regardless of the reason, these dogs are also rejected.

The tester gives no commands as he walks along. He does not attempt to teach or correct the dog in any way. He is looking for an animal that tends to pull ahead, or one that keeps a pace or two ahead while looking about with interest. These are signs of initiative and confidence. A lagging, balking, skittish, or seemingly dull dog will be rejected.

Although no commands are given, the tester talks to the animal and watches for the dog's reactions to this verbal communication. Every animal will show some confusion and concern as it is taken from the donor, but it should almost immediately adapt to the new situation, relating to the tester in a positive fashion. It might be playful, exhibiting enthusiasm and joy at being taken for a walk, or it may be quite subdued, moving along with a quiet demeanor, depending on its individual character. The dog, however, should indicate in some fashion that it is constantly aware of the tester and does not mind being with him.

Some dogs move out to the end of the leash and investigate on their own, sniff the ground, and otherwise ignore the person walking with them. Such animals are exhibiting an independent streak that is counterproductive to a training program where intense interest in people and willingness to please are more important than canine interests.

Test 5. Rapidly Changing Environment—Noise—Traffic

As the tester moves along, he observes the dog's reactions to the things they are passing and the noises around them. Two highways are adjacent to the school, and the environment changes rapidly from the quiet parking lot to the highway shoulder with heavy, fast-moving traffic. The dog should be aware of all moving vehicles, but should not fear them. The animal should be alert, indicating by the way it moves on the leash that it would not mindlessly walk out in front of speeding traffic. At no time should the dog exhibit nervousness or fear of any of the things it sees, hears or passes.

Test 6. Body Sensitivity—Physical Faults

While the dog and tester are together, the animal's basic physical condition is noted. Does it appear healthy? Does it seem to have good eyesight and hearing? Is the coat in good condition? Does it have a weak or sway back? Is the gait wobbly? Is there any sign of limping? Are the leg bones strong and equally well-proportioned? Are the feet and pasterns strong? Does the dog appear tired? Does it look as if it has stamina? Is it well-balanced?

Stopping, the tester runs his hands over the dog's entire body, noting the depth of chest, lung capacity, and bone structure.

A dog guide's hearing and eyesight must be good. It must have stamina, adequate lung capacity, and good bone structure. Its job will require a great deal of walking while leaning into a harness, and its back, legs, and feet are very important. A sway back or wobbly gait will be cause for rejection. "Flat feet" might be an occupational hazard in a few human professions, but a dog guide school will reject dogs with broken-down pasterns, weak feet or pads.

While this brief examination is conducted, the tester notes the dog's reactions to touch on various parts of the body. Does the animal accept this examination, or does it fear or resent any part of it? The latter dogs are rejected.

Continuing the walk, the tester reaches down and notes the dog's reactions to sudden touch on the head, back, and hip from behind. Some dogs startle at touch or gestures originating behind them. Others are sensitive to touch on certain parts of their bodies. Dogs with such body sensitivity are poor candidates for guide work, as are dogs that startle at movements behind them. They are untrustworthy in all but carefully monitored situations.

Test 7. Reinforcement of Confidence—Willingness

Returning to the school, the tester has a good idea of the basic character and general physical condition of the dog. He also has learned a great deal about the dog's intelligence and interest simply through observation.

As one last test, however, he walks the dog up a metal, open-backed staircase. Some dogs move up without the slightest hesitation. Others will hold back, sniff the stairs, and then slowly begin ascending with encouragement. Both reactions are acceptable as they indicate a willingness to follow human direction in a situation the average dog would rather avoid. A few dogs will panic, pulling backwards on the lead and struggling to free themselves. The latter dogs are rejected. They may refuse to guide their blind masters over unusual footings or into unusual environments.

These seven tests, lasting ten to fifteen minutes, are based completely on observation. If the tester is uncertain as to a given response, he will request a back-up analysis from a second tester. Rejected dogs are given back to the donors with a brief explanation. Although such donors are disappointed, a few border on belligerence, accusing the school of being unfair and giving a cursory exam. Some feel the tester should have tried to teach the dog in some capacity. Others state their pets simply need a day or two to acclimate themselves and then will behave perfectly.

The school tries to be as tactful as possible. There is no leeway allowed. A dog guide school will not start with any indication of pretraining problems in hopes training or time will solve things.

The swiftness with which judgment is passed on incoming animals amazes most people. In this brief period of time the tester eliminates dogs with obvious physical disabilities and character deficiencies. Those accepted will appear healthy and structurally sound. They are friendly, confident and seem intelligent and willing to please.

Accepted dogs are turned over to the school and legal papers are signed to this effect. Should any dog be rejected during the program, it will be returned to the donor, or, if the donor prefers, it will be turned over to someone on the school's waiting list for such animals. Rejection can and does occur at any time as the work becomes more complex and unforeseen problem areas become apparent.

The donor also agrees to allow the school to castrate or spay his animal during advanced training. Some dogs are rejected for various reasons after these operations, and donors must be aware of all aspects surrounding donation.

After the legal papers are signed, the accepted dogs are moved into quarantine. The school now hopefully will be their home for the next five to six months.

Quarantine is not a particularly happy time for most dogs. The lethargic Golden Retriever and her two kennel companions that had recently been accepted were undergoing a great deal of stress as they tried to adjust to the new things occurring in their lives. Jim Henderson explained the school's experiences with dogs during this period of time, which usually lasts ten days to two weeks. As he did so, he placed the Golden Retriever in the exercise yard, watching as she walked slowly to a corner, curled up and listlessly closed her eyes.

The majority of dogs perk up within a day or two, just as the majority of household dogs left at boarding kennels adapt to their new world. Some, however, cannot cope with the switch in environment. They brood, mope, refuse to eat, show no interest in their surroundings, and display signs of altered temperament. Once in awhile, the school has sent dogs home whose behavior had switched overnight to the point where they could be termed fear-biters (dogs that bite irrationally through fear). Since these dogs must live several months in a kennel atmosphere for training purposes, it is important that they adjust rapidly or the school will be unsuccessful in training them. Dogs that cannot make this adjustment are rejected before training begins.

As soon as an accepted dog enters quarantine it is given a medicated bath to ensure no external parasites are brought onto the premises. It is then subjected to an exhaustive physical examination by Dr. Eastman. Every conceivable laboratory and physical test is given, and it is x-rayed for bone deformities such as hip dysplasia as well as lung and heart defects through utilization of a unique, rotating, sling x-ray machine.

These tests often turn up both major and minor problems of which donors were unaware. Animals with bone deformities or other serious physical defects will be rejected. Once in awhile, however, Dr. Eastman will accept and treat animals with minor, correctable problems if treatment time will not be lengthy.

The long stay in quarantine helps ensure that no incubating virus or communicable disease is spread to the dogs in training. Dog guide schools fear any sort of infection going through their kennels, and all have a close working relationship with university and laboratory research programs in efforts to isolate and develop vaccines for contagious diseases.

While in quarantine, undesirable character traits may become evident that could not be noted during initial testing. A few dogs, for example, become aggressive when eating. They do not want anyone to approach them or their food. This behavior usually originates during early puppyhood when litter mates growl at each other to secure a better spot without interruptions at meal time. If this behavior is left uncorrected, many dogs reach maturity thinking it is perfectly permissible to threaten anyone who approaches while they are eating. It is a trait usually seen in dominant dogs with a high level of protective instinct. It cannot be tolerated in a dog guide, and staff members test for it while dogs are in quarantine. Someone will place his hands quickly in the dog's food dish while it is eating. Any animal that snarls, growls, snaps, or attempts to bite is rejected.

Dogs in quarantine are eased into group exercise. Potential fighters are rejected. The others utilize exercise time by playing together. They quickly form kennel friendships which help them adjust to the changes in their lives.

The kennel staff and trainers spend as much time as possible with the new recruits. It is not unusual to find one of the trainers, on his lunch hour, in the quarantine section playing with the new dogs. He is not only helping to ease the stress surrounding the quarantine period, but is also making mental notes on each dog's character and response. If he is scheduled for an upcoming beginner's group, he is already deciding how he will begin working with each animal.

A walk up an open staircase.

Moving up with encourgement.

Coming down without fear.

Quarantine can be a stressful time as dogs adjust to a new lifestyle, but kennel friendships are quickly formed. The school rejects dogs that can't get along with other animals.

Once the dogs have settled down to kennel life, have passed all physical tests, and Dr. Eastman feels incubation periods for any diseases or viruses have passed, they are moved into the Beginners' Kennel where they await placement with an upcoming "string." Their training days are about to begin.

Two of the three dogs visited that day in quarantine, as Jim Henderson and I discussed and observed the school's incoming tests, went on to become guides. The third was rejected in beginner's training.

If you think the sad, mopey Golden Retriever would be the one rejected, you're as wrong as I was. The dog adjusted quickly, went on to enjoy her new life and work, and soon formed warm friendships with the staff. She was a serious, willing worker and undertook every facet of her job with interest and thoroughness.

The confident, alert, male German Shepherd Dog also went on to become a guide. He learned quickly, bringing a tireless dedication to his job.

It was the bouncy, happy, lop-eared German Shepherd-mix that was rejected. The very traits that made him so appealing to his sighted admirers caused his rejection. His main interest in people was to play and have his ears scratched. He had no intention of actually working.

69

Puppy at Guide Dogs for the Blind is tested for response to sudden noise, in this case a gun shot. Future dog guides must not fear sudden, loud sounds. Tests differ from school to school. Both Leader Dogs and Guide Dogs are showing approximately 60–65 percent acceptance at adulthood from among foster puppies.

Chapter 5

Science Helps Dog Guide Breeding and Puppy Programs

"Take a look at what's in the yard off the kennel!" Ed Lange called on his way to the office. He and I walked over to the fenced yard, but I could see nothing except a dog house, a few bushes and grass. Then a general squirming began under the largest bush, and seven Golden Retriever puppies, who had been sleeping in a heap, gradually woke up and scrambled over each other in their hurry to greet their visitors. By name this was Litter #283, bred for the school and born six weeks previously. Ed explained that they were to be given physicals and then to be temperament tested, and he asked if I would help.

The ease with which Ed talked about these puppies and the confidence he expressed in the accuracy of the tests we were about to perform made me wonder how people from the early years of service work and especially dog guide training would react to what we were about to do. It was a dream shared by all early breeders and trainers, but up until 1946 it remained largely a dream. How could anyone predict with any accuracy that a six-week-old puppy had the potential to be a dog guide?

The early German schools felt the German Shepherd Dog was one breed apt to possess the qualities needed in a dog guide or any other service field. The history of modern service dog programs, in fact, is interwoven with the interesting history of this one breed of dog, developed almost single-handedly by a German cavalry captain, Max von Stephanitz (1950).

In 1899, Rittmeister von Stephanitz and a friend, Artur Meyer, attended one of Germany's first organized dog shows in Karlsruhe. A working farm dog, named Hektor Linksrheim, caught von Stephanitz's eye as being one of the finest specimens of native German herding dogs he had ever seen. Von Stephanitz had long appreciated the working qualities of these dogs and had been breeding them for several years, hoping to embody in one strain all the finest characteristics of the various herding types found throughout Germany. Hektor was promptly purchased and renamed Horand von Grafrath. Von

Stephanitz saw in him the ideal foundation sire for the type of dog he envisioned.

Shortly afterwards, von Stephanitz and a few friends who were also interested in German herding dogs formed a society named the Verein fur Deutsche Schaferhund (S.V.) which became the German parent club for the German Shepherd Dog. Today it has over fifty thousand members, and its records date back to the purchase of Horand, whose name is followed by SZ I.

Max von Stephanitz devoted the remainder of his life to the German Shepherd Dog, while studying and comparing all European breeds. He culled ruthlessly within his breeding program, keeping only those dogs who could prove themselves through training at maturity to be both mentally and physically sound.

Within a few years, von Stephanitz's theories and breeding practices proved correct. The German Shepherd Dog quickly developed from numerous homogenous strains into the major and distinctive breed we know today. Dog shows were becoming popular in Germany, and von Stephanitz insisted on stringent, adult temperament tests for his increasingly popular breed. He had no use for either shy dogs or overly aggressive ones. By the time Konrad Most began training dogs for service work in World War I, the German Shepherd Dog was considered one of the best working breeds in the world.

Max von Stephanitz had foreseen changing lifestyles in Germany and the resulting displacement of dogs that had their origins in herding work. People were leaving rural areas in increasing numbers and moving to cities, bringing the herding dogs of their childhoods with them. Just as human lifestyles change, so the lifestyles of dogs would have to change.

Von Stephanitz incorporated his dogs into the environment in which they lived. If they could no longer guard flocks, they could use the same abilities to guard homes and families and aid the police in the apprehension of criminals. If they could no longer use their noses to track wandering sheep, they could use their highly developed sense of smell to track criminals, lost children, or seek victims of disasters buried under rubble or in an avalanche. If they could no longer work independently in the fields, they could use their initiative, intelligence, and common sense to serve as message carriers in the army, patrol dogs, and search and rescue dogs. The possibilities were numerous, and to von Stephanitz's delight the German Shepherd Dog rose to each task.

To Max von Stephanitz, the unpardonable sin was to allow this breed to be useless. He noted a marked deterioration in character among individuals left to mature in kennels with little or nothing to do. If a dog had no legitimate job, then jobs must be created! As a result, he devised a series of obedience, tracking, and protection tests which allowed non-working dogs to utilize and prove their abilities in some capacity. Eventually, no dog in his Verein could participate in adult conformation classes at dog shows or have its progeny properly registered without first proving its worth by either working in a service field or passing working tests. These tests developed into today's German "Schutzhund" (Protection Dog) titles, with von Stephanitz's policies continuing to this day in Germany and many other countries as well.

Dorothy Harrison Eustis (Humphrey and Warner, 1934) also preferred the German Shepherd Dog as a working breed, and the Fortunate Fields program was devoted exclusively to its breeding and training. As with any program of this scope, there was limited space for puppies, and they were boarded with local families until maturity, when they were brought back to the school. The adult dogs were then placed in various fields of work. As long as litters had several options at adulthood the system worked well. At Fortunate Fields the goal was to find a suitable place for every animal, as traits which meant failure in one area of work were often assets in another.

Eventually, through careful record-keeping, analysis, and observational study, the Fortunate Fields' staff could pinpoint characteristics which indicated aptitudes for specific tasks before dogs were started in training. By the time The Seeing Eye was established in the United States, adult dogs with high potential for this work were selected on the basis of several screening tests.

It is interesting that the development of service dog programs and the subsequent need for breeders and trainers to correctly analyze canine character and abilities roughly parallels the emergence of the scientific disciplines of both ethology and comparative psychology in the early decades of this century. Ethology is the study of animal gestures, movements and rituals for the purpose of interpreting animal behavior and character. Comparative psychology is primarily the study of animals for the purpose of learning more about human behavior and character. Scientists around the world, dog breeders, and trainers were beginning to thoroughly investigate and interpret canine behavior and character at about the same periods of time. Many of the theories of astute breeders and trainers, such as von Stephanitz's observation concerning character deterioration in kennel dogs, were proved correct and were backed up with thorough scientific data. Even more exciting was that scientific research pinpointed why, how, and when this type of character deterioration occurred and what could be done to avoid it. The secret lay, for the most part, in early puppyhood.

One person who brought much of this data into the practical world of breeding and training dogs, and especially the breeding and selection of dog guides, was Clarence Pfaffenberger (1963). During World War II, at the Dog Training and Reception Center for Dogs for Defense and the Army, in San Carlos, California, Pfaffenberger, serving as regional director, laboriously screened over six thousand donated dogs before finding eighteen hundred suitable for service work. He noticed that dogs had a better chance of passing the tests if they had been raised in an environment where they shared their masters' lives and had close associations with people. Yet many of these animals failed when placed into training programs. Seemingly similar animals were not similar at all when it came to working performance! He wondered why. Perhaps differences in upbringing resulted in the wide variance in adult working behavior and capabilities. He asked Dogs for Defense to begin some sort of research program but the immediate needs of the war effort made such a program unrealistic.

As the war continued, Dogs for Defense supplied a few prescreened dogs for use by blinded veterans to The Seeing Eye and took an active interest in supplying prescreened dogs to the newly formed Guide Dogs for the Blind in California. By the time the war was over, Clarence Pfaffenberger was serving on the board of directors at Guide Dogs for the Blind. He eventually assumed a vice presidency, a post held until his death in 1967.

Guide Dogs for the Blind immediately discovered what Leader Dogs and The Seeing Eye already knew—that securing a steady supply of suitable dogs for applicants was not an easy task. A breeding program was started at once, with the first litter registered in the autumn of 1942. In spite of this, Guide Dogs for the Blind graduated fewer than thirty-five dogs in its first five years of existence.

Pfaffenberger wondered again why so few prescreened dogs succeeded in training. Were the tests at fault, were they breeding the wrong type of dog, or were there factors in the raising of these animals that influenced performance later in life? The school decided to seek out current scientific information on breeding and raising dogs, with emphasis on puppy selection and upbringing in order to determine inherited characteristics and potential as early in life as possible.

After seeking advice from several sources, Pfaffenberger, in 1946, was directed to Dr. John Paul Scott at the Roscoe B. Jackson Memorial Laboratory in Bar Harbor, Maine, where some of the nation's foremost geneticists, sociologists, and comparative psychologists were beginning what was to become an intensive thirteen-year research project involving the effects of heredity and subsequent environmental influences on the behavior of the dog.

When Pfaffenberger arrived at the Jackson Laboratory the research project had been under way for only ten months but was already producing a wealth of new information on the formation of behavioral patterns in dogs. Dr. Scott and his associates offered to share their findings with Pfaffenberger, as well as help with Guide Dogs' breeding and puppy raising program. This association and friendship continued until Pfaffenberger's death, long after the original scientists had gone on to various research facilities and universities to expand on their newly acquired knowledge.

At the Jackson Laboratory, scientists had chosen five breeds of dogs to study, selected on the basis of size for ease in handling, as well as characters roughly similar to human character types. These were the Wirehair Fox Terrier, inheriting bold, aggressive tendencies; the Cocker Spaniel, willing to please and sociable; the Basenji, aloof, independent and quite primitive or wild in nature; the Shetland Sheepdog, sensitive and needing approval; the Beagle, sociable yet independent. Each breed and later cross-breed was studied from birth to adulthood under controlled environmental conditions.

One of the first major discoveries at the Jackson Laboratory (Scott & Fuller, 1965) was that genetic behavioral differences in dogs exist, but these do not appear spontaneously in a finished form. They develop under and are highly influenced by environmental factors. In addition, as a puppy matures it passes through several developmental periods during which "critical periods" may occur. Scientists define a "critical period" as a special time in life when an organizational process is under way, proceeding rapidly and open to change or modification. Even limited experiences during these "critical periods" will almost invariably modify and have effects on an animal's later behavior in keeping with the genetic predisposition of each individual.

Research at the Jackson Laboratory eventually encompassed a detailed study of each period in the dog's development with emphasis on what occurs during the "critical periods." This research not only helped scientists in the study of human behavior, but later proved invaluable to dog guide schools, service dog centers and all people interested in dogs.

For Pfaffenberger some nagging thoughts were put to rest. The Jackson Laboratory research proved that past experiences do indeed influence adult performance and capabilities, and especially if they occur during the special "critical periods."

For the staff at Guide Dogs for the Blind, this data indicated that dogs inherit capabilities or tendencies, but these develop under and may be altered or modified by experience. It followed, therefore, that it might be possible to channel behavior through careful upbringing, especially if one knows how to utilize the periods when behavioral development is most highly influenced.

Scientists and Guide Dogs for the Blind concluded that puppies should be bred from the best stock and then raised for the express purpose of becoming guides. This would help direct all behavior towards a specific adult goal. The breeding program was improved, utilizing animals with working backgrounds, and special puppy selection tests were formulated under the guidance of Dr. Scott and his associates. The tradition of placing puppies until adulthood with local families was expanded to include a comprehensive introduction to the various situations and environments a future dog guide would be apt to encounter.

The results were dramatic and almost instantaneous! Within three years the percentage of accepted puppies at adulthood at Guide Dogs for the Blind had skyrocketed to 60 percent! This was felt to be the combined result of the improved breeding and testing programs, utilization of the puppy's developmental periods to best advantage, combined with guidance for the foster families, and cooperation among the school's staff. This figure of approximately 60 percent acceptance has remained fairly constant to this date.

The discoveries at the Jackson Laboratory have explained how, why, and when the dog bonds to man, and how experiences or lack of them can create behavioral differences in genetically similar animals. These developmental periods are categorized by scientists, as per the research of Dr. John Paul Scott, Dr. John L. Fuller and their associates (Scott and Fuller, 1965) as follows:

Developmental Period 1—Neonatal Period

This period lasts from birth to approximately two weeks of age and is considered by scientists to be a critical one from a physical standpoint for the establishment of the neonatal pattern of nutrition, the acquisition of antibodies from the mother's milk, and for physical survival. The puppy comes into life blind, deaf, and unable to adequately control its body temperature. It is completely dependent on the care of its dam (or substitute) for survival. Food, protection, care, and warmth all must be supplied or the puppy will die. The newborn is capable of only a few activities: a sucking reflex (nursing), crawling (accompanied by a rooting motion of the head used to orient itself to the mother's body for warmth and food), elimination (which cannot take place unless the body is stimulated by the mother's tongue), and vocalization (indicating pain, cold or hunger and to which the dam responds).

The puppy's existence revolves around the dam, and it is not psychologically influenced by its environment or even its litter mates except for whatever group warmth these may supply. Unable to physically or mentally function in a self-sufficient manner, the behavior of the puppy is uniquely organized towards the dam and the requirements of neonatal existence. The dam rarely leaves her puppies during this period but remains nearby to ensure that all needs are met.

The puppy's brain, sense organs, and motor organs are all undeveloped. Movements and responses are slow and clumsy. The ability to learn at this age is very limited. The puppy primarily grows and gathers strength. To human onlookers, a puppy at this age seems to be another species as its behavior is so different from that to come.

Developmental Period 2—Transition Period

This period begins when the eyes fully open at approximately two weeks of age. It ends when the ears are completely functional at approximately three weeks of age. During this one short week the puppy undergoes major, rapid biological changes, from a dependent newborn to a more adult type of animal. As the eyes open, the puppy begins to focus on its immediate environment and can better orient its movements, crawling both backwards and forwards. By three weeks of age it responds to people, other animals and objects at a distance.

At two weeks the puppy is able to lap milk from a dish. By three weeks it can stand and eat in an adult fashion, although the newly emerging teeth limit chewing ability and food must be a semi-liquid type.

By the third week of life, the puppy is better able to control its body temperature and is walking, although clumsily. It begins to venture away from its sleeping area to eliminate and the stimulation of the mother's tongue is no longer necessary to accomplish this latter function.

As the puppy's eyesight develops it expands its social relationships to include its litter mates. Tail wagging begins, as does play fighting, which is the foundation of the dominance order within the litter. The mother's constant care begins to gradually decrease. Her relationship to the puppy is about to alter. At the time of weaning she begins to discipline her offspring by utilizing threatening behavior.

The ears open completely at about twenty days of age (an average of nineteen and a half days), and the puppy exhibits its first startle reaction to sound. Since this response is easily seen by observers, scientists use it as the signal that the transition period is ending. At about the same period of time, the puppy shows distress when moved to a strange location even a short distance from the litter box or nest area, whereas previously it was quiet in such a situation as long as well-fed and warm. The puppy is bonding to a particular spot or environment as well as the things or individuals in it and becoming emotionally upset when removed.

At the end of the transition period (usually between eighteen and twenty-one days of age), the puppy develops a sudden ability to be conditioned or taught through experience in an adult fashion. Puppies in the early neonatal period can learn in connection with their sucking behavior, and research (Fox, 1971) indicates that there is a gradual increase in the ability to learn throughout the neonatal and transitional periods, although very slowly and perhaps not permanently. At the end of the transition period, however, there is a definite change in the speed with which puppies can be taught, and their responses become quite stable.

By the end of the transition period, the puppy has the capacities to see, hear, move, eat, and respond to stimuli in an adult fashion. Up to this point, the puppy has been largely insulated from a psychological standpoint from its environment, but now all its senses are operating and preparing it for the next critical period. The puppy becomes acutely sensitive to all experiences it is encountering or about to encounter. These initial experiences will have profound effects on the puppy's future behavior. If they were to occur at any other time in life, they would have different effects.

Developmental Period 3—Period of Socialization

This period begins at approximately twenty-one days of age and extends to approximately twelve weeks of age, at which time a puppy readily begins to explore areas beyond twenty-five to thirty feet from the nest or litter box. FROM A BEHAVIORAL STANDPOINT THIS CRITICAL PERIOD IS THE MOST IMPORTANT ONE IN A DOG'S LIFE.

During these nine weeks the puppy forms emotional attachments towards those who will be its future close associates. Other dogs, animals and human beings all enter into the process if the puppy has exposure to them throughout the period. Researchers at the Jackson Laboratory discovered that only twenty minutes per week is adequate for satisfactory socialization to take place during this period.

The socialization process proceeds rapidly in the early part of the period, peaks around seven weeks of age, then decreases just as rapidly throughout the latter part of the period (see Figure 3) when two developing factors interfere. First of all, at about seven weeks of age the puppy begins to develop increasing fear reactions to strange individuals and objects. This trait is necessary for survival in a natural state. In addition, the puppy is already emotionally attached to familiar objects and individuals and will prefer these to the unknown and strange.

The Jackson Laboratory scientists discovered that if individual socialization is lacking during this period, puppies will be unable to form completely satisfactory relationships later in life. If they are raised without any human contact whatsoever until twelve weeks of age, they will react like fearful, wild animals when approached and are unable to form close associations with people. If raised in complete isolation from other dogs, they are unable to interact with them in a normal fashion as adults, exhibiting varying degrees of intolerance, avoidance or an inability to mate. Although these are extremes in lack of socialization, it is easy to understand how limiting or expanding the socialization process during this period can have permanent effects on adult behavior. By giving each puppy optimal socialization experiences during these weeks, it is possible to help shape future behavior in the most positive fashion.

Besides individuals, the puppy is forming strong emotional attachments to its environment and the inanimate objects in it. This emotional attachment increases towards the end of the socialization period and is intensified by the development of fear reactions starting at seven weeks compounded by the puppy's experiences or lack of them in

Figure 3—Time Relationships of Certain Developmental Processes in the Dog

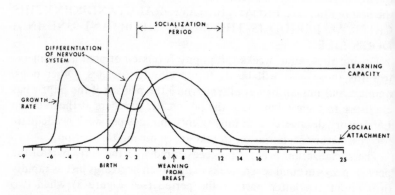

Processes are indicated semidiagrammatically in terms of weeks prior to and after birth.

new environments. Just as with social relationships, the puppy will prefer a familiar environment and the things in it. Unless the environment is expanded during this time, the puppy may be unable to cope with a shift in environment later in life. The Jackson Laboratory research showed that any dog, regardless of breed, kept in a confined existence beyond twelve weeks of age will show increasing, persistent timidity and lack of confidence with unfamiliar situations and environments later in life. By offering optimal experiences outside the initial environment, it is possible to help ensure that a puppy's future behavior is organized to include the confident acceptance of new objects and environments. This involves introducing the puppy to as many new environments as possible, even if only a short distance from the litter box.

Scientists feel that the best time for a puppy to permanently switch environments is about seven weeks of age when the socialization process is at its peak. At this age the puppy has not had too much interference from developing fears and can still readily make social adjustments of all kinds. The older the puppy becomes, the more risks are involved.

During the latter portion of the socialization period (weeks eight to twelve) the puppy is physically and mentally ready, in fact eager, to cope with problem solving and disciplined learning situations. THESE

80

WEEKS ARE CONSIDERED CRITICAL ONES FOR INTRO-
DUCING THE PUPPY TO ITS FUTURE ADULT ROLE IN LIFE,
ALWAYS BEARING IN MIND THE PUPPY'S CLUMSY MOTOR
ABILITIES AND SHORT ATTENTION SPAN. If this type of
instruction is not started at this time, it becomes increasingly difficult to
introduce later. Scientists feel that certain preliminary experiences are
necessary during this period in order for the dog to later learn various
tasks. If these are not forthcoming, the puppy may teach itself that
learning anything outside the first, simple environment is not
important. Attempting to train such a dog later in life for consistency of
action when performing various tasks can be a frustrating experience.
Depriving a puppy of mental stimulation during this period will have
varying effects on future performance.

By the time the puppy is twelve weeks of age, it has largely organized
its behavior. If the puppy has had many successful experiences involving all aspects of the socialization process and comes from sound genetic stock, it will be prepared to mature into a well-adjusted, confident
adult.

Developmental Period 4—Juvenile Period

This period begins at approximately twelve weeks of age, when the
puppy readily explores at greater distances from its nest or litter box,
and ends at sexual maturity which may occur anytime between five
months and a year-and-a-half, depending on the individual dog. During
this period the puppy slowly continues to grow, increasing in strength
and motor skills. It investigates as much as possible, learning from the
environment as it does so. The foundation for future behavior has been
established and now stabilizes, although behavioral development does
continue throughout the dog's life, past experiences serving as a basis
for response.

During the juvenile period, guidance must continue to ensure that the
puppy is directed towards suitable adult behavior. By fifteen weeks of
age, the puppy is showing patterns of behavior typical of adults. In a
natural state the dominance order within the litter or pack is already
well established, and increasing intolerance is seen towards strange
animals entering the territory. These territorial defense reactions inhibit
further attachment between adult dog and adult dog, adult dog and
people.

The period ends with the first estrus cycle in the female or the
emergence of adult sexual behavior in both sexes.

Forced training at the Jackson Laboratory as a puppy is taught to remain on the scales while weighed.

Outside runs where the puppies lived from 16 to 52 weeks of age. In the background is the nursery wing of Behavior Lab.

In this first problem-solving experience, the puppy must go away from the goal on the side of the barrier in order to reach it.

Nursery room interior. Shetland Sheepdog female carries a puppy in a retrieving test.

Developmental Period 5—Pubertal Period

This period begins at sexual maturity and ends when the dog becomes sexually active. It is often a short period as females will usually mate during their first estrus cycle if allowed to do so.

Developmental Period 6—Parental Period

This period begins with the conception of the young. Reproductive activity continues for many years, ending about the age of eight in females and much later in males, while physical vigor gradually declines over the years. During the parental period the dog exhibits behavioral patterns having to do with care of the young, and the life cycle repeats itself.

Since Guide Dogs for the Blind as well as The Seeing Eye bred their own stock, they immediately benefited from the research at the Jackson Laboratory. Guide Dogs for the Blind subsequently had the benefit of nearly twenty years' advice from some of the nation's top scientific minds as it organized its breeding, selection, and foster raising program. Leader Dogs, meanwhile, was successful in meeting its canine quota through donations, and although interested in the other schools' results, did not feel the need for a similar program.

By 1970, however, things began to change. Increasing numbers of visually handicapped individuals wanted guides from Leader Dogs. These students, in time, wanted replacements. With a 70-80 percent rejection figure among donated adult dogs, the possibility of piloting a

Clarence Pfaffenberger, who brought scientific discoveries into the practical world of breeding and training dogs, especially dog guides.

84

A puppy tester at Guide Dogs for the Blind. Future dog guides must be friendly and confident around people.

puppy program began to take shape. It was seen as a viable way to meet the demand for Leader Dogs.

The program was started in 1973 after a study of research data and evaluation of what other dog guide schools were doing with similar programs. During that year sixty-seven puppies were donated to the program and placed with 4-H club members. The following year forty-one of these puppies went on to become guides.

The school was encouraged with the results and decided to continue the project. The following year the program was expanded to one hundred fifteen puppies. Of these, seventy-seven went on to become guides. Increasing practical experience helped shape the preselection process, and statistics were kept on top-producing kennel stock. The 4-H program continued to improve as did liaison with the school. Even those members of the office staff who had been concerned about the paper work and time spent in keeping tabs on so many puppies had to agree that the program was worth it. Today, statistics show that 62 percent of puppies bred for the school are accepted at adulthood. This figure is in keeping with the incoming percentages of puppies accepted at adulthood at other dog guide schools.

The breeding and raising program at Leader Dogs operates within the framework of the research of Dr. John Paul Scott and his associates. Knowing something about this research helps anyone interested in dogs in general or dog guides in particular understand what occurs as puppies are born, tested, and raised for a dog guide school.

Above, the best way to identify each puppy is to shave a portion of the legs.

Above, this puppy scores well in retrieving by showing interest in the ball.

Above, confidence and willingness are shown by this puppy in the recall test.

Below, a perfect response is given by this puppy to the toe pinch test.

Chapter 6

Puppy Tests

In their outdoor yard the seven Golden Retriever puppies Ed Lange and I were about to test seemed identical. They not only looked alike, they appeared equally playful, inquisitive, and friendly. At first glance their behavior did not seem to emanate from seven individuals but from one litter unit. As soon as one puppy happened to see something new and began to investigate, the others immediately followed. Scientists call this "allelomimetic behavior," with animals reacting as a pack rather than as individuals. They may run, lie down, sleep, walk, investigate, and perform other activities as a group.

A misleading impression might be obtained by briefly observing puppies together. They often appear to draw strengths and weaknesses from each other through imitative behavior. Differences are apparent when puppies are observed individually, and they become pronounced when specific tests are administered to pinpoint characteristics that might otherwise remain undetected until later in life.

How different from each other were these puppies going to be? Ed must have had similar thoughts as he said, "They really look and act alike, don't they? It will be interesting to see how they test out."

Our first stop was Dr. Eastman's office where each puppy was examined and given shots for distemper, hepatitis, leptospirosis, and parainfluenza. This particular litter had had one major disadvantage to date. The dam had been ill and could not properly nurse them. This required supplemental bottle feeding, and the entire litter was small for its age.

While we carried puppies back and forth to the play yard, Ed commented on how composed and quiet they were. Not a single puppy seemed afraid of any of the new experiences. Each puppy looked about with interest, settled comfortably into our arms and underwent the brief indignity of the physical with aplomb.

"We breed for a specific type of temperament so this is not unusual," Ed said. "Our litters are born in homes and are given human socialization and experiences on the premises, so these puppies don't find what we're doing out of the ordinary. Remember too, they had to adjust to the car ride, the puppy yard and the immediate separation from their old environment. So far they've had a stressful day, but they're doing fine!"

As the puppies finished their physicals, Ed explained what we would be looking for within the tests and why. "By bringing in our puppies at the end of their sixth week of life, we capitalize on the peak of the socialization period," he said. "They're emotionally and physically ready for a life away from the dam and each other. They're eager for new experiences and have not had much time to form impressions based on environmental factors. We feel we can pinpoint inherited character traits not yet influenced by experience.

"The tests we use are conducted only once. Each dog guide school develops a system it feels is best for its purposes. Guide Dogs for the Blind, for example, prefers keeping its puppies until ten weeks of age, running tests on a weekly basis. We like to place puppies at seven weeks of age so that the entire environment will be similar to the final one in which the dog will live as a guide. Host raisers can also concentrate on slight problem areas. All in all, the system has worked well for us.

"The tests differ from those given adult dogs and each puppy undergoes the adult tests when coming back to the school at maturity. We're looking for confidence, inquisitiveness, interest in people, willingness, attentiveness, and intelligence. We don't want a puppy that might give us emotional problems in the future—one that is overly sensitive, fearful, or aggressive. These tests help us pinpoint potential."

The puppies were to be tested in the kennel office, a small room measuring perhaps twelve by fourteen feet, sparsely furnished with a desk, a few chairs and other basic office equipment. One door leads directly outdoors and another into the kennel. To a puppy six weeks old this would be a large, new, interesting area.

Ed organized his testing materials before we started. A scale was placed on the desk and an electric shaver. "We need to identify each puppy, and we've found that the best way to do this is to shave a portion of the legs," Ed explained. "We tried yarn collars in different colors and indelible inks, but these had a way of disappearing. There's no doubt who's who with our current method."

Reaching into a desk drawer he brought out a small rubber ball and a crumpled empty cigarette package to which was attached a long string. He placed these on the desk alongside a score sheet.

"There are seven tests," Ed explained, "and the puppy is scored as to response: 1—excellent; 2—good; 3—fair; 4—poor. We then total the results. A total of seven points would be a perfect score, and a total of twenty-eight points would, in theory, be the poorest possible score. Failing any test, however, does not necessarily mean a rejected puppy. We'll discuss that as we go along."

These seven tests were listed across the top of the score sheet: Come, Fetch, Recall, Toe Pinch, On Back, Noise, Moving Object. "There's room in the result section to jot down little things we might see during the tests," Ed added. "Sometimes we notice an unusual factor in a puppy's response, and we make a note of it. This information can be valuable in the future.

"All tests are important, as each one brings out different facets of a puppy's character. The 'toe pinch' and 'on back' tests are good barometers of future emotional stability, so we are very interested in these scores. Puppies that fail these tests as well as the recall tests usually fail as adults. The other tests give us a good idea of intelligence, willingness, interest in people, and so on. However, we always look at the overall response to all tests and make our evaluation accordingly."

Two members of the school's staff conduct the tests, bringing in a third party's opinion if they are uncertain as to a puppy's response. If they feel a particular puppy is not feeling well, it will be tested on a subsequent day.

Ed went out to the yard and brought back the first puppy, a male who weighed in at 4½ pounds. He sat quietly on the scale, looking around with interest. Ed then shaved off a portion of coat on the puppy's right front leg. I had thought the sound and feel of the razor might cause a fearful reaction, but the puppy seemed not to notice anything was happening at all.

Test 1—Come (Social Attraction—Environmental Confidence—Curiosity)

"O.K!" Ed said as he jotted the puppy's weight, sex and identification on the chart. "We're about to start. I'm going to place the puppy on the floor. You and I will remain absolutely still and simply observe his actions. He should begin investigating the room with confidence. Any puppy that appears fearful, panics, tries to run back outside, cowers, quivers, or whines will be giving us an extremely negative response. We'll allow this little guy to do whatever he wants without distracting him for about fifteen seconds. At that point, I'm going to move about the room, calling him to come to my side. We are looking for a puppy that immediately stops investigating and follows me without growling, grabbing my pants' legs or shoes, or otherwise being openly aggressive. At no time do we justify a puppy's behavior, compare it to that of any other animal, or otherwise allow leeway."

Ed placed Puppy #1 on the floor. The puppy immediately began sniffing the area and moved confidently around the desk as he quickly investigated each new object. So far, his response was excellent.

After the fifteen-second interval, Ed called the puppy and began walking slowly around the room. "C'mon puppy!" he coaxed. "That's a good boy!" Puppy #1 looked up but immediately turned back to exploring the room. Ed coaxed harder. Tapping his thigh, he made his voice sound exciting. "Hey puppy—look at that! Come on!" This time the puppy walked over to Ed, but remained at his side for only a second or two. He then turned aside to sniff something else in the room. Ed reached down to pet him and moved to the score sheet.

"That's a '3—fair,' " he said. "I would have liked to see him drop all interest in investigating as soon as he heard my voice and saw my movements. He finally responded, but it took too much effort."

Since Puppy #1 did not respond quickly to a human voice and movement, there was an indication that he was currently more interested in objects than people. Such a puppy could develop with an independent streak that many dog owners erroneously call "stubborn."

"When placed with a family that understands this point, effort can be made to encourage this puppy to find people more fun than objects," Ed said. "The high inquisitiveness can then be an asset. What could become independence can hopefully be shaped into a deeper strength of character. The ability to react in an independent fashion is necessary in a dog guide, but the animal must place its master's interests before its own."

The test had been conducted in a relaxed fashion, and a casual observer might have misread the puppy's actions. Ed, however, had learned a great deal about this animal's basic character. There was a high level of confidence in the strange environment, a great deal of bold curiosity, and no fear of the testers. The negative factor, and it was a major one, was the initial disinterest in responding to the call to come. The response was late, brief, and occurred only after repeated coaxing. At six to seven weeks of age, a puppy should readily approach strangers when invited to do so, as this is the peak of the socialization period. Because of this, the test could not be scored "excellent" or even "good."

Test 2—Fetch (Chase Instinct—Intelligence—Willingness—Confidence)

As Puppy #1 continued his investigation of the room, Ed took the small ball and waited until the puppy moved closer. He then rolled the ball past the puppy's nose. "We place high emphasis on our retrieving score," he said as the puppy instantly looked up and watched the ball move towards the wall. "At this age, though, we never expect the puppy to bring the ball back, or even pick it up. We're looking for interest."

Puppy #1 happily chased the ball across the floor. It bounced off the wall, rolled under the desk and the puppy ducked his head and went under in pursuit.

"That's great!" Ed exclaimed. "Some dogs are afraid of overhanging objects and this can be a cause of rejection in an adult dog. This puppy isn't concerned."

Ed rolled the ball four times in four different directions and the puppy responded eagerly each time. He showed no hesitation as he batted the ball with his paws, gnawed it, and chased it as it bounced off various objects. At one point he put the ball in his mouth, lifting head and tail high as he pranced around the room. As all this was going on, Ed encouraged him. "Hey, that's great! That's a good puppy!" He then took the chart and marked "1—excellent" under the retrieving test. "Obviously his interest and attitude indicates an excellent score," he commented with a smile.

"We mark each puppy in the same way, but we're apt to see different attitudes in different breeds," Ed added. "I'd almost expect a high retrieving score with Retrievers, but German Shepherds may react differently. They use their abilities in different ways. A six-week-old German Shepherd may show interest in the ball but hesitate to go after it. He may appear to be more interested in what the tester does with the ball rather than involving himself in the action. It's interesting, but we can already see the differences in breed character. Of course, we also have German Shepherds that react like this puppy. Each one is an individual."

Guide Dogs for the Blind (Pfaffenberger, 1963) in its original work with Dr. Scott at the Jackson Laboratory had noted a high correlation between puppies that passed the retrieving test and adult dogs that went on to become guides. This test was subsequently considered extremely important by that school. Ed had commented that Leader Dogs also places high emphasis on the retrieving score. What relationship does retrieving have with performance as dog guides?

"The retrieving instinct is linked to intelligence and willingness, and it is inherited," Ed explained. "A puppy with a high level of retrieving instinct is usually enthusiastic about doing things with people, and is full of energy, curiosity, and confidence. A timid dog will be afraid to move after a moving object in a strange place, and a dull dog will probably show no interest at all.

"In testing, we always make sure that a puppy has seen the ball being rolled, and we use one that is small enough to pick up comfortably. If the initial response is excellent, we vary the toss so that the puppy can be observed as he follows the ball into different areas, such as under the desk, among other items, or as it hits something. Every action has a bearing on the final score."

Many people feel a dog must run after an object, pick it up, and immediately return with it to the person who had tossed it to possess a high retrieving instinct. It is the interest in the object that indicates the retrieving instinct rather than a specific set of actions. In time the puppy will learn to pick up objects and return them. To begin, the object may be simply chased or pawed.

Test 3—Recall (Social Attraction—Social Confidence—Willingness)

In this test the puppy is called back and forth twice between the two testers. The puppy is held by one tester who crouches or kneels while the other tester, also crouching, calls the puppy from a distance of perhaps eight feet. The puppy is encouraged to respond through voice and hands. The testers otherwise remain still and do not reach forward to touch a hesitant puppy.

I held Puppy #1 as Ed crouched and tapped the floor with his finger tips. "Come on, puppy!" he called. Without any hesitation, Puppy #1 willingly ran to Ed with his tail held high. Ed praised and petted him, then turned him around to face me as the action was repeated.

On each call the puppy ran quickly back and forth between us. The test seemed to be a game to him. He was fascinated with our fingers, following their movements with great interest. As he approached he nuzzled them gently with his nose. Ed was pleased with the results as he placed a "1—excellent" on the score sheet.

He then analyzed this test in relationship to the first one, which had rated only a fair response. In the initial test, the call to come was given in an upright position. The testers had been still, with movement brought in as a calculated distraction when the puppy was deeply involved in investigation. In Test #3, the entire time span of the test was directed towards the puppy. By crouching, the testers came down to the dog's eye level—a more interesting posture. With the differences in human posture and approach towards the test, Puppy #1 indicated both willingness and enthusiasm. He responded completely to people who responded completely to him. There was also a possibility that the puppy had satisfied his curiosity about the environment within the first test and was ready to devote attention to the people in the room, especially since the retrieving test with them had been fun.

Had Puppy #1 dashed off to further investigate the room, we would have had stronger evidence to support the independence noted during the initial test. Had the puppy elected to watch us or to move only a portion of the way towards us, we would have been observing a tendency towards wariness or timidity. Had the puppy run forward and growled or nipped at our hands, we would have had evidence of over-aggressiveness. As it was, Puppy #1 had turned in the school's ideal of a perfect performance.

"Now you see how we analyze overall performance," Ed commented. "We never modify test results, but there is the possibility that actions can be explained. I'm interested now in the next tests."

Test 4—Toe Pinch (Body Sensitivity—Forgiveness—Dominance/ Submission)

Ed picked up the puppy and cradled him in his arms. "The next test involves taking a front paw and exerting a steady, firm pressure for about ten seconds with the thumb and middle finger on the skin between the toes," he said. "We are interested in the puppy's reaction to this kind of pressure.

"At this age, the pressure I'm going to use should bring little or no reaction. I'm *not* going to use my fingernails or exert an increasing amount of pressure until the puppy shows signs of pain. I'm testing for what should be a subdued response under the circumstances. Any puppy that struggles, whines or cries, exhibits extreme evidence of pain, or attempts to bite, fails.

"This test pinpoints the dog with unusually high body sensitivity or one that cannot forgive the tester for a mild discomfort. Puppies that fail tend to show up with emotional problems as adults. Sometimes they're shy, nervous, fearful, panicky, insecure, or simply cannot respond positively to training corrections."

The test also pinpoints dominant, overly aggressive puppies. These animals usually resent being held for even a short period of time and will struggle to free themselves. Such puppies may also resent any pressure between the toes and attempt to bite.

Ed stroked Puppy #1's head and told him he was a good boy. He then reached between the toes of one paw and began squeezing, using the pads of his fingers rather than the nails. The puppy looked calmly around the room without showing any sign of distress or discomfort. After ten seconds, Ed placed the puppy on the floor. He moved to the score sheet and marked "1—excellent" in the alloted space.

"That was a perfect response!" he said. "Should he have tried to bite or struggle, I would have stopped the test at once and failed him."

Test 5—On Back (Dominance/Submission—Trust)

This test is also seen by Ed as a good indicator of inherited character. Puppies that fail also tend to fail as adults. In this test the puppy is lifted from the floor and then slowly rotated in the hands until it is lying on its back. One hand supports the neck and the other the body. It is held in this inverted position for approximately ten seconds.

"Some puppies struggle as soon as we begin turning them," Ed explained. "We don't continue the test with any puppy that is upset or tries to bite. We're looking for acceptance of the position which gives us an excellent idea of basic submission and trust."

Ed lifted Puppy #1 under the front legs, and slowly turned him on his back. When the puppy did not struggle, he gradually stood up holding the puppy slightly away from his body.

Puppy #1 relaxed, becoming limp in Ed's hands. His legs extended sideways to expose his pink stomach, and his tiny head lolled backwards as the eyes partially closed. "This is the response I want," Ed said. "This little guy is showing absolute acceptance, submission and trust." Lowering the puppy to the floor, he marked the score sheet "1—excellent."

94

Test 6—Noise (Sound Sensitivity)

"A dog guide must not be sound shy," Ed said as he explained the next test. "What we are going to do now is repeat Test #3 in which the puppy is called back and forth between us. Just as the puppy passes the edge of the desk, I'm going to tip over the empty waste paper basket.

"The sound of a falling waste paper basket should be acceptable to a puppy this age. If he accepts this sound, he will probably mature to cope with office machines, household appliances, traffic, even gunshots if exposed in a gradual fashion. We don't see the purpose in starting with a gunshot or some monstrous, falling object. If the puppy is genetically oversensitive to sound, we'll catch it without using extremes.

"If he panics, cowers, urinates in fear, or dashes across the floor to run from the sound, he'll be failed. If he tucks tail and seems concerned but holds his own, I'll probably score him 'fair.' If he ignores the sound, turns to see what fell, or walks over to investigate the source of the sound, I'll probably mark him 'good' to 'excellent.' "

We both crouched on the floor and began the recall with the puppy. As he happily responded and passed the desk, Ed pushed over the plastic waste paper basket which thudded to the floor less than two feet from the puppy's hind legs. The puppy stopped and looked behind him. Since he showed no fear his response was excellent. The sound had broken his attention span, however, and he needed to be reminded that someone had called him.

The recall was repeated with exactly the same response. Ed was pleased. "That's a '1—excellent,' " he said as he petted the puppy who responded with a violently wagging tail.

"Testing for sound shyness can be tricky," Ed added. "You'll find some temperament testers who think a puppy should completely ignore any sound and continue on with a given action. This is unreasonable, and especially so in potential dog guides. (Authors note: Dr. John Paul Scott, in going over material for this chapter commented that lack of reaction to sound might indicate deafness.) These dogs must be aware of everything going on in the immediate environment and react accordingly. The ideal puppy will alert, perhaps pause and momentarily put his ears back, but won't show fear. Some puppies may want to investigate the source of the sound, which is also an excellent response. We don't expect a puppy of this age to remember what he was doing when the sound came. This puppy's reminder to continue his recall shouldn't make anyone think he was 'shook up' because of the noise. You can see confidence in the body posture and attitude of a puppy."

The falling waste paper basket also served another purpose. The puppy was aware of the sudden movement behind him as Ed reached towards the basket and tipped it. Many dogs are skittish of fast movements behind their backs. Ed's gesture would probably have bothered such a puppy and been reflected in the score.

It is interesting to note that the basket was tipped close to the puppy, and the sound came from behind rather than in front of the animal. Many puppies appear composed if facing the source of a sound, or if the sound emanates from a distance, yet the same puppies may panic when the sound comes from close behind. Dog guides, of course, must remain composed in all situations.

Test 7—Moving Object (Chase Instinct—Willingness—Curiosity—Enthusiasm

"This last test," Ed said, "is similar to the retrieving test, and we're looking for the puppy's interest in doing something close to and with a person. German Shepherd puppies sometimes show more interest in this test than retrieving. All we do is move around and drag an object on a string, encouraging the puppy to run after it and play in some fashion. If the puppy shows no interest or is frightened, it's failed."

Ed took the crumpled cigarette package with the attached string from the desk. "Notice we don't feel it's necessary to invest in specialized testing equipment," he said with a laugh. Ed then walked past Puppy #1 while pulling the empty package behind him. The puppy immediately followed the package, pawed at it, pounced on it, and otherwise indicated great interest. Ed raised the package slightly off the floor and the puppy leaped up after it. Throughout the test, which lasted about ten seconds, the puppy moved close to Ed's left side, following the movements of the package with excitement. "That's a '1—excellent,'" Ed said. "This little guy scored well on both retrieving and this test. Sometimes we'll get a puppy that scores well on one and not the other, and sometimes we'll get a puppy that scores poorly on both. We closely evaluate total test scores in those cases."

Ed tallied Puppy #1's final score, which came to 9. "That's an excellent score," he said. "I think now you can see how unfair it would have been to gauge his potential from just the first test. Sometimes a tester may subconsciously be overly critical of a puppy that scores poorly on the first test or two. We try to be careful of that, so that no test reflects on the score of any other. Using two testers definitely helps, and by using members of the staff who are familiar with the entire dog guide training program, we feel our results are accurate."

Puppy #1 was taken out to the play yard and Puppy #2 was brought in. I looked at my watch. Approximately ten minutes had passed since the start of the tests.

Puppy #2, also a male, seemed identical to Puppy #1, except for size. Puppy #2 was larger. He responded quietly to his weigh-in and as a portion of coat was shaved off his left front leg. The testing started and we were in for a few surprises.

The puppy responded perfectly to both tests 1 and 2. During the first test he explored the room with interest but instantly left his investigation to run to Ed's side when called. During the retrieving test he not only chased the ball but indicated that he knew the action stemmed from the tester. After pouncing on the ball he turned to look at Ed as if asking for further directions. Undoubtedly, I thought, this puppy will receive a perfect score on all tests.

During Test 3, however, something unusual happened. The puppy started his recall to either party but stopped just outside arm's reach and quietly watched, although he eventually moved to us with vocal coaxing and fingers tapping the floor. "That's a '3—fair,'" Ed noted with a touch of disappointment in his voice. "Here's a case again where the foster family can help by stressing personal contact on a one-to-one basis. This puppy has no basic fear of people, as we've seen during the first test and his attitude around us, but he should be responding without hesitancy. It could be our body postures, or perhaps someone made a grabbing motion towards him in this position and it frightened him. Whatever the reason, though, we score them as we see them."

We were still discussing the response to this test as Ed cradled the puppy to his chest and initiated the toe pinch test. Almost at once Puppy #2 lowered his head to Ed's pressing fingers and opened his mouth to emit a shocked, pint-sized grunt. As the test continued, the puppy gradually lifted his head and started squirming. Ed praised him and lowered him to the floor. "That's a '3—fair,'" he said in a noncommittal tone. "I'd like to see less body sensitivity than that although the reaction wasn't extreme. He did not struggle violently or bite."

Ed then lifted the puppy from the floor and began the fourth test in which the puppy is turned on the back. Puppy #2 squirmed slightly as he was rotated, but relaxed. Towards the end of the test, he again began squirming and showing minor irritation at being in such a position. Ed lowered him to the floor. "That's a '3—fair,'" he commented. "A failure wouldn't give us that many seconds of relaxation."

This puppy went on to receive a score of "1—excellent" on the noise test. Although he persisted in stopping short of us when called, he exhibited no fear when the waste paper basket fell over. Ed based this score on the puppy's reaction to the sound alone and considered the recall portion of the test as incidental.

During the last test the puppy showed interest in the moving object but not as much as was shown in the retrieving. Ed marked this score a "2—good."

He then tallied the score. Puppy #2 came up with 14 points. "That's a borderline reject," he commented. "When we get up to 14 or 15 points we're concerned. A puppy over that number of points will be rejected. If that's the case, we usually keep the papers and place the puppy in a home as a pet. We have a waiting list of families.

"Of course," he added quickly, "we're talking about dogs that will make good house pets and simply don't match up to the extremely high standards required of a dog guide.

"What I think we'll do with this puppy, however, is inform the raiser of the problem areas. The family can work on the recall and help build confidence and trust. The body sensitivity may or may not be a deciding factor. We'll see as he matures."

Puppy #2 was taken out to the play yard. As I watched him go I realized again how unfair it would have been to gauge this puppy on the basis of the first two tests or on observation alone. It was only through the entire testing process that his weak characteristics had come to light.

The testing continued until each puppy had finished. Ed and I then went over the score sheet. Each puppy had presented a unique personality, usually exhibiting problem areas we would never have noticed otherwise. No puppy tested with the perfect score of 7, although Puppy #4 came close with an 8. She performed each test perfectly until the last one when her interest in following the moving object rated a secondary "good" rather than "excellent." Ed then summarized his thoughts on each puppy.

Puppy #1, scoring a 9, was considered an excellent prospect. His host family would be told to work on orienting his interest towards people rather than objects.

Puppy #2, with a total score of 14, had several problem areas and was a borderline reject. Ed noted that the puppy had followed on the call to come when the tester was standing and moving but showed hesitancy when the testers were still, crouched and concentrating completely on the puppy. This uncertainty indicated a lack of both confidence and trust. Lack of these traits again showed up in intensified form when the puppy began to squirm when held in an inverted position. In neither test, however, were the results so extreme as to earn a failing score, and Ed felt the host family could help develop the puppy's character in a positive fashion. Ed's major concern involved the relatively high body sensitivity. If confidence and trust could be developed, however, this level of body sensitivity might be acceptable at adulthood.

Puppy #3, a female, with a score of 12 also exhibited hesitancy on the recall tests. She refused to move to Ed without coaxing. She responded quickly to my call but did so with a lowered head and tail indicating uncertainty and a bit too much submission. Ed commented that this puppy may not have been exposed to many men and needed much more socialization around people to build confidence. The host family could concentrate on this.

This puppy also showed no interest in retrieving. She watched the ball for only a fraction of a second before going back to exploring the room. She did, however, score a "1—excellent" on the moving object test. Ed felt she needed time and encouragement to enjoy retrieving and doing things with people, and the host family could help.

Puppy #4, a female, with 8 points, performed almost perfectly. Ed felt she had no problem areas at all.

Puppy #5, female, with a score of 15 points, was also a borderline reject. Her score was poorest of the entire litter. She showed no interest in either retrieving or following a moving object, failing both tests. Ed felt the host family might help develop this puppy's enthusiasm and desire to do things with people.

This puppy came quickly when called but exhibited a slight tuck of the tail and lowered head when responding to Ed. Ed commented that two puppies out of seven showing a marked difference in attitude towards a man indicated all puppies needed more socialization around people of both sexes and all ages.

Puppy #5 also exhibited relatively high body sensitivity, scoring a "3—fair" on the toe pinch test. This was offset, however, by the puppy's submission and trust when held in an inverted position. Ed thought this was encouraging, and that by overcoming other problem areas, the fairly high body sensitivity might be acceptable at adulthood.

Puppies #6 and #7, scoring 10 and 11 respectively, could have scored higher in retrieving and Ed felt the host families should concentrate on building enthusiasm and desire to do things with people. The overall scores of both puppies were good and Ed had high hopes for them.

After analyzing each puppy's tests in relationship to others in the litter Ed felt all puppies should be placed in foster homes with emphasis given to human socialization and problem areas. He jotted a notation to this effect on the bottom of the score sheet.

"As many as 33 percent of our borderline puppies go on to become successful Leader Dogs," Ed said. "There's a great deal the host family can do to work with certain problems, especially since we place puppies at the peak of the socialization period when they are still highly adaptable."

Leader Dogs does not place puppies that fail all tests or exhibit responses such as excessive timidity, over-aggressiveness, continual vocalization, or attempting to flee the testing area. Chances are slim that such puppies would overcome problems and mature into acceptable adults. They would only disappoint the host families who want to raise potential "winners." Emphasis is always on placing those puppies that score best or have a good chance of overcoming problems.

The borderline puppies serve as the school's control group. As puppies mature, the school checks progress against test scores. In this fashion the accuracy of the tests and the testers' opinions are confirmed. If, for example, it were discovered that an overwhelming majority of puppies that fail particular tests later go on to become Leader Dogs these tests would not have predictive value. They would then be modified or replaced with others. Through the accumulation of data on both high and low scoring dogs, the school feels that its current tests and scoring procedures produce an accurate analysis of a puppy's potential.

Potential and success at adulthood are two different things, however. Scoring well on all puppy tests is no guarantee that a particular animal will become a Leader Dog. A great deal can happen during the maturing and raising processes which we will discuss in the next chapter.

The school's breeding program currently includes Golden Retrievers, Labrador Retrievers, and German Shepherd Dogs. Approximately 50 percent of the breeding stock is owned by the school although placed in private homes. The other 50 percent is owned by private individuals with stud service and/or litters donated to the school. In every instance, breeding animals are raised as house pets. New breeding stock is selected on the basis of the school's incoming adult tests, training evaluation, physical condition, and pedigree.

The school has accumulated data on both stud dogs and brood bitches that have produced a high percentage of accepted puppies. These animals are currently being line-bred, similar bloodlines being used in order to establish type. Common ancestors pop up in the pedigrees with increasing frequency as the school attempts to preserve the genes of outstanding producers so that they can exert as strong an influence as possible on each generation of puppies. "The linebreeding program is quite successful," Ed stated with confidence. "We're at the point where we've had 100 percent litters [Ed. note: all puppies going on to become Leader Dogs], and we're disappointed if we have below 50 percent acceptance within a litter at adulthood."

In-breeding on top producing lines will start soon. In-breeding involves mating very close relatives such as sister to brother, mother to son, etc., and is practiced by careful breeders when the genetic backgrounds of all individuals are well-known, and it is felt that outstanding, genetically acquired family traits overshadow deleterious ones.

Leader Dogs is currently placing slightly over two hundred puppies a year in its foster program. The long-range goal is to place four hundred per year. This will come about gradually as the school expands its dormitory and kennel space.

Of the breeds produced by the school, the Labrador Retriever is placing first in order of acceptance at adulthood; the Golden Retriever, second; and the German Shepherd Dog, third. Interestingly enough, Guide Dogs for the Blind in California places these three breeds in identical order. The Seeing Eye in New Jersey, a traditional user of only the German Shepherd Dog for many years due to its Fortunate Fields' ties, now includes approximately 24 percent Labrador Retrievers and 24 percent Golden Retrievers, with the remaining percentage composed of German Shepherd Dogs and a sprinkling of other breeds.

Is the German Shepherd Dog, the breed that proved dogs could successfully lead the blind, losing its popularity? Not so, say all three schools. It is just that other breeds can perform dog guide work equally as well and are being utilized.

The seven Golden Retriever puppies we had tested had homes waiting for them with members of 4-H clubs approved to participate in the Leader Dog Puppy Program. Before leaving the premises, the puppies

Its hesitancy to approach the tester made this puppy a borderline reject.

would be issued identification number tags which would be affixed to collars, and contracts would be drawn up for the host families to sign.

The foster families would have the fun of selecting call names, although Ed would explain that these "should be dignified, please!" They would also have first option on keeping any puppies as pets that might be rejected from the program, although Leader Dogs would retain The American Kennel Club registration papers.

Ed was about to begin the necessary paper work when he received a phone call from a woman who owned a four-month-old German Shepherd puppy she was planning on donating to the school at adulthood. Before she invested a year's time in the raising process, she wanted an analysis of the dog's potential. Ed offered to test the dog, although testing puppies other than those belonging to the school is not ordinarily done, and an appointment was made for later in the day.

Its foster family worked on this puppy's social confidence to help it become a guide.

Since this puppy was four months old and exhibiting adult characteristics, Ed would use the adult tests rather than the puppy tests.

"If you like this puppy, will it become part of your official puppy program?" I asked.

"No!" Ed replied. "Our program involves puppies we have placed ourselves. We never discourage people from raising dogs for us, but we don't have the time or manpower to help those outside our program. There are many puppies being raised independently for us and we hope they're all successful, but the raising families are usually on their own until the dogs are mature and come in for testing."

Later that day, after Ed had told me the four-month-old puppy looked like a potential "winner," I stood outside the puppy yard and watched the seven Golden Retriever puppies. Except for the various spots on the legs where the coat had been shaved for identification purposes, they once again looked and acted alike. Yet I had seen differences in character ranging from the school's concept of ideal to near failure. I could not see these differences now. I could only see the puppies relating to each other as they raced around the bushes, chewed on each other's coats and otherwise had fun. Through such seemingly irrelevant and simple actions as throwing a ball, squeezing between toes, tipping a waste paper basket, pulling an object on a string, I had seen the embryonic character traits that spelled possible success or failure as Leader Dogs. The differences in puppies were subtle, but they were there, and it was only through testing that they could be easily seen. Ten weeks later the same tests would no longer be used. By four months of age potential Leader Dogs are treated and tested as adults. What, I wondered, would Rittmeister Max von Stephanitz, Konrad Most, Dorothy Harrison Eustis, and other early breeders and trainers have to say about all this? Probably something similar to what I said as I reached down and petted seven soft heads—"Amazing!"

In August 1980, the seven Golden Retriever puppies from Litter #283 were returned to Leader Dogs. Puppy #1 was accepted. Puppy #2 (borderline reject) was rejected due to shyness and nervousness. Puppy #3 was accepted. Puppy #4 was accepted. Puppy #5 (borderline reject) was rejected due to shyness and high body sensitivity. Puppy #6 was accepted. Puppy #7 was accepted. The puppy tests had proved 100 percent accurate, as had Ed's analysis of the borderline rejects, whose foster families, in these cases, had been unable to overcome problems.

This Golden Retriever, "Jerry," was donated to the puppy program by former President and Mrs. Ford, and raised by Lisa Jensen.

Lapeer Leader Dog puppies and their foster raisers visit the Birmingham airport.

Chapter 7

Foster Families—More Than a Helping Hand

We were in the meeting room of the Lapeer, Michigan, 4-H Club. It had been a long, tiring day. Participants in the Leader Dog Puppy Program had just returned from a visit to the Birmingham airport. Two Labrador and five Golden Retriever puppies, ranging in age from three to seven months, played with each other in the center of the room, while their host raisers, youngsters between nine and twelve years old, all tried to talk at the same time. Program leaders, Nan Nellenbach and Pat Brauer, had just asked them how they enjoyed their day. "It was great!" "Wow!" "It was noisy!"

Pat encouraged each child to share his or her impressions of the airport. "How did your puppies like the day?" Pat asked. Each child answered that his or her puppy had had a wonderful time, enjoying all the new experiences, sounds, and attention from strangers. The conversation continued as the youngsters' mothers, who had joined the day's outing, looked at their watches and made plans for a late dinner. It was already after six o'clock.

The meeting finally broke up and tired mothers herded youngsters and puppies towards home. Pat then took the time to explain the structure of the 4-H Leader Dog program. "These children come from the area," she said, "and most of their families own and operate farms. The youngster, who will be entrusted with the puppy, must be a member of the 4-H and at least nine years old. However, there must be cooperation from the entire family. The parents are involved in our meetings and are expected to offer support and follow-through. Puppies three months old are easier to handle than animals close to a year of age. If a child can't control a big dog, the parents must give a helping hand. However, it is the child's reponsibility to care for the animal, groom it, feed it, take it to public places at least twice a week, and spend about fifteen minutes a day teaching simple obedience commands."

The 4-H (the 4 "H"s stand for health, hands, head and heart) is the youth program division of the Cooperative Extension Service of the United States Department of Agriculture. There are over one hundred fifty major 4-H activities from which to choose, or participants may develop their own projects. An interested person merely has to contact the nearest Cooperative Extension Service or County 4-H office. New groups can be started by finding an adult volunteer leader and several young people interested in the same project. The 4-H, although connected to the Department of Agriculture, is not confined to rural or farming areas. There are active groups in cities, suburbs, and towns across the nation as well as abroad.

Animal projects have been popular since the organization's inception in 1914. Leaders working with livestock and pet care programs have traditionally been experts in relating their subject material to youngsters while securing the cooperation of families. This special ability helps to ensure that the care and raising of animals is seen as a serious and continuing responsibility rather than a temporary amusement. With this type of intelligent approach to animal care, the 4-H has been a logical place for dog guide schools to turn for help in raising puppies. In return the 4-H has responded with dedication and enthusiasm.

Leader Dogs works closely with the 4-H, giving approval to groups within a comfortable driving distance from Rochester. "We want to be sure of our leaders," Ed Lange explained, "and we want to be close enough to puppies so that we can quickly handle any situation that may arise on a personal basis. If a group or foster family is five or six hundred miles away, we lose touch. If someone from outside our immediate area wants to raise a puppy, we may elect to place one, but this is considered an 'outside' project. If interested families can't locate a group in their area, they should contact us for information."

Although tax deductible, expenses incurred in raising a puppy are borne by the family, including food, medical care, and equipment such as leashes and collars. In most areas, however, Lions Clubs have come forward to defray expenses, working hand-in-hand with approved groups to make the program a success. Numerous veterinarians, including Dr. Eastman at Leader Dogs, donate basic services. Feed manufacturers often supply food. Communities, once aware of an active Leader Dog program in their midsts, usually help in whatever ways they can.

Raising a puppy for a dog guide school has changed since the early days when schools were interested in locating homes so that kennel space could be saved for dogs being trained. The importance of the enriched environment found in a home was not realized until the esearch of Drs. Scott and Fuller (1965) at the Jackson Laboratory. Today a foster home is more than a nice place for a puppy to live. It supplies a complete atmosphere in which to prepare an animal for life as a dog guide. As each puppy completes its critical period of socialization and moves into the adolescent period, the family helps shape behavior through a structured program involving household discipline, exposure to people, places, things, and other animals, and introduction to simple obedience commands.

A monthly inventory and training report is sent to every 4-H leader. Accompanying this report is any new information available on the project along with suggestions for improving programs. Leaders are encouraged to contact the school if problems arise, and the staff meets twice a year with leaders to discuss the general program.

The Lapeer 4-H is typical of an active program, and Pat Brauer is a typical leader. "I don't see myself as a replacement for anyone on the staff at Leader Dogs," she states emphatically. "All leaders feel the same way. If we suspect a serious problem with a puppy or a host raiser, we always take our problems to the school. They're the experts!"

Ed Lange described some of these problems: "Maybe a dog is maturing with hip dysplasia or some other physical problem. Maybe a puppy is becoming overly timid or aggressive. Maybe a host family just isn't doing the job. We want to handle problems such as these directly from the school. If a puppy is obviously going to be rejected as an adult, we'll remove it from the program immediately. In most cases such a puppy can be placed with someone on our waiting list as a house pet, although the foster family always has the option of keeping the puppy and often does this. Once in awhile we discover a puppy having problems in a particular household. If we think the family and puppy are mismatched, we may place the puppy with another family. This has been quite successful."

The Lapeer 4-H Leader Dog group meets regularly, and puppies are handled by everyone and play together. Pat and Nan arrange for socialization trips and demonstrate obedience commands to be worked on at home. Youngsters are told that they should teach just enough obedience to secure control.

The main purpose of the 4-H program is to introduce the puppy to situations it will be likely to encounter as a dog guide. Confidence and initiative are fostered while shaping the character of the animal.

4-H meetings are not classes or drill sessions. An overly zealous raiser or a leader who uses an improper training approach can break down canine enthusiasm, initiative, and confidence. If the leader has very little experience as a dog trainer, no obedience is introduced at all. In such a case the puppy raiser follows the program outlined in the 4-H puppy orientation booklet. If obedience is introduced, the leader follows the guidelines in the leader's guide. Commands are demonstrated to the group and are for use at home.

Whenever a puppy is raised, there is danger of the animal overbonding to the host raiser or family in general. An overly dependent dog will be rejected at adulthood.

The school emphasizes that the puppy should be a family dog and not the sole responsibility of one person. Initiative is encouraged by allowing the puppy freedom to investigate and learn without the family being overly protective. Short visits to the homes of other people, overnight trips, or a day or two in a boarding kennel are encouraged—all situations in which the puppy is without the constant presence of the foster family. These things help the puppy develop confidence.

Puppies that had weak areas in testing are observed by leaders as families work on problems. Suggestions are made, usually after checking with the school, on how to improve the puppy's response to new situations and learning experiences.

Leaders notify community officials and shop owners that foster puppies are in the area, securing permission to enter stores, office buildings, churches, and to ride buses and trains. Participants carry identification or wear identifying jackets, and foster puppies are soon usually welcome everywhere. Local Lions Clubs also help with the socialization process, making arrangements for puppies to visit schools, convalescent homes, libraries, community clubs, and participate in parades and other local activities. Within a short time puppies are familiar with city, suburban, and rural environments and all the sounds that go with them. They have been exposed to crowded streets, heavy traffic, railroad stations, bus terminals, and airports. They have had the experience of riding buses and trains, being on elevators, moving up and down different types of stairs, walking through several kinds of doors, and over different footings. They are encouraged to be friendly and accept the attention of people of all ages. Unlike most dogs, familiar only with the routines of home and yard, Leader Dogs are expected to be familiar with the experiences that make up the world of man.

While socialization continues, families concentrate on teaching puppies to be trustworthy house pets. Leaders lecture on pet care and household control at meetings. Housebreaking, mouthing, chewing, chasing other animals, jumping, begging at the table, and similar subjects are covered, in addition to grooming, diet, and disease prevention. Puppies returning to the school at adulthood are expected to be healthy, well-groomed, and have no bad household habits. Behavioral problems such as destructive chewing, animal distraction, and lapses in housebreaking will mean rejection. As anyone who has raised a puppy knows, the kind of household dependability required of prospective Leader Dogs within a year's time involves a great deal of patience, time, and discipline.

Sometimes a participating family wants to become involved in the school's breeding program. Selected stock is then placed in the home. These animals come under the supervision of the 4-H program although breeding decisions are made by Leader Dogs.

One of the highlights of the year for Michigan puppy raisers is the statewide 4-H dog show held every summer at Michigan State University. The Leader Dog class is divided into competitive (placings are selected) and non-competitive (everyone participating receives a ribbon) sections. After being judged on grooming and general condition, each puppy accompanies his handler in and out of buildings, through swinging doors, up and down stairs, across slippery floors, through heavy traffic, and finally is put through an obstacle course. This involves reactions to uncommon situations and sounds. As the puppy and handler move along, someone suddenly opens an umbrella close to the puppy, someone else pops a balloon in the puppy's face, and someone shakes a can filled with pebbles. The puppy should not exhibit fear in any of these situations. The puppy and handler are then required to enter and leave an automobile, and finally, the puppy is asked to sit quietly as the handler eats a cookie.

Everyone enjoys the annual dog show, and the tests indicate where additional work is needed. A puppy may need more exposure to stairs, slippery floors, doors, or crowds; or perhaps the problem may be more serious, indicating a fear of sounds in a strange environment, timidity, or insecurity. Feedback to the school can often help, so that no child is disappointed in the future because of a rejected puppy.

Even with the best testing and raising programs puppies are rejected for numerous reasons when returned to the school. Ed Lange cites some of them: "Physical problems often do not become apparent until the puppy is maturing. Unfortunately, rejections occur because of them.

"Many rejections from a character standpoint come from among our borderline puppies. Although we are about 33 percent successful with these puppies, we are also 67 percent unsuccessful. It may be high body sensitivity, disinterest in people, or timidity. Sometimes the family couldn't work out the problems or more effort could have been made. Once in awhile we'll have a host raiser who does a fantastic job but doesn't extend the environment beyond the immediate town and area. The puppy may be confident in these places but cannot relax elsewhere. Sometimes a puppy will overbond to a family in spite of precaution and cannot adjust to a switch in environment.

"Being distracted by other animals is another cause of rejection. Leader Dogs must not only ignore stray dogs and cats, but also birds, rabbits, squirrels, and livestock. It's easy to overlook a chasing problem especially when puppies are small and free on the premises. We also don't want puppies used as hunting dogs as this is not going to be their working purpose."

Another major cause for rejection at all dog guide schools among both foster puppies and donated dogs is the inability to take initiative. This characteristic is not detectable until animals begin training. Guide Dogs for the Blind (Pfaffenberger, 1963), in its research work with Dr. John Paul Scott, felt that factors in early upbringing had a deleterious effect on an animal's ability to make later independent decisions and take initiative. An overly long kennel stay in puppyhood resulting in a nonstimulating environment appeared to be a major factor at Guide Dogs. This school now attempts to place puppies in homes at ten weeks of age (Pfaffenberger, et al., 1976) rather than wait beyond the end of the critical period of socialization (i.e. twelve weeks). This has helped the school but has not completely solved the problem.

Leader Dogs feels there are other factors beyond a nonstimulating environment that can hinder a puppy's developing initiative. Extensive obedience training or utilization of harsh training methods at too early an age may dampen a puppy's desire to attempt decision making. An overly solicitous or protective host raiser may unwittingly teach a puppy that decisions must never be made without supervision and approval. When later expected to act on its own without continual direction, such a puppy lacks confidence to function.

Time goes by quickly for foster families, and puppies soon mature. Even unskilled eyes can detect possible problems in the dog's characters and physical structures. Behavior has solidified, with puppies exhibiting

110

he characteristics of the dogs they are, as opposed to the potential seen
within the puppy tests. Every youngster hopes that his or her puppy will
match or go beyond puppy expectations, and become a "winner."

Emotions run high at the end of a year's time when Leader Dogs
notifies a 4-H leader that a particular puppy is due back at the school.
For many youngsters this will be life's first painful experience with loss
and sorrow. It is difficult to part with an animal that has shared a
family's life for a year and to which so much attention, time, and love
have been devoted. There are always tears when parting with a puppy
accepted by the school at adulthood. Later, barring unforeseen
rejection, there will be tears of pride and joy when the puppy graduates
as a Leader Dog. By that time the host raiser is most likely hard at work
raising another puppy. The time, emotional involvement, and tears are
worth it.

- - - - -

Two booklets published by the 4-H Youth Programs, Cooperative
Extension Service at Michigan State University are invaluable to
everyone involved in the puppy raising program. They are: *Leader Dog
Puppy Orientation for 4-H Members*, which is given to every youngster participating in the program; and *Leader's Guide: Leader Dog
Puppy Orientation*, which is given to every leader. Both were written by
members of the State 4-H Leader Dog Developmental Committee in
cooperation with the school.

These booklets help youngsters raise puppies with specific goals in
mind and aid leaders to work out a progressive program of socialization
and canine control without danger of over-training or misusing
techniques. Information is included on feeding, grooming, house
training, bad habits, exercise requirements, health, and basic use of
leash and collar.

Leader Dog in leash, collar and harness.

The harness room. Equipment is custom made at the school.

Leader Dogs in training van ready for a day's work.

112

Chapter 8

Beginning Dog—Beginning Trainer

It was seven forty-five on a cool, rainy morning and my first working day with dogs-in-training. Team captain, Harold "Smitty" Smith greeted me above the clatter of food dishes and yips from excited dogs as I entered the kennel. He and the other trainers had already groomed, fed, and exercised their dogs, and the vans were waiting to leave.

Smitty cautioned me to stand aside as he walked down a row of stalls and flipped open gates. The dogs dashed out, rounded the corner at full gallop, and disappeared out the side door where they leaped into the back of the waiting van. "They learn that in just a few days," Smitty said with a smile when he saw the look of surprise on my face. "They enjoy that little touch of freedom, and it sure saves time!"

"These dogs have had street training for only three days, so they're beginners," he explained as we climbed into the van. "Since you're a dog trainer, and your time at the school is limited, we thought we'd start you at the point where you observe what we do and critique it."

In the van the dogs were placed on a down-stay command and attached by bench chains to the side of the vehicle. Eventually they would learn to down-stay on the floor of cars, buses, trains, and airplanes.

The dogs must remain quiet in the van and wait patiently at the training site. A few barked once or twice at the stranger in their midst, and Smitty silenced them with a clipped "Quiet!" command. Those nearest the door reached out to sniff and lick my hands.

As we drove into Rochester, Smitty explained the dogs' training up to this point. Several days earlier the team of four trainers had run down the line-up of waiting dogs. Each trainer works with eight animals, selected by number rather than choice, and the initial thirty-two are called a "string." Dogs are never switched among trainers once the program starts, although once in awhile a trainer may sense that a good dog would respond better to another instructor, in which case the new instructor will finish the training program.

As soon as dogs are selected, they are retested by their trainers in order to weed out any animals that may have undergone subtle character changes while waiting for a new class to start. A few days are then spent watching the dogs' actions. Each trainer makes notes on the personalities he sees, observing how the animals react to vocal tone, praise, petting, and hand movements. This pretraining observation helps ensure that teaching techniques are tailored to each animal. Initial corrections that are too harsh or too soft may result in rejected dogs, and trainers never want to misjudge their animals.

"Sometimes it takes several days before a dog is relaxed with us," Smitty explained, "but we never rush things. The dog has to be mentally ready to begin work. We then start basic obedience commands on leash such as 'sit,' 'down,' 'come,' 'stay,' and the dog guide's concept of 'heel' which involves moving slightly ahead of the handler. We may spend a week or more on these before we feel the dog is ready for introduction of the harness.

"We never train dogs on the premises. An intelligent animal reacts quickly to a set-up environment. The best way is to get out in everyday life and teach as the situations present themselves. Who wants a dog that works only in one or two locations?"

We were nearing the downtown area of Rochester and the school's in-town training headquarters. The dogs would be worked along a few side streets ending with a brief walk through the main shopping area.

After we parked, Smitty looked over the waiting group of dogs and mentioned that two from this string had already been rejected as being too sensitive and hesitant to lead out. He then selected a very strong, muscular, female black Labrador to start the day. "Meet Belle!" he said. "Let's get to work!"

Belle rushed to greet me as Smitty snapped on her leash. Before she left the van, he asked her to sit, giving one soft-spoken command. Almost immediately he jerked up on her collar and pushed on her rear so that she responded quickly. He praised her, then allowed her to leave the van, his hands ready to jerk her back if she pulled too much.

Leader Dogs work in leash, collar, and harness. Even when fully trained and placed, the lead and collar are always attached although not readily discernible to the casual onlooker.

The collar is a large oval link metal choke chain made in Germany. The school has studied various weights and link sizes in collars and thinks this particular one is best for training breeds used for guide work. Its width and weight ensures the proper correction, whereas narrower collars tend to cut into the flesh and coat when repeatedly jerked.

Leashes are custom-made for the school. They _are leather, approximately five-eighths of an inch in width with clips at both ends. When the dog is working in harness the leash is doubled and clipped to an extra ring near the collar. It may also be clipped to a ring about eight inches from the handler's end to form a loop handle and a leash approximately five feet in length. When doubled it is less than three feet long.

The harness is also custom-made and comes in three sizes. The handle is steel, covered with a soft, durable, plasticized cover for comfort. It is held in the left hand with fingers curled on top and thumb under. The grip must be light with the arm relaxed. This is the only way the dog's muscles, lungs and movements can telegraph up to the handler the signals he needs as he moves. It is also the only way the dog can take initiative. When the dog is trained, the lead is run up and tucked loosely under the index finger of the left hand.

Belle's harness was attached after she left the van. She sensed its meaning, settling down in preparation for her working session. While buckling the harness, Smitty placed her on his left side and lined her up on the sidewalk in the direction they were going to go. This, he explained, is a very important point. A dog will move in the direction it is facing. A blind handler must give his dog the benefit of a correct direction, otherwise he has no one to blame but himself if he is led into a confusing situation. A dog guide is intelligent but not a mind reader—a fact driven home again and again as I worked at the school.

Smitty then explained the commands the dog was learning and the basic rules of correction and praise. She would be expected to move forward on command and signal, walk at a steady pace without weaving while keeping slightly to right center of the walk, find curbs on command, break pace and halt upon reaching them, and move to right or left upon command and signal.

The harness is never used to correct the dog or as an aid in teaching. Either the leash and collar are used to teach or, if the situation warrants, objects are used. These latter corrections are discussed in Chapter 10. When correcting through leash and collar, the trainer initially drops the harness handle and uses either the right or left hand to jerk the leash. Timing is off by approximately one second if a left handed correction is used since this hand is already holding the harness. For this reason the majority of trainers keep the right hand lightly on the leash and use that hand to correct the beginning dog.

A dog guide moves in what is called the "master position." The dog's thigh remains next to the handler's left leg. If the dog moves too far back (lagging), the harness jams down into its ribs and the handler cannot feel the critical signals the dog's body is sending. If the dog pulls too hard (forging), the handler loses balance and control. Ideally the harness is slightly taut, and the handler moves with his forearm comfortably lowered, wrist flexed upwards, body relaxed. The dogs prefer to move quickly, although they learn to pace themselves to their handlers.

Belle was ready to begin work. Smitty commanded, "Belle, forward!" and simultaneously scooped his right hand straight ahead, palm down. Belle moved off and I followed them, watching foot and hand movements and listening to Smitty's running conversation. His voice was a mastery of vocal control—enthusiastic praise broken by firmer command and correction. All trainers utilize this approach. "It's fun to watch the reactions of people when they see us," Smitty said. "Some of them have never owned a dog in their lives. Here we are, walking down the street talking away for all we're worth, and then the next minute we're jerking the lead or banging on car hoods. Sometimes people come up and say, '*What* are you *doing*?' The reactions are priceless. Yet when we tell an apprentice how we expect him to talk to and praise his dogs he will say, 'Really? I can really do that?' and he's pleased he can be so demonstrative."

We were approaching a curb, and I wondered what would happen. Smitty seemed to read my thoughts. "A beginning dog is taught to sit when reaching a curb or step," he said. "A sit is a definite action. We use the command, 'Find the curb!' as we approach and begin reaching forward with the right foot past the dog's nose while slowing down. If the dog misses it and goes over, even one paw, it's corrected. Once the dog begins halting at a curb, we stop enforcing the sit and the dog simply slows down and stands."

Belle was cautioned to, "Find the curb!" Smitty's right hand was on the lead, ready to correct, but both lead and harness were relaxed. Belle slowed pace. This is an excellent sign, Smitty said softly. It shows the command has meaning after only three days. Later she will inform her blind master that a curb or step is ahead by breaking pace in just this way. Smitty's right foot inched forward and touched the curb. Belle paused at his side and then put her right front paw in the street. "*No!*" she was told in a low, firm tone. Smitty jerked her back into place, then reached down and tapped the curb with both his hand and right foot. "Curb, Belle! Find the curb!" he repeated several times in a quiet, calm tone. Belle showed no remorse but calmly gazed across the street. Smitty made no effort to get her attention as he spoke and I wondered if she were listening.

We waited for traffic to pass. "The curb is important," Smitty explained. "If she puts one paw over, the next day she'll put two, and the next day might walk out into the street. In this work a dog must be precise within our guidelines. As for traffic—we listen. If all is quiet, we cross. If traffic is moving, we wait. At lights, if we come to a crossing in our favor, we wait for the next full light cycle. At all times, though, once we're in the street we keep on going—even if we made a mistake. Dogs do not read lights. They move with traffic flow. The handler must know where traffic is coming from and where it is going. He has to learn to listen."

On command, "Belle, forward!" we moved into the street. The correction was forgotten. Belle was moving well and Smitty reached down and patted her backside. "Hey, what a good girl, Belle!" he said with enthusiasm in his voice. About midway in the street he repeated, "Find the curb, Belle!" Remembering her previous correction Belle instantly slowed down. "Good girl, find the curb!" Belle was now lagging in the middle of the street. She certainly *had* been listening, I thought. Smitty reached in front of her nose and wiggled his fingers, then snapped them. "Hup-up, Belle!" he said in an encouraging voice. Belle nosed slightly forward. "Hey, good girl! Hup-up! Find the curb!" Belle was barely moving as Smitty's right foot reached ahead of her nose. They were only a few inches short of the "up-curb," which must be touched with the foot before the dog is praised and the maneuver completed. At no time, however, did Smitty use the leash to pull Belle forward. She was made to move, even though slowly, through his voice and fingers alone. Smitty's toe finally touched the curb and remained there. He reached over and hugged her. "Good dog, Belle! Find the curb!"

He straightened up and commanded, "Belle, forward!" They moved up onto the curb. At once Smitty commanded, "Belle, left!" At the same time his right hand swung in front of her nose, close and fast enough so that her head moved in that direction to avoid contact with his hand. "Good girl, left!" he said happily as he turned to take advantage of her head movement. We were on the intersecting sidewalk. "Belle, find the curb!" he repeated, and we prepared to cross another street.

The dog guide does not move without directions. Although the trained dog will learn familiar routes by rote, it needs guidance in

117

strange places. Its master must know where he is going and how to get there. If his route calls for two blocks down, then one block left and half a block right, just next door to the restaurant, he must count street crossings and curbs and keep track of right and left turns. He may use his sense of smell to tell when he is at the restaurant, knowing the building he wants is next door, or he will need to count paces from the corner to his location. Because of this required concentration, dog guide schools try to educate the public in the importance of ignoring a working dog guide and master. Coming up to offer assistance or asking to pet the dog may break the handler's train of thought. A team should be approached only if the handler appears confused or has dropped the harness which is a tell-tale signal that the dog is not under a command.

After we passed the center of town, Smitty stopped and handed Belle to me. "Okay," he said, "Do your thing!" I had not been told I would handle dogs, especially so soon in the program, and I felt one hundred feet tall and absolutely incompetent at the same time. Belle looked quizzically at me and then at Smitty as I fumbled with the harness and leash. I scratched her ears and hoped for the best. "Belle, forward!" I commanded, trying to imitate Smitty's vocal tone and hand signal. I was amazed when she responded.

This had looked easy when I followed Smitty and watched him. Now I was struggling with an untrained dog, new commands, new signals, and new methods of teaching. The harness and lead seemed to be in the wrong places at the wrong times. The standard techniques and timing I had used for years in training house pets and AKC competition dogs were out of place. I gave corrections too soon, which did not allow Belle time to think. I stepped out without waiting for her to take the initiative. I guided her with the harness. It felt awkward to use my right hand to give leash corrections. I found it difficult to keep her moving at a steady pace, in a straight line, while watching for distractions, such as squirrels or stray dogs, which would change the training situation. The simple act of crossing a street turned into a series of complicated commands and maneuvers.

Through it all, Smitty walked at my side and did not miss a single mistake. By the time we returned to the training building, his criticism had accompanied me across several streets, through many curb halts, right and left turns. I felt inept and wondered if I would be asked to handle any more animals. I patted Belle as Smitty removed her harness. "Just between us, Belle," I said, "I made more mistakes than you did." Belle wagged her tail and Smitty just smiled.

I was surprised when he returned with a female German Shepherd named Nikki and announced, "We'll repeat what we just did. I'll take her out through the main street, and you'll bring her back."

This time I could fully appreciate what Smitty said as he again explained the commands and how to enforce them. I watched everything more carefully—foot work, hand signals, turns, timing. As I watched Nikki's mistakes, I tried to time my mental corrections to Smitty's physical ones.

Nikki was more agile than Belle, and she responded quickly to the slightest correction. Smitty's training approach was also different. Corrections were not as hard, but there were more of them. Nikki had a tendency to look around as she moved, alerting to things Belle had ignored. She had to be corrected numerous times as she watched pedestrians enter and leave stores on the main street of town.

As we returned to the training building, I felt more confident. The mechanics of curb halts, street crossings, keeping to right center of the sidewalk, moving at a steady pace, making right and left turns were falling into place. I could concentrate on canine response as Smitty explained the importance of the commands we were learning. "A steady pace is important," he said. "The dog that speeds up and slows down without a reason is not performing properly. When the dog slows down, something should be coming up. Maybe pedestrians are blocking the sidewalk or footing is bad. If the dog stops, the handler knows there is something immediately ahead that drastically changes footing or blocks progress. When this happens, the handler must stop and ascertain why. That's why we're reaching forward with the foot to find the curb. The blind handler will do the same thing. If he can't feel anything with his foot he will sweep his right arm up and out. Once he knows why his dog stopped, he can command accordingly.

"Moving in a straight line is also important. The dog should move with pedestrian flow and not angle off course except for a reason. Who wants a dog that wanders around from left to right on a sidewalk? The dog must also move in a straight line when there is no sidewalk or path to follow. For example, what if the dog were to cross a street and lead his handler into the cross street? This would mean a complete loss of orientation. Whenever the dog veers to avoid an obstacle, it should return to the original path. It's up to the handler to feel this and make sure it's done or know why it isn't done.

"Sometimes handlers unwittingly set their dogs up to make mistakes in direction. I showed you with Belle how we line up in the direction we want to go. Let's see what happens at the next corner if the handler makes a mistake."

At the next corner Nikki broke pace and stopped with only the slightest help. Smitty did not correct us, and I assumed we had done a nice job. I dropped the harness and petted her using my left hand on her left shoulder. She leaned against my leg. When I stood upright and picked up the harness, she was angling slightly to the right.

"Look what you did!" Smitty pointed out. "You didn't even know you were doing it! If this were a trained dog and you were blind, you'd follow her when you gave the command, 'Forward!' and she might move out at that angle. You'd end up away from the opposite curb and wonder where you were. We keep the right foot on the curb or step while we praise because this keeps the dog straight. We then use the phrase, 'Find the curb!' once again when we're in the middle of the street. This helps keep the dog's mind on the opposite corner. Later, most dogs learn by rote to move from corner to corner in a straight line. Handlers, though, have to feel any shift in direction just in case the dog makes a mistake. Angling can become a serious problem if a handler allows it to happen."

As Nikki and I moved off the curb into the street, Smitty had more criticism. "You're still stepping out with the dog rather than allowing her to take the initiative," he said. "That might not seem important to you because you can see, but a blind person hasn't any idea what's beyond that curb. For all he knows there might be a drop-off or a series of steps.

Leader Dog moves out in the "master position."

Leader Dog stops at an "up-curb."

120

Dogs are taught to stop and sit at curb or step.

Trainer Harold Smith teaches a left turn.

He won't chance moving until the dog is under way. The angle of the harness and the amount of pull are his clues as to what to expect. By moving with the dog, you're teaching her to expect the same response from any future handler. She then may not move at all when the command is given."

I thought about the points raised by Smitty as we walked back to the training building. Each step we took had new meaning and importance. It wasn't enough to learn new commands and techniques in order to train dog guides. I had to learn how it felt to be blind—to know what is important and what isn't in a world without vision. Dog guide trainers cannot teach without this knowledge. With a jolt I realized that my lifetime of sighted standards did not apply here.

This dog's angling must be corrected.

Angling can be a serious problem.

"Heel!" One of the students enters the dormitory. His Leader Dog moves in the master position with the harness off. Trainer is at right.

Chapter 9

More on Basic Training

By the time we drove back to the school for lunch, we had walked approximately four miles in a cold drizzle and trained four dogs. The routing and commands had remained the same for each animal, and I wondered if the afternoon's assignment would be similar. Yes, Smitty said, as the van bounced over a few pot-holes, although new commands would be introduced as the environment warranted them. He also planned to run the afternoon dogs through basic obedience exercises. He then handed me a set of index cards. "Here! Take a look at these!" he said. "I think they'll help you understand what we'll be doing on a daily basis."

The cards were divided by days under headings indicating which commands had been used, which stores or restaurants had been visited, and how each dog responded.

"All trainers have some sort of system," Smitty explained, "although not necessarily identical. I like to jot down what I did every day so that no dog is short-changed. By the time these dogs finish basic training, they'll be familiar with every command they'll need and have been everywhere in town. We'll talk more about the breakdown of the program at lunch."

Lunch hour is usually a hurried affair for the trainers. Each dog is worked approximately thirty to forty minutes a day, although some lessons run as long as an hour. There's also driving time to and from training locations. Back at the school the dogs must be exercised and put in their stalls. Most trainers pop into the school's kitchen, grab a sandwich, and are gone again.

Several trainers were seated at the large table in the kitchen, and they crowded together to make room for us. Everyone wanted to know what I thought about the morning's work and if I was finding dog guide training different from initial expectations.

I commented that I had expected new techniques, but nothing had prepared me for a new way of thinking. It had not occurred to me, and I doubted if it occurred to other sighted individuals, that dog guides are trained by non-visual standards. I had a lot to learn.

Everyone assured me that things would fall into place. I would begin to envision things and even move as a blind person. If I had a difficult time, they would blindfold me—a common experience for apprentices.

Smitty explained that not only was each command taught from an unsighted person's point of view but that the dogs would have numerous lessons in which the trainers would pretend they were blind, either closing their eyes or working under blindfold. Each dog's work is checked in this fashion, and the lessons also serve as an introduction to the animal in working for a visually handicapped master.

"Every day we expect the dogs to make a little more progress," Smitty said. "Once they begin to respond to commands, and that's already starting as you saw, we begin fading into the background, allowing them to take initiative. Then it's just a matter of experience."

The dogs' training program lasts four months, although one week is a vacation period following neutering which occurs sometime after the second month in training. Approximately two weeks are alloted at the beginning of the program for retesting and introduction to basic obedience commands. Once the harness is introduced, progress is rapid. Six weeks later, basic training, which takes place primarily in and around Rochester, is finished. The dogs then move up to the advanced training kennel. The next four weeks involve use of the commands in surrounding cities and countryside. The final four weeks involve polishing the dogs' performances and seeking out complicated routings.

After lunch Smitty showed me the staff library which includes hundreds of books on blindness, animal behavior, and dog training. "We expect the apprentices to use these," he said simply. As we walked out to the kennel, he added that Dr. Eastman also helped educate the apprentices. The trainers were expected to recognize signs of illness and vitamin deficiencies, be proficient in canine first aid, and scrub-up to participate in surgery when their dogs were neutered.

As we drove back into town with the afternoon dogs, Smitty mentioned that routings would vary for each dog on the following day. "Right now they're having their first introduction to the center of town, but we're going to start visits to stores, the post office, and so on. Some dogs will be ready for more experiences sooner than others."

At the training site he selected a male Golden Retriever. "I told you this morning that two dogs have already been rejected from this string. This will probably be our third. His name is Brandy."

After the harness was attached and Brandy was aimed down the street Smitty commanded, "Brandy, forward!" Brandy looked up and hesitated. Wiggling his fingers in front of Brandy's nose, Smitty encouraged, "Hup-up, Brandy!" Brandy moved ahead a few inches and Smitty followed him, "Good boy! Forward!" Brandy, however, did not lead out, but walked with his shoulder firmly at Smitty's knee. Smitty reached in front of the dog's nose and tried again to encourage him to move ahead, but Brandy could not be enticed. His previous owner had taught him to "heel" by American Kennel Club standards, and he had learned the exercise well. He was determined to follow his handler.

"I had hoped that he'd begin leading out within a few days, especially when he was in harness, but it just isn't working," Smitty said with disappointment. "He's a perfect example why dogs should only be familiar with obedience commands before we get them. Once a habit like this is formed, it's hard to change. This dog just isn't going to take initiative."

Since the working requirements for dog guides vary from those of ordinary dogs, any pretraining can be detrimental. For this reason, even foster puppy programs discourage formalized obedience work of any kind. "We've had too many cases," Smitty said, "where well-meaning people tried to 'help us out' by pretraining animals only to end up ruining them. I remember one otherwise good dog. His owner was very proud of the fact that he had taught him to stop at curbs. His corrections had been too hard and this dog would slink up to corners. This isn't the image we want in a dog guide, and we had to reject him."

Rejections in basic training are common. Leader Dogs does not like placing these into categories which tend to group together a wide variety of similar but not identical problems. A dog that is rejected because it constantly sniffs the pavement is different from one that cannot be controlled when it sees squirrels, yet both are classified under the general heading of "distraction prone." A dog that fails to take initiative only in a specific situation is different from one such as Brandy who refused to take a single step without guidance, yet both are classified under the general heading, "fails to take initiative." Sometimes, too, rejections stem from more than one factor and neatly categorizing these dogs is impossible. Once training starts, however, failure to take initiative in some capacity is the major cause for rejection, followed by being overly distracted or exhibiting some sort of negative training attitude. Unfortunately these characteristics usually cannot be detected until the program actually begins.

Each case is slightly different. The dogs test out well, and then problems become evident on a day-to-day basis. Besides being unable to take initiative or being distraction prone, several are overly sensitive to correction or exhibit signs of stress as the work becomes more complicated. Others resist or resent teaching efforts. A few have playful or immature attitudes towards the work. Still others may vacillate, working well one day and exhibiting disinterest and boredom the next. Several of these problems are suspected in advance through the foster program, although some families don't recognize them, and early detection is not possible with donated dogs.

Isolated fears show up as the work progresses, and these also can be cause for rejection. Smitty had the opportunity to show me how these are handled when he began working a male yellow Labrador Retriever named Star. We made a left turn onto a street just off the center of town and noticed some barricades up ahead partially blocking the sidewalk. "Good!" Smitty exclaimed. "We'll see how he leads me around them." As we moved closer a workman set up a pneumatic drill and began breaking up the sidewalk. The sound was deafening, but it was too late to turn back. Smitty told me to watch what he would do. Dropping the harness, he moved forward with Star, encouraging the dog with his voice while lightly holding the leash. Star put his tail between his legs and moved in a semi-crouch. The barricades came closer and the only way he could pass them would be to move closer to the drill. He did this, eyeing the workman and drill as he moved slowly past. "Hey, good dog!" Smitty yelled above the noise. He didn't dwell on the praise but immediately lifted the harness as they continued ahead. It wasn't until we reached the corner that he stopped and turned to me. "We both saw that he was frightened," he said. "I'm going to gamble that the fear stems from lack of experience. He didn't panic or try to bolt. When he reached the barricade he didn't try to move away from the sound. He actually went towards it. We'll bring him back here tomorrow and see how he does. I think his response was good. If he had tried to bolt or become panic-stricken, I'd say we had a real problem."

Numerous dogs are accepted by dog guide schools having never been exposed to various sounds, types of footings, revolving doors, elevators, etc. Initial uncertainty and confusion in these cases may not be reason for rejection. The manner in which each dog responds is analyzed. A few days may then be spent on the problem. If the dog cannot adjust with confidence within that time, it will be rejected. In Star's case rejection was not necessary. Two days later he was passing the area with barely a sideward glance.

Each of the afternoon dogs spent several minutes practicing obedience commands which are introduced on leash during the two initial weeks of training. By the time work begins in harness, the dogs are familiar with several commands. If no opportunities arise during the day's lesson to use them, the trainers usually stop somewhere and review. Smitty selected one of the residential streets and explained the exercises as each dog practiced.

"The dog guide isn't always in a harness," Smitty explained, "so we teach commands both in harness and on leash. Obedience commands are similar to the ones dogs learn in a public obedience class although we don't use American Kennel Club standards of performance."

MASTER POSITION

The dog guide works both on leash and in harness from the "master position." This is always at the handler's left side with the dog facing in the same direction as the handler, its right thigh even with the handler's left leg. Any variation from this position will be forging, lagging, or angling. This position differs from The American Kennel Club's "heel position" in which the dog's head to shoulder remains in line with the handler's left hip. The master position is taught to the dog by simply placing it in this position before any work begins.

"NO!"

The word "no" is one of the most important commands taught at Leader Dogs. It is given in a quiet, patient, but clipped tone whenever the dog is in the act of making a mistake. It is immediately followed by the appropriate command. Correction follows if the dog does not respond. The dog soon realizes that the utterance of this word means something is not quite right. With the following command it is given the solution to the problem. If it does not correct itself, it is corrected.

Many public dog trainers shun the word "no" from their training vocabularies, insisting its use is deflating to the dog attempting to learn. This is true only if the word is bellowed in exasperation by a handler exhibiting a lack of patience or used repeatedly without a counter-command to help the dog select the proper action.

When used as a command in a business-like tone of voice, the effects are startling. With the beginning Leader Dog the time lapse during the sequence of "no"—command—correction—praise is very fast, but as the dog progresses the time lapse becomes longer between the "no"—

command and correction—praise portions of the cycle so that the dog has sufficient time to correct itself.

By the time dogs reach advanced training, they respond to the word "no" with unusual willingness and alacrity, wagging their tails and attempting to remember what was originally requested before the counter-command is given. This type of teaching builds initiative.

"HEEL!"

It surprised me that Leader Dogs are taught to heel on leash. When the harness is attached the command is, "Forward!" but when the leash alone is attached the command changes to, "Heel!" On the command the dog steps out in the master position with just enough pull to exert an element of control over its master while listening for commands to move right or left. This command will be used when the harness is off even if it is just to move around the house or yard or when someone other than the master walks the dog. The introduction of this exercise with leash and collar prepares the dog for the "forward" command in harness.

The most difficult aspect of this exercise is to teach the dog to initiate movement before the handler. Trainers use an excited tone of voice, jiggle the leash, and reach in front of the nose to wiggle or snap fingers. The leash is never jerked forward to force a dog to move. This creates distrust of both handler and leash, serving to break down willingness and initiative.

Once the dog moves, the handler steps out and enforces the exercise by jerking back on the leash when the dog is forging (using a "No, steady!" command prior to correction), jerking sideways when the dog is veering from a straight line without reason (using a "No, straight!" command prior to correction), and using the command, "Hup-up!" to encourage forward movement when the dog is lagging.

"HUP-UP!"

This command is used to entice a dog to move forward on its own volition. After giving the command, the handler uses vocal tone, sounds, jingling the leash, wiggling or snapping the fingers in front of the dog's nose, or tapping the left thigh to encourage response. It is used repeatedly as the dog nears obstructions, curbs and doors or whenever the dog slows down in training without reason.

"LEFT!"

This is a ninety degree turn to the left, taught by vocal command and hand signal. The command, "Left!" is given while the right hand swings in front of the dog's muzzle to the left creating a sideward turn of the head. The handler then pivots into the turn with the dog. Care is usually taken not to touch the dog on this turn although some animals initially require some body contact to complete the turn. As soon as the dog responds on its own, the excessive body movements and exaggerated hand signal are phased out. The dog then turns on command accompanied by a simple right hand gesture across the body to the left. A hand signal alone may be used in a noisy environment.

"RIGHT!"

This is a ninety degree turn to the right, taught by vocal command and hand signal. The command, "Right!" is given while the right hand swings to the right. The handler then pivots right and jerks the leash as he turns to bring the dog with him. As soon as the dog responds on its own, the leash jerk and exaggerated hand signal are phased out. The dog then turns on command accompanied by a simple right hand gesture to the right. A hand signal alone may be used in a noisy environment.

"SIT!"

Most animals coming to Leader Dogs already know this exercise although many have to be taught that immediate response is expected.

If a dog has never been taught to sit, the trainer utilizes a jackknife technique to introduce the exercise. The dog is placed in the master position. The leash is then held in the right hand very close to the collar, taut behind the dog's head. The left arm then comes behind both rear legs. Following the command, the left arm creates a forward pressure on the rear legs while the right hand jerks up and slightly backward on the leash. The dog sits on the handler's arm. In a few days the jackknife technique is phased out, and the dog is expected to sit on command only. If it doesn't, the right hand brings the leash short behind the dog's head. An upward jerk on the leash is then given while the left hand pushes on the dog's rear.

"Sit" is also taught from a down position while the dog is in the master position. The command is given with hand signal, vocal command or both. The signal is a slap on the handler's left thigh. The majority of dogs rise on the sound alone; if not, the leash is used to jerk the dog up into a sitting position.

"DOWN!"

With the dog seated in the master position, the leash is held short in the right hand close to the dog's collar, which is often lifted high behind the ears and under the chin. After the command is given, the leash is jerked hard towards the ground. Should the dog balk at this technique, the trainer uses his left hand to exert downward pressure on the dog's shoulders while his right arm comes behind both front legs and flips them forward. No matter which technique is used to teach the exercise, the reaction time in placing the dogs is very fast so that animals learn after a few lessons to descend as soon as the command is given. Once the dog is responding on its own, a down signal is incorporated, which is the handler's left hand, angled sidewards, palm down, in front of the dog's nose.

"STAND!"

This command is introduced while the dog is being groomed and later is repeated while the harness is being buckled and removed. It is taught for familiarity, and the dog is not expected to remain in a rigid pose. Holding the dog upright with a hand braced at one of the back flanks is usually sufficient to teach the dog what is wanted.

"STAY!"

A stay command is taught in both a sit and down position. Response is expected only at leash's length since dog guides are rarely placed on these commands at any distance from their masters. With the dog in the master position, in either a sit or down position, the trainer gives the command, "Stay!" accompanied by a hand signal. The signal is the left palm coming in front of the dog's eyes, fingers pointed down. A stay signal is also used once the trainer is in front of the dog, which is the left palm facing the animal.

Once the command and signal are given the trainer pivots in front of the dog's nose, pauses for a few seconds, then pivots back to the master position. The dog is instantly replaced following a, "No! Sit! Stay!" command if it breaks position. Once the dog understands the exercise the trainer adds on time and begins moving towards the end of the leash.

To return to the dog from leash's length, the trainer runs his left hand down the leash to guide him back towards the dog's head. He then pivots back to the master position. The dog's master will use this same technique to locate his dog after a stay command. This differs from American Kennel Club standards in which handlers return to the heel position by circling around their dogs' backs.

This Labrador
Retriever will be
corrected for sniff-
ing the sidewalk.

Trainer observes
this dog's reaction
to construction
noise.

This Leader Dog
stops at the
change of footing
ahead of him.

"COME!"

The dog guide is taught to come by approaching the handler's right side and circling around his back to the master position where it sits automatically. This differs from The American Kennel Club's concept of "come" which requires the dog to move directly in front of the handler and sit facing him.

To teach this exercise the handler places the dog on leash in a sit-stay position while he moves to leash's length. The dog is then called to come. If response is not immediate, the leash is jerked and the dog encouraged to approach the handler without further correction. Once the dog reaches the handler, it is brought past the right side. The leash changes hands behind the back and the dog is encouraged forward into the master position as it moves alongside the handler's left side. While the dog is circling, body contact is kept at all times so that the master will feel the dog as it goes around his back. Once in the master position the dog is commanded to sit.

"Around!" Leader Dog trainer shifts dog from left to right side of the body when entering or leaving doors that swing from the right.

"AROUND"

This command is used to bring the dog from the master position to the right side of the handler. There are times when a dog guide must be on the handler's right, especially when going through doors which swing from right to left. In cases such as these, a dog on the left will move in front of the handler in order to lead him and, by crossing in front of him, may create confusion or accident. Handlers must ascertain at every door which way it swings and move the dog around to the right side if necessary. Once the doorway is passed, the handler commands his dog, "Heel!" and moves it around his back to the master position. This exercise is taught by passing the dog behind the back and switching the leash, or leash and harness, behind the back to the opposite hand.

———

Since basic obedience commands are incorporated in daily work, it doesn't take more than a few days for animals to realize that they must be obeyed in spite of distractions or location.

"We don't look for a certain working style," Smitty said as he reviewed exercises with a female Golden Retriever named Mindy. "I'm not going to criticize her work if she happens to go down slowly or sits by rolling over on one hip. These dogs must understand the commands and obey them everywhere, but we're not going to mold dogs to fit a sighted ideal of a perfect performance."

Early rush hour traffic was heavy as we drove back to Leader Dogs at half-past four. Smitty mentioned that the next day, we would work in the center of town with emphasis on curb halts and steps, right and left turns, and visits into some of the local stores. In reality, he said, the majority of "walking commands" had already been introduced including, "forward," "straight," "steady," "hup-up," "right," "left," and the introduction of the phrase "find the _____," which would be built on with several nouns as the weeks went by, the dogs already learning, "Find the curb!" and "Find the stairs!" When these commands were incorporated with the basic obedience exercises, the foundation the dogs already had was evident.

Many dog guide manuevers do not have a command phrase. The animal is expected to perform in a given fashion when a situation calls for a specific response. An unsighted person cannot command his dog, "Avoid the tree trunk up ahead!" or, "Slow down! The footing looks bad!" yet the dog must respond as if commands had been given. Responses to specific situations are taught through repetition and soon become part of the dog's performance.

"You'll see!" Smitty assured me as we pulled into the school's parking lot. "These dogs will be ready for advanced training in a few weeks!"

I was inwardly skeptical but Smitty was right. The dogs learned much faster than I expected.

Leader Dog trainer Mickey Loesser "far-sights" or pretends he is blind. Mickey will "read" his dog through muscle tone and breathing rather than through vision.

Chapter 10

Putting It All Together

"Smitty, she's aiming me into that car! What should I do?"

"I'd say you're going to scrape your right side. When it happens, give the hood a whomp you wouldn't believe!"

I tried to relax. It could be worse, I thought. At least the car was stopped for a light and wasn't moving. The dog angled quickly to avoid the front bumper but I caught my right leg and winced. "No!" I commanded as I whacked the car hood with my right hand, giving the driver an apologetic look. She stared back in disbelief, mouth slightly open. The dog sidestepped quickly and glanced with alert suspicion at the car. As we walked by, Smitty leaned over the car hood and smiled. "Thank you very much!" he said happily. The woman stared back at us. I wondered what she was thinking. I knew what I was thinking. I had one sore leg, one sore palm, and a dog that had been corrected without being touched. Hopefully, she had learned new respect for cars in relationship to her handler.

———

"Mickey, do you see those tree branches up ahead? Should I duck them?"

"Of course not!" Mickey Loesser casually said. "Let him walk you right into them if that's what he's planning."

There had been a heavy rain the night before and the thick, wet branches hung down about four feet above the walk.

"Unreal!" I moaned as they slapped into my face.

"Okay," Mickey said, "halt and shake those branches until I say 'Stop!' and keep saying 'No!' in a calm, low voice over and over again."

I shook the branches as hard as I could. The dog seemed to enjoy the entire performance.

"Come back about fifteen feet and try again," my instructor finally said. "I'd be surprised if he does the same thing twice."

"Mickey?" This time my voice had a pleading quality. The dog had pulled forward at a fast clip and was aiming directly towards the same branches.

This German Shepherd has moved his trainer too close to a trash container and the dog is corrected.

The same dog moves over to avoid a mail box and is praised for initiative.

The dog eyes the trash container as he progresses forward.

"Well, what do you know!" Mickey exclaimed with surprise. "He's going to do it again!"

"Unreal!" I said with desperation as the branches smashed into my face for the second time.

Once more the branches shook with a frenzy, and we backed up to try again. Two corrections did it, saving one tree and one apprentice's face. Next time, the dog moved forward and angled around the area.

———

"Jim, he's getting close to these store fronts, but I might break something if I hit the glass."

"Tell him, 'No! Straight!' and hit your right thigh with your right hand."

I had seen the trainers do this and it seemed easy. When I tried, however, my hand barely made a sound. I wasn't hitting hard enough. "He's got to hear the slap of your hand against your leg and be a little afraid of it," Jim said. "It's got to really be hard!" Next time, my hand and leg stung for ten minutes, but my instructor was happy. The dog responded as expected by sidestepping away from the building.

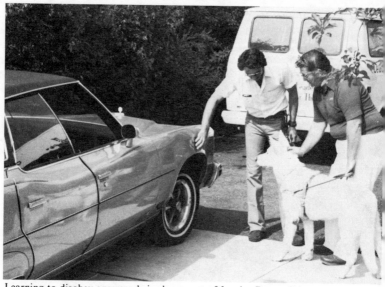

Learning to disobey commands is also a part of Leader Dog training.

Teaching the dog to avoid obstacles, overhanging objects and protrusions in order to compensate for the handler is considered by the trainers to be one of the most difficult portions of dog guide training, at least to experience. As I rubbed my sore palms and gazed at the growing number of black and blue marks, it was easy to understand why they feel this way. They must allow themselves to be led into situations through which they can correct. It is not unusual for a dog guide trainer to find himself bumping into people, falling over car hoods, brushing into buildings, tripping over sidewalk toys and bicycles, stumbling into and over parking meters, mail boxes and fire hydrants. When a trainer sees situations like these coming up he must try to relax, just as a blind person would be relaxed, so that his tenseness does not telegraph through the harness that something is amiss.

Since the blind handler is unable to either duck to avoid something or move his dog out of the way, it is up to the animal to learn to skirt objects within a certain radius to the side or above him. These are shaken or hit, depending on their type. The dog is never touched. It is the trainer who suffers the knocks, bruises and scratches. Some trainers wear a ring on the right hand to make a sharper sound as they hit a building corner, parking meter, mail box and similar objects. Awnings, tree limbs and shrubbery are shaken. Whenever an object cannot be touched such as a plate glass window or a person, the handler hits his right thigh. Once handler compensation is mastered, the dogs gauge, almost to the inch, the height and width of their trainers. They alert from as far away as fifteen or twenty feet that something is coming up but tend to maneuver around these objects with as few extra steps as possible.

It was interesting to observe the same dogs after they were placed. Trainers are invariably of a slim, athletic build and the dogs adjust accordingly. If placed with heavy-set or very tall individuals the dogs made a few errors in compensation before they readjusted to the new bodily dimensions.

The training days moved along quickly and progress was rapid. The basic walking commands were used repeatedly throughout each working session. Every square inch of Rochester was covered again and yet again. Beginning with short three or four block walks along quiet, residental streets, the dogs soon became familiar with the entire business district.

Within a few weeks the beginners were moving well in harness, keeping to right center of the walk. They were breaking pace and halting at obstructions, steps and curbs. They were beginning to move automatically to right or left on command and signal, were learning to avoid projections and overhangs, and were moving around obstacles on their own if there was enough room for both dog and handler to do so. They kept their minds on their work when they encountered people, cats, dogs, squirrels, birds, moving vehicles, fire hydrants, and other interesting distractions. Whenever they had veered off course to investigate someone or something, their instructors had commanded, "No! Straight!" before dropping the harness and jerking them back into place. As their noses descended to sniff the pavement, they had been just as strongly corrected with an upward jerk on the leash. These corrections were harder than others since bad habits had to be quickly broken.

Every day the routes grew more complex. Each dog was soon worked a few paces behind another one in the string, and both were expected to keep their minds on the task at hand. Trainers would pass each other in groups at crossings or in town, and no canine socializing was allowed.

Every office building and store had been entered for familiarization purposes. New experiences became harder to find as trainers actively sought out obstructions, construction areas, and unusual footings. At lunch everyone discussed interesting areas they had discovered so that the others could try them.

As the work became more familiar to me, so did Rochester. Because of the training progam, I began to envision a city composed of geometric blocks with so many up-curbs, down-curbs, straight line walks, and obstacles to encounter to move from one location to any other. I knew where I would be apt to encounter children, toys left in driveways, broken sidewalks or no sidewalks, houses with cats, tall trees with squirrels, yards with fence-running, yapping dogs, and low awnings. I no longer had to see these things. I knew they were there from experience. The cliche, "I could find my way blindfolded," was taking on real meaning. I was beginning to understand how a blind person envisions or maps out his environment as he moves.

I was no longer interested in things as far as my eyes could see but only the immediate space around my body. Things at a distance were important only if they were about to infringe on my moving space and create problems in maneuvering. My mind was busy cataloging information having to do with lines, angles, footings, obstructions, sounds, and precise locations based on counting paces and street corners. I no longer was aware of architecture, landscaping, colors, people, distant traffic, or window displays. These things existed, but they were not imprinted in my mind. My concentration was elsewhere.

In similar fashion, step by step, the visually handicapped person becomes familiar with his locale so that a five or six block walk in any direction offers few surprises. He counts paces and blocks and knows how many up-curbs and down-curbs he must cross to reach any destination. He concentrates on sounds and their directions, a sometimes difficult task depending on weather conditions, wind direction and velocity, buildings or lack of them. In crowded environments he moves through an ocean of conflicting sounds that come and go, with important ones not necessarily the loudest. In using a dog guide, he learns to "read" the animal through the harness and can sense by the dog's breathing, pause in gait, and muscle tone exactly what is happening around him. He must concentrate on his dog's actions and know why there is a shift in direction, aiding his animal, if need be, to resume the initial direction by giving commands to move right or left. He must think, "To pass that car, she took me five paces left, then went right for four paces. Now I have to return five paces right and then go left again to be on the proper path."

In time, the dog guide will learn specific routes through repetition. "Let's go home, Lady!" will be used in the handler's familiar neighborhood. The dog will also probably learn the route used to go to and from work, guiding its master to the correct building and office with very little direction. Just like people, some dogs have a better sense of direction than others, learning routes, buildings and general areas very quickly. Others require more guidance.

In strange areas, however, the dog guide always needs firm, careful direction from its master. The human portion of the team must know where he is going and how to get there.

As the training days continued, it became evident that the dogs were becoming just as familiar with their routes and routines as the trainers. As the commands solidified in the dogs' minds, the trainers began giving them increasing responsibility. This was a gradual process depending on the individual dog and its progress. As soon as possible, each dog was encouraged to make its own decisions and perform without guidance.

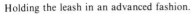

Holding the leash in an advanced fashion.

"Training attitude has a lot to do with it," Smitty said. "The dog has to be confident and relaxed while learning, and this means the trainer must be confident and relaxed while teaching."

The school's general training philosophy, however, involves more than requiring each trainer to be relaxed and confident. It respects the individuality of each animal while adhering to a basic teaching approach.

1. Never shout at a dog. Use vocal tone but never volume. Commands should be given in a business-like tone of voice.

2. Each command must be enforced.

3. Never lose patience or become angry. You can't control a dog if you can't control yourself.

4. Never hit dogs with hands or objects, or use feet to push or kick.

5. Break down each exercise into steps. Take each step slowly; never rush.

6. Never justify a dog's actions; correct if necessary.

7. Know each dog's capabilties and limitations.

8. Correct and praise each dog according to the animal's likes and dislikes.

Some dogs like vocal praise but are not fond of physical praise. Others respond to touch but prefer little vocalization. A few require both an exuberant tone of voice and a great deal of physical touch. Some dogs need a firm collar correction, while others can be controlled by voice. Some can be motivated by withdrawing praise or affection for a short period of time. Others find such denial confusing and stressful. Each dog must be properly motivated to succeed.

One form of motivation that is quite popular among public dog trainers but never used in dog guide training is use of food as an inducement to perform a given action. The dog guide is trained to ignore food except at meal time, a necessary requirement for an animal that will visit restaurants and food stores frequently and that must be trustworthy around counter and table tops without supervision.

Because animals are treated as individuals as they learn, they progress with trust in their trainers and confidence in their work. As soon as commands are learned, instructors expect response without insisting on a stylized performance. It is then time for the dogs to make their own decisions and learn from their mistakes. The instructors fade into the background, correcting if wrong, praising if right. Excessive body motions and exaggerated hand signals are gradually replaced with

Correcting for canine socializing.

normal postures and business-like gestures. Praise becomes more subdued. Correction is delayed in certain circumstances in order to give each animal time to think and make decisions, while in other situations—when disobedience is obvious—it is faster and firmer. Although this point in training varies for each dog, it is reached towards the end of the dog's first month working in harness.

At this time the most fascinating aspects of the dog's work begin to emerge—the ability to select safe routings without help and the ability to disobey a command for safety's sake. Both are based on a combination of canine intelligence, common sense, survival instinct, and training.

Mickey demonstrated the emergence of the ability to select a safe route with a black Labrador named Kelly. He purposely selected an area where there was some construction, with barricades blocking one sidewalk and stretching around a wide trench several feet deep in the adjoining street. As we neared the barricade, Kelly slowed down and stopped. Mickey reached forward with foot and hand, found the barricade and praised him. He then commanded, "Kelly, forward!" Kelly looked up and hesitated. When no guidance was forthcoming, he tentatively took a short step to the left. Mickey praised him. Responding to the praise Kelly slowly moved around the barricade, crossing onto the parkway grass in order to do so. He stopped at the down-curb of the street, once again earning Mickey's praise. On the command, "Kelly, forward!" he hesitantly moved around the trench and finally picked up speed to cross the street. Mickey again praised him

and then turned to me. "All the decisions were his and he made them. H
could see that he could get around the barricades. All he had to do wa
select which way he wanted to go, right or left. If a dog understand
the command, 'Forward!' he will attempt to pass an obstruction if it
possible. If it isn't, the dog waits for further instruction. A lot depend
on solid foundation training, initiative, intelligence, and common sens
There's some survival instinct at work, too. No dog is going to walk off
subway platform or into a ditch if he can help it, regardless o
command."

The ability, therefore, to disobey commands for the sake of safety
based on the same combination of training, initiative, intelligenc
common sense and survival instinct. However, the decision to di
obey is not always made in such obvious situations as being poise
at the edge of a subway platform or precipice. In some situations speci
training is necessary. For example, this ability will be called upon r
peatedly in traffic, and the general public regards the trained dog
response as extraordinary. The master will give a "Forward!" com
mand, and the dog will steadfastly refuse to obey because traffic ha
begun to move.

Smitty showed me how this type of training is accomplished. We too
the school's station wagon into Rochester during an ordinary workin
day for the express purpose of cutting off unwary trainers and dogs a
they were about to cross streets. As with all other aspects of th
program, trainers had to be relaxed so that animals suspected nothing
Parking near corners and patiently waiting for the precise momen
when trainers and dogs were stepping off curbs, Smitty drove forwar
and braked to a screeching halt as close to the team as possible. Th
dogs reacted with shock, coming to a rigid stop. Trainers then banged o
the side of the wagon with their hands while commanding, "No!" Afte
several tests on subsequent days, the dogs became observant to an
movement before stepping out with confidence. The command
"Forward!" now had a new twist. It was to be obeyed but only i
conditions were right. It was up to the dog alone to ascertain if it wa
safe to move. Survival depended on it. The wagon was also used to cu
off trainers and dogs in mid-street. Gunning the engine, Smitty drov
forward and sped past them coming as close as possible. The dog
reacted once again by coming to a fast halt. Lessons such as thes
are not easily forgotten. They would be utilized and thus reinforced in
the dogs' future lives.

Not all dogs, however, progress as expected during this portion of training. Through failure to take initiative and use caution when necessary, they must be rejected.

After the walking commands were mastered and trainers were fairly sure of the dogs' responses in the familiar Rochester area, they began to "far sight" or pretend they were blind. A person who is blind moves with his head and body erect and eyes focused forward. His steps are hesitant as the dog breaks pace for obstacles, and he does not lean over and look at the animal as he moves, gives commands, or praises. Since dogs learn largely through body postures and movements, they must learn, before being placed, to work for a "blind" person.

The trainers began moving as though they were day-dreaming, with heads and bodies erect and eyes focused ahead. At the same time, they made mental notes on each animal's movements and signals as felt through the harness. A dog reacts a bit differently to each object, person, or animal sighted. By observing the dog visually the trainers measured what they felt through the harness, concentrating on muscle tone, breathing, and subtle pauses or changes in gait.

Canine behaviorists such as Dr. Michael Fox (1972) have given us excellent studies on canine facial expressions and body postures to help us visually gauge an animal's feelings. However, a blind person cannot use this information. He cannot see if the dog's ears move forward (alert) or backward (submissive or fearful), if hackles are up (aggressive), if the mouth is open or closed with lips pulled back in a "submissive grin" or corners pushed forward in an aggressive manner, if tail is wagging or still, up (alert) or down (submissive or fearful). He must rely on other information. When he receives his dog, the trainer will explain how the animal reacts to variables in the environment and what signals will be telegraphed up through the harness. The blind handler must recognize these signals so that he can correct or praise, and be sure of his response. "Reading" dogs in this fashion is a skill all trainers possess. They *feel* as accurately as they *see*—able to gauge an animal's mood, action, and even anticipated action without visual help.

By the time the dogs enter their second month of training in harness, they are apt to be worked for short periods of time along the Rochester streets with the trainer's eyes closed. The accuracy of basic work is checked as well as the dog's ability to take initiative. There is always a risk while training that dogs are responding to some body movement that only a sighted person would give—an almost imperceptible tenseness while holding the harness, a way of walking or looking in advance in the direction one intends to go. Once in awhile a dog that appears to be taking initiative fails to perform when the trainer closes his eyes or uses a blindfold. By analyzing movements or gestures at this time, trainers can often correct problems.

Suzie, a German Shepherd-Alaskan Malamute mix, was the first dog I handled with my eyes closed. She was a confident animal and had learned all the basic commands very quickly. We had walked into the center of town and along one of the adjoining side streets and now would reverse the routing and go back to the training headquarters. For one of those blocks Jim asked me to close my eyes.

It was a quiet residential street with no foreseeable problems. I organized the leash and harness, closed my eyes and gave the command, "Suzie, forward!" Suzie moved out, and I was immediately aware of two things I had never noticed with my eyes open—the speed with which I was moving and the combined feel of muscle, bone, lungs, and animation against the harness. I could feel Suzie's slightest movement, even her breathing. I knew when she intended to speed up or slow down by the pull of her initial step before her foot touched the ground. I could feel the slightest shift to right or left as the harness moved in the palm of my hand. The sensation of moving so quickly with my eyes closed was both exciting and confusing. My mind could not register what was occurring or what we might be passing. There was no time to orient myself or plan my next step. Suzie had taken over and was doing it all.

As we moved along, I became aware of something else I had never noticed before—the sounds around me. With my eyes open, I would be walking down a quiet street—no more, no less. With my eyes closed, I found myself listening to the soft rhythmic pad of Suzie's paws, my footsteps, Jim's heavier ones, traffic sounds, a dog barking in the distance, a door slamming behind me across the street, a car coming closer, closer and louder, louder, passing with the sounds of engine and tires against pavement coupled with the faint smell of exhaust, then receding into the distance. I heard the wind in the trees and knew we were passing some very tall ones off the parkway by the sound in the upper branches. If I had had my eyes open, my other senses would probably have blocked out all these incidents. I wanted to concentrate on these sounds, but Suzie slowed down and I wondered why. I felt an uneven surface under my right foot and remembered that the sidewalk was broken along this street at a place where tree roots were pushing up the pavement. Suzie was picking her way through the rough section. I wondered where she was on the sidewalk. I had not felt a shift in direction, but I might have missed it in my concentration on the sounds around me. I reached out to the side with my right foot and located the edge of the walk, with earth beyond. She had elected to walk directly through the broken section of walk close to the parkway rather than skirt it. "Hey! Good girl, Suzie!" I heard myself saying, realizing that I had been so busy concentrating on my new sensations that I had all but forgotten her. I could feel her respond to the praise with a turn of her head to the right, a slightly faster step, and what must have been her tail wagging, as the feel through the harness was a side-to-side motion.

We were now midway down the block, and I could hear children's voices and some clattering up ahead to my left. They must have been playing with wagons or tricycles. The sounds grew louder as we came closer. Suzie's gait picked up and she began breathing faster, but we passed the spot without any problem. I could feel through the harness that she was looking left. The shrill voices and sounds receded behind us, and I found myself relieved that neither had stopped as we passed. I would have been uncomfortable, even embarrassed, to know children had stopped what they were doing and were staring at me. Not being able to see them, I felt unusually vulnerable. Later I learned this is a sensation shared by all visually handicapped individuals who often find conversations abruptly stopping and actions ceasing as they move along. Besides these obvious individuals who else might be silently watching? It is a creepy feeling, a rude feeling, yet one that must be lived with daily.

I tried to forget it and concentrate on all the other new impressions and sensations as we completed the block. Why is it that I had never used my ears like this before? Why had I never noticed the texture of things under my feet? I could even feel the cracks in the sidewalk, but this, too, was blocked out with my eyes open. I was fascinated with the signals coming up through the harness. For someone whose only experience moving without vision was to stumble through a dark room, the speed with which I was moving was akin to flying. Were my feelings similar to those of the visually handicapped? I later learned they were, with one addition—for someone who had no vision, the initial walk with a dog guide, once the nervousness passed, produced the major sensation of freedom, freedom to move quickly and naturally without pondering and probing each forward step.

Locating the door by following the dog's nose.

Blind handlers must be careful of their dogs' safety when using revolving doors.

Chapter 11

Country and City—Coffee Breaks and Shopping Trips

During the second month of training, the Rochester routes were expanded beyond the town. We went into the country where commands were used in a rural setting, along gravel, dirt, and cinder paths, highway shoulders, and vast expanses of green turf. "Country training" instantly exposed differences in canine characters not noticeable in the residential areas of Rochester. The Retrievers initially proved more difficult to manage as the inbred attraction to open space rose to the surface. Nostrils quivering in the air and muscles taut under harnesses, the urge to run and flush birds played counterpoint to commands. Some of the Working breeds, however, found country training only mildly interesting and then rather boring. They preferred the commotion and rapidly changing situations to be found in town. These differences would have a bearing on the future placement of each animal.

We also went to office complexes where the dogs had to deal with revolving doors, elevators, slippery stairways, and waxed tile floors; and we visited neighboring towns and indoor shopping malls where plate glass window displays stretched from floor to ceiling, almost indistinguishable by sighted person or dog from open shop doorways. Store managers watched silently as dogs were introduced to the intricacies of moving through confined space, an especially hazardous lesson in gift shops where crystal and china were within reach of every tail. Such trips were nearly everyday occurrences.

There were also visits to banks, grocery stores, post offices, even barber shops. Unlike the early weeks when dogs were primarily introduced to entering and immediately leaving stores, the trainers now waited in lines and took care of errands so that animals would have full working experiences in these locations. The index card system received full use as extensive exposure to as many different places as possible is necessary for every dog. Lessons began to last nearly an hour.

In the business district of Rochester, the dogs already had learned the location of major stores. This "homing-in" ability is something sighted persons do not ordinarily observe in their dogs as they are rarely allowed in buildings. The ever-present sign, "NO DOGS ALLOWED," offers no choice. By the second month of training, the Leader Dog perks up at the sight of the business district and then slows down as it passes shop after shop. If it is a place visited many times, the dog will glance back to see if its handler is interested in entering. This ability will be utilized in its new life. Each dog will learn its home town, down to the last door, and come to know the places frequented. If its master works out a set route and repeats the names of places before entering, the dog will learn to, "Find the bakery!" or "Find the post office!"

Knapps Coffee Shop in Rochester is a great favorite. At ten in the morning and two in the afternoon coffee is not only a break for trainers but a time for special training. Knapps is one of the first places visited by all Leader Dogs-in-training, with animals rotated on a daily basis so that all have several visits.

By the time dogs reach the advanced level, they are familiar with the restaurant routine, and trainers test them by far-sighting. This is what Jim intended to do with Daisy, a gentle, submissive Golden Retriever. "Daisy, right! Find the door!" Jim commanded, carefully keeping his eyes and body facing straight ahead. Daisy immediately turned her head to the right but saw no door. It was a few yards farther ahead, and she confidently continued straight for a few feet before turning. "Hey! Good girl!" Jim said enthusiastically at this display of initiative. Daisy moved towards the door, broke pace and stopped. Jim closed his eyes before reaching forward with his right hand to locate Daisy's muzzle. He then reached ahead of her nose with his hand and attempted to locate the door knob. Every former house dog has learned to "point" a door. Many actually touch the knob with their noses, but most look up expectantly and wait. Reach beyond the dog's nose with your hand and you'll find the door, is the rule. In this case, however, Daisy had stopped too soon and Jim could not reach the door. "Hup-up, Daisy!" he commanded softly. Daisy inched ahead very slowly and stopped. Jim, eyes still closed, inched with her. Now following the direction indicated by her muzzle with his right hand, he touched the doorframe. He fumbled up and down a few inches and grasped the knob. "What a good girl, Daisy!" he said happily. Daisy wiggled all over with pleasure. Jim ascertained that the door swung from left to right. Daisy could, therefore, remain on his left side as they entered. He opened the door and commanded firmly, "Daisy, forward!" and we entered the restaurant. Jim kept his eyes focused straight ahead as he spoke to me. "I'm going to let her do all the work. Let's see what happens."

Still obeying her forward command, Daisy led Jim into the restaurant. She paused briefly at the scene in front of her. There were endless tables and booths filled with people. Waitresses scurried past. No one looked at us or offered to help. Jim commanded, "Daisy, forward! Find a chair!" Daisy knew the routine from previous visits. Initially Jim had dropped her harness and guided her on leash when he gave the command, "Find a chair!" as he led her to a vacant seat. Later, he had followed her while holding the harness. Daisy now moved ahead, walking very slowly, weaving carefully around the crowded tables, compensating for Jim at all times, pausing as someone stepped into her path before resuming her slow pace. Several other trainers and their dogs were seated at a large table. They watched us in silence. Jim, who was now far-sighting, saw them, too, and ignored them. Daisy had selected a chair at the far side of the room. She halted when she reached her obstacle and Jim, who had again closed his eyes as they moved forward, reached out with his right foot and hand, fumbling for the back of the chair and then the seat. As he sat down, he petted Daisy who was already sitting. "What a good girl to find a chair!"

Jim dropped the harness and looked around the room. We decided to join the other trainers. This time he gave Daisy a simple, "Heel!" command, and we moved to the other table. Daisy was told to, "Down! Stay!" to Jim's left. No Leader Dog is allowed to sit next to a table or beg for food. In fact, whenever his master is seated, the dog must lie down.

Rich Guzik had a beginning dog with him, a playful, male Golden Retriever. Everytime the dog was placed down, he immediately popped up and peered eagerly at everyone around the table. He was playing a game and had to be corrected firmly before a bad habit was formed. Rich, however, was at a severe disadvantage. He was in a public place, among countless people who knew nothing at all about dog training or canine behavior.

"You can see what kind of correction he really needed," Jim said. "Unfortunately, the public is always analyzing. There are people who consider a jerk on the collar the ultimate in cruelty. Some will come up on the street and say, 'You are cruel trainers.' We always have to smile and be polite. In this type of service work, it's just that way. The school's image is of paramount importance, and that image must meet the public's standards."

Over coffee, the trainers discuss their current dogs and which routes hold new and interesting distractions. The dogs usually fall asleep, leads safely tucked under the trainers' thighs, just in case. This allows the trainer free use of hands, gives the dog a feeling of freedom, yet signals up any movement.

When we finished coffee, Jim reached down and took Daisy's harness. "Let's go, Daisy!" he said quietly. He rose and moved away from the chair, turning around before he commanded, "Daisy, forward! Find the counter!" Daisy, secure in her coffee shop routine, moved confidently among the tables to the cashier where she broke pace and stopped. Jim located the counter and paid his bill. He then commanded, "Daisy, right!" With this turn Daisy had a full view of the door. "Daisy, forward! Find the door!" he commanded, and Daisy moved towards her goal.

When Daisy stopped, Jim followed her muzzle direction with his hand, ascertaining that this time the door swung from right to left. In order to leave, Daisy had to move to his right hand side so that she could lead out without stepping in front of him. Jim calmly commanded, "Daisy, around!" and moved her behind his back into a right master position. He then grasped the harness with his right hand, opened the door and commanded, "Daisy, forward!" Once outdoors, he moved her back to his left side on the command, "Daisy, heel!" The coffee break had gone perfectly. Daisy had responded well, obeying each spoken command and a few unspoken ones, such as moving slowly indoors and remaining quiet.

The Leader Dog is introduced to the phrase, "Find the _____!" during the first day of training in harness. It is cautioned to "Find the *curb*!" and halt upon reaching it. This foundation phrase will be used throughout the working life of the dog. Everytime its master senses he is near a corner, he will use this command, repeating it when crossing a street so that the dog "sights" the opposite curb and leads him directly there. Within a day or two, stairs are introduced and the beginning dog is taught to "Find the *stairs*!" in exactly the same way—by moving to the first step and halting. "Find the *door*!" is next, and most dogs respond quickly as they are eager to enter places. When using this phrase, however, the blind handler must be certain he is entering the correct place. If he gives the command to turn, "Right! Find the door!" his dog will turn and point the nearest entry to the right, even though the handler may want a building farther down the street. (Once again, counting on the handler's part is important as well as an accurate sense of distance.) Other nouns are later added to the phrase, "Find the _____!" All dogs are taught to "Find a *chair*!" (vacant), "Find the *ounter!*" (used in all department stores, banks, post office, small shops, etc.), "Find the *window*!" and "Find the *table*!" These are phrases the handler will use repeatedly.

Public dog trainers rarely incorporate nouns into their training vocabularies, relying on commands which are verbs. If nouns are attempted, they are usually introduced with retrieving—the dog may be taught to fetch its leash or the morning paper. Through repetition a dog that retrieves well can be taught to fetch all sorts of articles, although there is always difficulty in teaching noun discrimination. If an animal is taught to fetch its food dish at meal time, fetch the car keys before going for a ride, and fetch the paper, it will respond with alacrity if the entire scenario fits the command but will, without careful discriminatory training, exhibit confusion if the sequence of events surrounding the command is altered. If, for example, the master stands at the front door and opens it to give a clear view of the driveway—an event in the dog's experience that precedes a retrieve of the newspaper— and then commands his dog to fetch its food bowl, the dog will most likely, without further training, run down the driveway in search of the paper. The same thing occurs if the master moves into the kitchen at meal time, takes out the dog food and starts preparation, but then commands the animal to fetch the car keys. Without further training, the dog will probably return with its food bowl. Initial response to these commands involves a set response in a given environment. The nouns are secondary to the routine involved.

The Leader Dog learns to "find" objects in the same way. Routines are played out repeatedly in specific surroundings. The trainer leads the animal to windows, doors, chairs, counters, curbs, and stairs on command. By altering the scene, the dog may "find" the wrong item. When Daisy entered the restaurant and had a view of the crowded room, if Jim had commanded, "Find the door!" when their backs were to it, Daisy would probably have moved towards the vacant chair, as that had always been her routine. She had not yet learned to differentiate thoroughly in her nouns. She had indicated some sort of understanding earlier by looking for a door a few paces farther ahead. She had not turned right when Jim had commanded as this would have led him towards a brick wall. However, the environment was also conducive to finding a door which could be seen ahead.

The following month, just prior to placement, I was amazed at the progress one dog had made in going beyond "routines" to actual "noun discrimination." New masters, however, would be told that solidification of these phrases would be one of their future jobs and never to expect their animals to learn a human vocabulary.

There are numerous possibilities surrounding the key phrase, "Find the _____!", and masters are limited only by their imaginations and desire to teach. Nearly everyone teaches, "Find the keys!" and/or "Find my purse!," and several mothers later told me they taught the dog to "find" their children when it was time for them to come in from outdoors. Retrieving becomes a natural extension to this command, as the handler teaches the dog to bring things to him rather than leading him to the required item and "pointing" it. For the visually handicapped master, part of the joy of having a dog guide is the fun of teaching it new things.

While working indoors, dogs must be careful of their movements. A dog moving slowly is not apt to be excited or have a gaily wagging tail. Leader Dogs are taught an automatic slow pace while indoors. This helps with footing, especially on slick surfaces, and also helps the dog to move through aisles in stores without inadvertently sweeping shelves clean with tails. If the command, "Find the counter!" is used or if the dog is required to wait for its master to finish shopping, it must remain still. Since the harness is made of steel, it could cause damage if the dog were to shake or scratch itself.

Dog guides do not ride escalators as this is considered too hazardous. On elevators, handlers are cautioned to move as far as possible to the rear for the dog's safety. When moving through revolving doors, the handler is responsible for his dog's safety. The dog is moved to the right hand side. The handler then enters the door, making sure the dog's tail and feet are completely inside before slowly moving forward.

As the dogs become proficient with indoor routines, they are introduced to the command, "Follow!" which is used whenever additional human help is needed or offered to locate a particular place. Initially someone walks ahead of the dog, encouraging it to move through vocal praise which is also emphasized by the trainer. Later the dog responds to the command while the trainer keeps up a conversation with the person to be followed.

I found indoor work fascinating and enjoyed the visits to shops, office buildings, and restaurants. I had expected some problems as the trainers attempted to teach in these new environments. I was surprised that the dogs were remarkably calm and well-mannered without specific training. They appeared relaxed and content as they learned their new commands and routines. The trainers feel this is a natural extension of he canine desire to be with his master. "This is a carry-over from the wild dog pack," Smitty said. "Dogs don't like to be left alone. When you take your dogs to town, they have to wait in the car. That's much harder on them emotionally than taking them everywhere. It's not difficult to teach these dogs the routines and behavior we want indoors. They're just happy to participate."

Indoors, outdoors, country, city—the familiar commands and phrases were repeated against the background of constantly shifting environments. Trainers were now interested in more complicated outings and difficult environments so that commands could be polished. Training days were spent in Birmingham, Pontiac, and Royal Oaks.

Towards the end of the second month and beginning of the third month—the process having been so gradual as to go unnoticed on a daily basis—we were working with advanced dogs rather than raw beginners. The dogs were exhibiting typical advanced working style, calmly and alertly performing their duties without any flashy visual displays of response. They were, for all practical purposes, dog guides. All they needed was experience. They would gather this throughout the remainder of the program, and then they would be placed. The trainers were looking forward to their upcoming class. I had not believed the dogs would learn so quickly. I now could not believe they would be placed so soon. "By the end of next month," Smitty assured me, "you'll know they're ready!" Once again, I was skeptical and Smitty was right.

Dogs must move slowly indoors   . . . and lie down in restaurants

155

Leader Dogs have experience in restaurants.

An active dog for an active person.

Praising for a curb halt.

Chapter 12

Ready for Placement

One day, after completing a working session, Smitty commented that the trainers were no longer doing much teaching or correcting. He asked if I had noticed. I had. "This is our peak," Smitty said. "From this point on we only repeat exercises even if they're in different places, and repetition is boring to the dog and handler. If we were to try to sharpen up a dog's response so that he reacts faster or performs with a style that pleases us, we would defeat our purpose. Once we attempt to create that type of animal, it would become 'our' dog. We have to train dogs to the point where they're still pliable. Call it a 'raw, finished product' if you want. It's up to the student to make the dog his own. What we accomplish is sometimes nothing to what teams accomplish when they leave. Every so often we have graduates come back with their dogs, and we're astonished at their teamwork and communication. In a sense, the real dog guide training starts when the 'unit' leaves."

During the last few weeks of training, the upcoming class of human students was foremost in every trainer's mind. He tried to envision the type of person—man or woman—who would enjoy each animal, dividing canine personalities to fit a wide range of human personalities and lifestyles. In order to ensure success, both personalities must be compatible.

When we talk about a dog guide we envision our own ideals of compatibility—the "perfect" dog—and let it go at that. Yet, what is perfect to one person may not be perfect to another. The dog guide trainer, therefore, never trains dogs to please himself but tries to foster traits he feels would be useful or enjoyable to upcoming students. Quite often the differences are so tiny they would go unnoticed in the world of ordinary household pets.

Jim wanted to know how I would like a particular, powerful, male black Labrador Retriever named Kelly. "Take him for a walk and tell me what you think," Jim said noncommittally. Kelly moved off like a freight train. He had little patience with me. Although he responded to commands and corrections, he would invariably look over his shoulder and give me looks that clearly said, "Listen lady, I'll do my job—you just hang in there!" Moving briskly through town, he respected the harness and he respected me, but he obviously would have preferred th company of . . . who?

Coming back to the training headquarters, we stopped for a dowr curb. Ahead of us, in the street, was a puddle of water. When I gave th command, "Forward!" Kelly moved ahead and sloshed happil through the puddle. I screwed up my face in distaste. "Isn't he suppose to skirt puddles?" I asked.

"Some dogs skirt puddles like that and some don't," Jim said with grin. "He could see it's a small puddle. He enjoyed it, I think."

I was silent. I didn't like wet shoes!

When we reached the training building, Kelly gave me a fast nuzzle then pushed his head deep into the watering bucket and began slurpin, water in a very loud, satisfied manner.

I laughed and shook my head when Jim asked, "Would he be a goo match for you?"

"I don't think so! I envision him with someone who smokes a pipe likes cold, wet weather, enjoys long walks in the woods, and doesn' mind wet shoes."

Jim nodded agreement. "He's also too big for you," he added. "Loo at the angle you had to hold the harness. That would make your arn sore in time. Even size-wise he's not your dog. There's no doubt that thi is a man's dog."

I watched as Kelly was placed on his bench chain in the van. Here wa perfect dog guide temperament, perfect willingness and dependability but not for me. I could enjoy training a dog like this, but we would botl be less than pleased if we had to live with each other.

(Kelly was placed with a university professor from New England wh wore tweeds, was six feet tall, and enjoyed walks in all kinds of weather.

Daisy was an altogether different animal—a submissive, feminin Golden Retriever. Her pull on the harness was so slight that one coulc barely feel it. Jim explained that this would become stronger as he confidence increased with experience. Daisy was a woman's dog destined for someone who would enjoy her gentle ways. This dog woulc be miserable if placed with a highly nervous person, or someone who would loudly reprimand her or physically correct her. To Daisy a whispered, "No!" was the ultimate in correction, a teeny flick on the leash a moment of shame. Here again was perfect dog guide temperament, yet future environment or past training techniques could have destroyed this fragile thing.

(Daisy was placed with a refined, middle-aged woman who was active in community affairs. She fit in perfectly with her quiet household.)

There was Bello, a super-alert, super-fast Belgian Tervuren. Here once more was perfect dog guide temperament but not for me. Moving at a brisk, happy pace through town. Bello was instantly aware of everything going on. Although he never faulted in his work, he was constantly alerting to things in his eager way. If leaves were blowing across the lawn, he would tell us so by a faster, prancing step felt through the harness. If he saw children up ahead, he would breathe a little faster and indicate how happy he was to see them. If he saw a cat or stray dog, he kept his eyes riveted on his work, but the tense signals were running up the harness. He was an exciting dog, a joy to work with—as long as my eyes were open. When I followed him for a block with my eyes closed, I found my nerves getting edgy. In time I would learn to read and discard most of his alerts, but I preferred a more subdued dog.

(Bello was matched with a large, jovial man who delighted in every muscle quiver this dog gave him. Bello gave him a new, unlimited zest for living, making him feel truly alive.)

At Leader Dogs I could walk into kennels filled with "perfect" dogs, yet, not all of them were perfect for me. Some dogs prefer the feel of grass underfoot and some enjoy the feel of concrete. There are city dogs and country dogs; dogs that definitely prefer women, and others, men. There are quiet personalities and exuberant ones, submissive characters and tougher, more dominant ones. Matching these dogs to human masters will be one of the keys to their success.

With only a week left in training, the trainers had a good idea of the type of person they had in mind for each animal, and training days were drawing to a close with much of the work conducted under blindfold or with the trainers' eyes closed. It was at this time that Mickey asked if I'd like to do some shopping.

"Let's do the whole thing with your eyes closed!" Mickey said enthusiastically. "We'll use Lady!" Lady was a quiet German Shepherd who fit her name perfectly.

Although I had handled dogs with my eyes closed, my experiences had always been outdoors with long, straight walks, a few stops and a turn or two. I had never attempted to handle any dog indoors in this fashion.

It would not be a matter of actually teaching Lady, Mickey assured me, as she knew all her indoor routines, " . . . but it would be a great experience for her to work with someone besides me at this point, and would be a good experience for you, too!" I agreed.

"Where would you like to go?" Mickey asked. "A person who is blind doesn't browse around and window shop. When he wants something he knows exactly where he is going and maps out his routing. Even neighborhood walk is thought out very carefully in advance."

I decided to shop for clothes and chose the largest department store i Rochester. I had never been inside and had only a vague idea of how t get there. Mickey gave me directions. I adjusted the harness and leas on Lady, gave her a pat on the head, watched her tail wag one last time closed my eyes and commanded, "Lady, forward!" We were on our way

Lady moved in the easy, ground-covering lope of her breed. She was fast worker due to her long stride. Nothing bothered or distracted her She had developed in the training program from a hesitant, submissiv dog into a confident, proud worker. She listened carefully t instructions and calmly obeyed. If Mickey had been the least b domineering or forceful in his training approach, her willingness woul probably have dissipated, and she could well have been rejected.

From the training headquarter's door it was only a few paces t the intersecting sidewalk. "Lady, left!" I commanded. She obeye promptly. "Good girl!" Lady was not one to become exuberant with praise. If she had wagged her tail, I couldn't feel it through the harness. strained my ears but couldn't hear Mickey's footsteps. I sensed hi presence rather than heard it.

Although I was on the sidewalk going towards the center of town, needed to know where Lady was on the walk. If she were in the center, would have seemingly endless sidewalk to either side of me. If she wer on the left, she would be walking into people. I reached out with m right foot and felt for the edge of the walk. She was where she should be the pavement ended about eighteen inches to my right. Three month ago the value of this precision movement hadn't assumed th importance it had now.

We were nearing the corner down-curb. I had neglected to count bu from experience knew it was close. Lady abruptly slowed down. "Fin the curb, Lady!" The command was an afterthought. She had already broken pace and stopped. I reached out with my right foot and located the edge of the pavement. "Good girl! Find the curb!"

There was no sound of traffic. It was, in fact, a very quiet day. Mos of the sounds were up ahead, near the center of town. "Lady, forward!

I had to concentrate on not moving on my own command, remembering what Smitty had said about the possibility of a ten foot drop-off. We moved into the street. There was no feel through the harness that Lady was veering off course. It was amazing that I didn't have to see to move in a straight line.

We crossed the street, and my confidence increased with each forward step. Within a few minutes we were approaching the business district of town. I could hear traffic and voices at the main intersection, and the area around me had changed in tone. Everything sounded louder, closer and more congested. I sensed buildings close to my left. I knew they were there by the change in sounds as compared to those on the preceding block where houses were set back off the pavement and had space and grass around them. I had noticed this echo effect before and imagined that with practice I might be able to tell how far away buildings actually were, and eventually envision any area I was in.

A door opened to the left of me, and I could hear three people fall in step behind me. They had been talking but now were silent. I knew they were watching me, and I felt the same uncomfortable feeling I had had the first time I handled a dog with my eyes closed.

I tried to concentrate on the increasing sounds as we approached the intersection. Lady's breathing picked up, and she broke pace. Then, just as abruptly, she picked up pace again. I heard voices in front of me, slightly to my right. Two people had evidently walked in front of us. I probably would have bumped into them if Lady hadn't slowed down. "Hey, good girl, Lady," I said in appreciation. The direction of the two voices indicated that we were at an intersecting sidewalk. This meant the curb would be just beyond. Almost on cue, Lady broke pace and stopped. Reaching out with my right foot, I located the curb and praised her.

This was a corner with a light and all was fairly quiet. The light was evidently in my favor, but I had no way of knowing if I had time to cross. I waited. The light changed and traffic began moving. I could sense people gathering around me waiting to cross. I tried to count them but couldn't. Everyone was silent. All of a sudden people began moving around me. They could see the light change and traffic stopping. Lady and I were last off the curb. She crossed well, stopping for the up-curb.

From our routing, I knew the department store was near the corner. I would have to turn left on the intersecting walk and go several paces before coming to the entrance. As soon as we had maneuvered the up-curb, I gave a left command and Lady obeyed, angling somewhat left to avoid some pedestrians. "Hey, good girl, Lady!" I said. Voices to my right stopped, and I could imagine heads turning to follow our progress.

I needed more experience in crowded environments. Maybe then I would be able to sort out distances, echos, the effect of wind and weather conditions. Right now every step produced an immediate area of sheer noise which receded behind me as new areas opened up.

I assumed we were near the department store entrance. "Right! Find the door, Lady!" I commanded, not really knowing where I was but hoping for the best. Lady's head turned right, but she continued ahead a few paces before angling across my body, breaking pace and coming to a halt.

I followed the direction indicated by her muzzle and located a glass door which pushed inwards. "Good girl! Find the door!" I pushed the door, commanded, "Forward!" and we entered.

My mind now went blank as I stopped. I wanted to find the women's clothing, but where would I go? I hadn't the faintest idea of the store's layout. Certainly the phrase, "Find the women's clothing department!" had not been part of Lady's indoor vocabulary.

A familiar voice came to my rescue. "Think!" Mickey said to my right. "What phrase does she know that could help you?" I shook my head. Nothing came to mind. Lady waited expectantly.

"The public is great," Mickey went on. "If you were actually blind, several people would probably ask if they could help, but you have a phrase you could use, 'Find the counter!'" Lady perked up. "You can use that phrase at a bank, post office, restaurant, department store—you name it. When she leads you there you would wait for help. Right now, though, I'm going to be a salesclerk. I want you to really pretend so the dog takes this seriously.

"Hello, madam! May I help you today?"

"Yes, please! Where are the women's clothes?"

"Right over here!"

Here? Where? I can't see, remember? My hesitancy paid off. My "salesclerk" quickly added, "May I show you? Come this way, please!"

I smiled in the general direction of the voice and waited expectantly, but no arm was forthcoming to guide me. How could I follow Mickey without help? I felt a slight shift in the harness. "Oh!" I exclaimed stupidly, "I forgot that she knows how to follow!"

"Well, give her the command!" Mickey said. "As long as we keep up a conversation she'll know I'm with you."

162

"Lady, follow!" I commanded. Mickey moved ahead of us. His voice asked, "What size please?"

We weaved around people and through the aisles. There seemed to be thousands of sounds around me. It was much worse than outdoors. It was difficult to keep up a conversation and concentrate on what the dog was doing. At each step, Mickey seemed to be getting farther away. Lady picked up pace—in fact, she seemed to be almost running. "Trust her!" I said as I gritted my teeth. It was almost impossible to hear Mickey over the sounds of cash registers, footsteps, voices of salesclerks and shoppers. The merchandise, counters, and walls muffled some sounds while echoing and amplifying others. I couldn't orient myself because Lady was moving so quickly. I could do little but hang on to the harness. Abruptly, Lady stopped, and I could tell by the commotion around me that we were in some sort of cross aisle. Something huge was rolled in front of me. I could hear wheels squeaking and turning heavily. I praised Lady, grateful for the brief pause.

Then a new worry set in. Where was Mickey? "Lady, forward!" I commanded and she slowly began moving. Would I create a spectacle of myself if I shouted, "Where are you, Mickey?" I was giving it some serious thought when the familiar, disembodied voice spoke at forehead level, "What color are you interested in?" "Lady, follow!" I gratefully said, and off we went again.

Mickey again receded in the distance, and Lady picked up pace. Although dog guides are trained to move slowly indoors, they must keep up with any person they are following. In my case, I had a salesclerk in a hurry. Lady turned abruptly right, then abruptly left, then right, and then a complete about turn. Soft materials brushed against my body. Finally we came to a halt.

"Here is your size," the "salesclerk" said.

"That was unbelievable!" I said, interjecting reality into our conversation. "I haven't moved that fast in ten years. Why did she stop in the main aisle?"

"Someone was pushing a dolly of clothing."

"And what was all the turning for just now?"

"Well, I was looking for your size and had to go from rack to rack to find it."

"The sounds inside make it difficult to concentrate," I admitted. "I'm completely disoriented."

I could imagine where I was and what was going on around me outdoors by drawing on past visual experiences, but the inside of the

163

store was new. I had to learn about it without eyes. I wasn't sure of what I was envisioning.

After a few seconds, Mickey said, "Let's pretend you're finished. Do you remember your routing in reverse so that you can find the door you entered?"

My mouth opened in protest. Surely no one could remember a reverse routing after moving at such incredible speed through so many turns, especially while carrying on an intelligent conversation among all those sounds! Mickey agreed that it was difficult, but in time I'd become more adept; many of my maneuvers would become second-nature, like driving a car.

"On second thought," he said suddenly, "instead of leaving, let's go up to the second floor and just walk around. I want to see how she does on stairs."

Lady followed and we weaved through aisles to the stairway, where she broke pace and stopped. My right foot told me the first step was perhaps six inches high. I praised her, "Good girl! Find the stairs!" and commanded, "Lady, forward!" She moved slowly up the steps. I remembered what Smitty had told me about the angle of the harness being an indicator of heights. I could tell instantly when she had reached the top step as the front portion of her body leveled off.

Mickey mentioned that we were in the housewares section and would walk up and down a few aisles before we left. We went left, then right, then left and left again. Finally he said, "Let's try something. Give her the command, 'Find the stairs!' and let's see what she does."

I did as I was told. Lady continued moving in the direction she was facing. Mickey moved back to my side. "Just see where she takes you," he said. I thought that she would probably continue straight ahead until we encountered a wall or a counter. To my astonishment she proceeded to the next aisle and then turned left on her own, confident that I would follow her. We proceeded in a straight line for what seemed a long time and then she turned right. "What's she doing?' I asked. "Just follow her!" Mickey said simply. Within a few seconds Lady calmly broke pace and halted. I couldn't help myself. I cheated and opened my eyes. There, looming straight down, were the stairs!

"I don't believe it!" I said incredulously. Lady looked up rather sheepishly, her ears flattened back against her head in a submissive position, her tail slowly wagging. I reached down to hug her. Mickey was grinning from ear to ear.

Since I had opened my eyes, he decided to take over to complete our shopping trip. "She's been up here before," he said after commanding Lady to move forward, "and she knows where the stairs are, but I wanted to see what she'd do when she wasn't lined up with them. That was something, wasn't it?"

Outside, Mickey asked how I had enjoyed the trip. "It wasn't as difficult as I thought it was going to be," I said, "although I don't think anyone will believe what she did upstairs. She really knew where she was going, didn't she?"

Mickey nodded. Here was a dog that picked up routings very quickly, evidently was learning noun discrimination, and would work with a minimum of direction while concentrating for long periods of time. Not all dogs in the string would locate stairs as she had just done, at least not yet. Mickey then repeated what Smitty had already said about the teamwork that would develop between dog and final master.

As we walked back to the training headquarters, all sorts of thoughts were going through my mind. It was the end of the training program, but the potential in each animal was just beginning to be tapped. The purpose of these dogs was only now coming into being. Imagine what things Lady and her new master would do and learn together over the years! Imagine what things all the dogs in this string and their new masters would learn and do together! In four months these dogs had changed from ordinary household pets into service dogs of the highest caliber. It had been a pleasure to participate in their training program and watch their individual personalities develop and complement their work. Their trainers had reason to be proud of them. I, for one, couldn't pinpoint the day it had occurred, as the metamorphosis had been a very gradual and individual thing, but today there was no doubt in my mind that Lady and her canine companions were trustworthy guides.

"Hey, what do you think?" Smitty yelled from the hallway into the trainers' lounge a little later. That question had become a standard phrase of greeting among the trainers whenever they saw me. They were always interested in how my experiences at the school compared to the public dog training with which I was familiar. I was still pondering my shopping trip with Lady, eager to discuss it with anyone who would listen, and Smitty was no exception. "You know," I finished, "I got the feeling today that the training here really is over. Her work was flawless, and she did things I really didn't expect her to do. You were right! These dogs are ready to be placed."

Left, an evening
snack in the
dormitory.

Right, trainers are
the link between
dogs and masters.

Left, even replace-
ment students
work hard.

Chapter 13

'No More Canes!'"

Proud Leader Dog—Lyrics for Leader Dog Tour Movie*

*Oh, you're a proud Leader Dog—And you've much to be proud of
You got where you are through praise—obedience and love—
Oh, you're a proud Leader Dog—As everyone can see—
I'm so proud we can walk together—knowing we are free.*

*There's no way to tell of the special things we share—
As we walk together with the pride beyond compare
There's no way to say what you have done for me—
I can walk everywhere—independent—and free.*

*Oh, you're a proud Leader Dog—And you've much to be proud of
You got where you are through praise—obedience and love—
Oh, you're a proud Leader Dog—As everyone can see—
I'm so proud we can walk together—knowing we are free.
I'm so proud we can walk together—knowing we are free.*

*Written and recorded by Leader Dog Graduate Janine Jamison, Richmond, Virginia.

Footsteps echoed along the dormitory corridors and through the deserted dining room and lounge. Every inch of the building had been dusted, vacuumed, scrubbed, and polished in preparation for the arrival Sunday of the new class. Trainers Larry Heflin, Steve Solwold, Randy Horn, and David Heins double-checked each room, making sure everything was in its place and working properly. They then replenished medicine cabinets, restocked canine grooming supplies, and checked new leashes, collars, harnesses, and bench chains for possible flaws. These tasks completed, they settled down at a table to study the office summary sheets on their upcoming class of twenty-six students—fourteen female and twelve male, ranging in age from sixteen to seventy-four, coming from thirteen states and the province of Ontario in Canada. Seventeen would be flying into Detroit on Sunday while others would be driven to the school. Flight times were noted and a pick-up schedule worked out. As usual, there would be several trips to the airport throughout the day. A rooming list was completed, and charts were prepared for assigned seating in the dining room and lounge. Everything that could be done in advance was finally finished. The instructors looked at their watches and headed for home. It would be a short weekend and Sunday would be a busy day.

The general public is largely ignorant of the role played by dog guide trainers in working with a class of blind students. The average person thinks of them as "dog trainers"—people who teach animals and then turn them over without second thought to blind individuals. Some workers for the visually handicapped actually share this opinion (Carroll, 1961). This viewpoint creates an erroneous, lopsided image of dog guide training, one in which the dog assumes more importance than the person who ultimately receives it. Few people understand that dog guides are taught from an unsighted person's point of view and are continually analyzed so that they match the personalities, interests, and lifestyles of the people with whom they will be placed. Few understand that the "dog trainers" go on to become "people trainers," changing from individuals who work with patience, physical skill, and natural rapport in teaching animals to individuals who teach human beings to handle these dogs while utilizing all the skill, patience, tact, and insight into human psychology this type of instruction requires. Only a minute percentage of the public realizes that dog guide trainers also understand the special problems of the visually handicapped, many of whom are tense, nervous, and frightened as they attempt this new and strange form of mobility. The trainers, in reality, are the indispensable links between dogs and masters, teaching both separately and then working tirelessly with them as uncoordinated teams until they learn to work together.

Not every visually handicapped person is eligible for a dog guide or has the attributes to be successful with one. One of the major prerequisites is that the person like dogs. Not everyone is suited to be a dog owner. Although most people appreciate this fact, some tend to view dog guides as working machines rather than animals that have individual personalities and needs, that shed, that do not automatically wipe their paws when they come in from outdoors, and that require food, regular exercise, time, grooming, veterinarian visits, and love. A dog guide owner must be willing to share life with a dog.

Leader Dogs has a few other basic requirements for students.

1. He or she must be at least 16 years of age.

2. He or she must be in good health, able and willing to give the dog adequate attention and exercise to keep it in top working condition.

3. He or she must have good hearing since orientation and commands are based on sounds and traffic flow.

4. He or she must be emotionally stable.

The successful dog guide owner is someone who has already come to terms with his handicap. He has no time for self-pity. He is an active individual who has had some sort of mobility training and now wants greater freedom of movement. He does not want to be slowed down by use of a cane alone. Neither does he want to rely continuously on other human beings. He already knows that he must be willing to work hard, even when tasks seem initially impossible, to learn from mistakes and to develop other senses to the fullest to help compensate for loss of vision.

This type of determination has no relationship to educational, financial or professional background. The students at Leader Dogs come from all walks of life and from all around the world. A check of the school's production records shows graduates throughout the United States (including Alaska), Canada, Mexico, Central and South America, Europe, India, and Israel. Interpreters are brought into the school whenever necessary and foreign students are taught to use English commands.

There is no charge for a Leader Dog. Neither does the student pay for room and board, equipment, or training while at the school. The only cost absorbed by the individual is that of transportation to and from the school. After graduation the blind handler owns the dog, but the school reserves the right to replace any animal not performing properly or to reclaim any dog being mistreated, used by any other person for guide work, or used for advertising or soliciting purposes.

By Sunday evening the entire new "class" has arrived. The instructors had been busy since early morning picking up students, greeting those who were driven, spending necessary time with relatives and friends, helping each student settle into his room, and giving an individual introduction to the dormitory layout.

"Okay, Sally*, we're entering the dormitory. There are just three paces from the door to a short flight of stairs—six altogether—leading

---

*In certain instances in this section of the book names have been changed to protect the privacy of individuals.

to the main level. Please follow the wall with your right hand as we move along. You're at the bottom step. At the top is a gate that is closed unless we're working. On the main floor, if you turn left at the stairs and go three paces, you'll locate the students' phone booth and guests' coat closet on the left. Directly across from the phone booth, a distance of about four paces, is the trainers' lounge. These two rooms flank the entrance to the dining room. We'll go that way later. Right now we're going to go straight ahead. Keep your hand on the wall. This is a long corridor with bedrooms to the right. Each room has a number and is also marked in braille. Your room is the third down. Here it is! As you enter there are closets with sliding doors to either side. After you pass the closets you come into the room itself. To your left, against the wall, is a desk and chair. Next, continuing around the room from left to right, is a twin bed. Next to the bed is a night table and lamp . . . "

Each step of the way Sally's fingers felt the location, shape and size of the various items mentioned in her tour. By the time the walk was over, she had a fairly good idea of the layout of her room and the dormitory itself. "Buzz the emergency button if you want anything," she was told as she was left to unpack and get acquainted with her fellow students.

Initial fears subsided as arriving students realized their instructors possessed the ability to put them at ease and understood their handicap without being condescending or overly solicitous. They were also relieved to hear that instructors and a housemother would be on the premises twenty-four hours a day throughout their stay. Within a few hours, most students were beginning to enjoy themselves, venturing out of their rooms towards the sound of voices in order to meet other new arrivals.

Replacement students eagerly began to relate past experiences with dogs to first-timers.

"I couldn't stand it when Rex died. I said to myself that no other dog could possibly take his place, and I waited a long time before I realized that I couldn't live without a replacement—at least live like I wanted—so I'm back."

"Oh, you'll have moments believe me! It's work! You'll see!"

"I hope they give me another black Labrador. That's what I want, and that's what I asked for. Of course, I only had one, but if they're all like her who would want anything else? We got to the point where I didn't have to say a thing; that dog just knew how I felt and what I wanted to do."

170

"Well, I'll tell you one thing. There's nothing like it! That's all I can say. There's nothing like it!"

"Wait until you see what these dogs can do! They're marvelous! They won't let you do anything foolish. They'll just absolutely refuse to obey you. It's unbelievable!"

The usual information on families, jobs and schools was exchanged. Then, hesitantly, politely, questions were asked about their mutual handicap. Some, they learned, had only recently lost their vision. Others had been blind from birth. A few had light perception, and one had enough residual vision to distinguish some vague shapes as through a heavy, thick fog.

As introductions were made and conversations started, the trainers seemed to be everywhere at once. They were already observing who seemed shy and indrawn, who appeared outgoing, who might be physically able to handle the livelier dogs in the string, and who might need the more placid animals. They were also noting any sort of dual handicap. A few students wore hearing aids. As long as hearing was adequate through use of an aid, this would not be a problem, but some individuals turn off a hearing aid when they prefer solitude and this can be dangerous. Some, too, do not realize the extent of a hearing loss. One instructor had already noticed that one person was frequently asking others to repeat themselves. This could be habit or nerves, or it could be an undetected and serious loss of hearing.

Students who had lost their eyesight due to diabetes would be observed as training got under way. Another side effect of diabetes is often a gradual loss of sensation in various parts of the body. "Diabetes is becoming the most common cause of blindness among our students," Steve said. "Since these people are apt to experience some loss of sensation over a long period of time, all dog guide schools are selecting dogs that will be easy for them to handle. We haven't found this to be much of a problem, but, obviously, a serious loss of sensation in the feet, for example, would disorient a blind individual. He wouldn't be able to feel changes in footing, curbs, and so on."

The trainers were also watchful for any individuals who were exhibiting unusual difficulty in maneuvering in their strange environment. If a student is unable to locate his way from his bed to the bathroom or cannot find his way to the dining room after repeated directions and help, he will probably be unsuccessful with a dog.

"I'd say we send home fewer than 1 percent of our students without a dog," Steve said, "but we do send home some. If a student has a serious hearing loss, cannot remember directions or routings, or has very little sensation in feet or hands, he or she will be unsuccessful as a handler. Once in awhile we also send home people who are really homesick or just can't emotionally cope with the training program. Sometimes we send home an individual who wants to leave as soon as he gets his dog, thinking he knows how to handle it without help. We tell these people to come back when they're ready.

"We make every effort, though, to help students," Steve went on. "If they can physically handle a dog, we'll work with them. We've had many students with dual handicaps such as artificial legs or only one arm. We even had a man who had lost his eyesight and both arms below the elbow in Vietnam. We made an extra long harness for him and modified our training somewhat, and it worked out fine."

Infrequently a visually handicapped individual is talked into applying for a dog when he or she really doesn't want one. Family members and friends often think a dog will automatically create a desire to be mobile or will lift a deep depression that actually requires psychiatric help. Fortunately, the school's staff can pinpoint these cases before placement is made, suggesting that the individual give a dog guide a great deal more thought. Quite often these people have been cared for in sheltered lifestyles where isolation, dependence and apathy have become desirable and comfortable ways of life. Family members and friends eventually realize something is wrong and hope a dog will help. A pet of some sort often can be of some therapeutic value, but a highly trained dog guide would be unused and unhappy. "We help if we can," Steve concluded, "but these people have to want to help themselves first."

The opening lecture for the class encompassed the organization of the school and the roles played by instructors and others on the staff. This was followed by a description of the premises and an explanation of the dormitory rules. An outline of the upcoming training program was given as well as a description of the following day's work which would involve Juno training—each student learning how to use equipment and begin giving commands while the instructors take the place of dogs.

"When do we get our dogs?" someone asked.

"If all goes well, on Wednesday afternoon."

A feeling of uneasiness permeated the room. This seemed like a long time to wait. Only the replacement students were fully aware of the work involved. The first-timers couldn't understand why they weren't given their dogs immediately. Handling a trained dog couldn't be difficult! The thought of spending several days in Juno sessions—looking silly and being embarrassed on city streets—was a blow to several egos and a disappointment to all. No one knew that the trainers themselves had undergone extensive Juno training in the course of becoming instructors and had also felt foolish and had been embarrassed. No one knew that this training protected dogs from ill-timed, incorrect, or harsh corrections from inexperienced handlers. No one really understood that trained dogs need proper handling in order to obey and that this involves practice and acquired skill. No one guessed that instructors could gauge motor ability, physical dexterity, and human character from a dog's point of view by assuming the role of the animal.

"When do we get our canes back?" someone asked.

A general murmuring of agreement broke out among others who had also had their canes taken upon entry to the dormitory. It would be easier to find their way around the premises if they had their canes.

"Your canes are right here and they're safe as can be," Steve said with a touch of humor in his voice. Then he became serious. "Right now, be careful while you're moving and don't leave objects lying around for others to trip on. Make sure drawers are closed and doors either open or shut completely. If you depend on a cane, you won't use a dog to full advantage. You came here because you wanted more mobility and freedom. Well, that's what you're going to get and that's why we took your canes. We'll return them when you leave, but I don't think you'll be using them."

There was a stunned silence. What Steve said made sense. They *had* come to Leader Dogs wanting more freedom. Now they were already complaining about giving up a part of their old lives. Maybe relinquishing their canes was a symbolic gesture; canes would obviously still be needed at times when a dog became ill and couldn't work, but the thought of a future without the constant presence of this metallic appendage sounded good. In fact, it sounded exciting! Smiles emerged on the faces of several people as spirits began to lift. "How about that!" someone said to no one in particular. "No more canes!"

Leader Dogs and new owners get acquainted.

"I think we're friends already!"

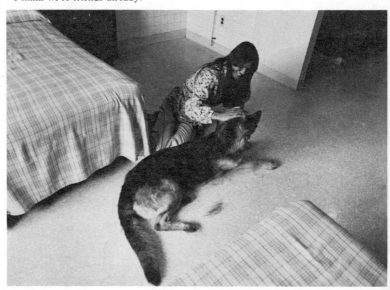

Chapter 14

No Time to Waste

A hush settled over the dormitory. Lunch was over and the students had gone back to their rooms. There would be no Juno session this afternoon. Instead, everyone waited with increasing anxiety. The sounds of knocking, doors opening and closing, and the tell-tale rattle of choke collars and dog tags could be heard further down the hall. Nevertheless, the sharp rap on the door was startling. "Mary?" Larry's voice played counterpart to the dog's movements and panting beside him. "This is Cindy. She's a Golden Retriever. Spend the afternoon with her, but don't allow her on your bed or up against the dresser, and have her lie down when you're seated."

Larry left, closing the door behind him, and Mary, a housewife in her thirties, was left with Cindy. The dog looked at her quizzically and proceeded to sniff the floor. Mary's hands ran over the honey-colored body, feeling the legs, tail, ears, head. Her fingers pulled away as they touched Cindy's open mouth and teeth. "That's a good girl, Cindy!" she said uncertainly. Cindy, expecting more action, impatiently allowed herself to be petted, closing her eyes as Mary's fingers moved over them and down her nose. She then whined softly, anxious to explore as she looked around the room. "What do I do with you for the next several hours?" Mary asked the dog. She had expected an animal that would curl up at her feet with automatic devotion. It didn't seem to be turning out that way. Mary's fingers entwined themselves in the dog's collar. She was afraid that if she lost physical contact with the dog, it would realize she couldn't see and take advantage of her by getting into things. "Cindy, down!" she commanded, pulling lightly on the choke collar. The dog braced against her pull—not so much out of defiance as out of disinterest. Mary sighed. She didn't know what Cindy wanted, but it obviously had little to do with her.

"This introduction period isn't always easy," Larry said. "The dogs have never been in the dormitory, and it's natural for them to want to investigate. The students are often afraid to give or enforce commands. Some have never owned dogs before. They expect an animal to make an instantaneous adjustment and become nervous when it doesn't occur. Within a few hours, though, everyone is feeling a bit more comfortable. They all manage."

At dinnertime, students moved slowly with dogs on tight leashes towards the dining room. It was no longer a matter of feeling along the wall for the turn at the end of the corridor; there was now a strange dog to control as well. The dogs were confused by half-hearted commands to heel. Their general reaction was to ignore the voices of their new masters and to strain at leashes while attempting to sniff the other dogs. The trainers watched quietly as everyone filed into the dining room. In three and-a-half weeks they would have to shape these dogs and handlers into teams.

Juno sessions had begun on Monday following lectures. Basic canine behavior had been explained, and descriptions of the town and the practice court on the school grounds had been given. No one would be expected to go beyond the curriculum; a few commands and maneuvers would be introduced at a time. Equipment had been passed out, and everyone examined leashes, collars, and harnesses with interest, listening as the instructors explained how leashes could be doubled or the end looped over to form an emergency muzzle.

Students and trainers circled a residential block in town and concentrated on right turns while learning how to praise and correct, and how to enforce the commands, "forward," "right," "steady," "straight," "hup-up," and "no." Each student worked individually. The instructors moved quickly, pointing out everyone's continuous errors.

Every student reacted differently. Some were hesitant, uncertain, afraid to ask questions, make corrections, or praise as the instructors tried to imitate the movements of the dogs they had trained. Others were overly anxious, eager to do things correctly and not appear inexperienced. The instructors, meanwhile, were gauging the feel of the people holding the harnesses behind them. By the time they had circled one square block, they had a good idea of bodily strength and general confidence. Some facts about character were becoming apparent as the instructors analyzed vocal tone and reactions to criticism and praise. By the time each walk was over, they knew what size dog each person required and its basic working style.

The morning's work was repeated in the afternoon, but this time the instructors purposely made mistakes, moving at an uneven pace, angling across the sidewalk into the grass, refusing to obey. "Correct,

Elizabeth! You can feel the grass under your right shoe, can't you? Didn't you feel the harness pull you to the right?"

"I thought you were passing around something."

"Did I break pace and slow down? Did you hear anything that would indicate a reason to move off course?"

"No!" Elizabeth admitted sheepishly.

"Then you should have commanded, 'No! Straight!' and corrected me."

There was an uneasy silence as they stopped, and Elizabeth, a young office worker from Pennsylvania, fumbled with the harness and leash. She felt foolish standing on someone's front lawn, holding on to a harness held by a person she barely knew. "Oh, well," she finally thought, "the people around here must have seen all this before." Then she commanded, "Juno, forward!" "Good dog!" she added quickly as Steve responded, then "No! Straight!" as she felt him about to move towards the grass. "That's good!" Steve said happily.

By evening the day's work had chipped away social barriers, and friendships were being formed among the students. Everyone was sharing the same experiences. When viewed as a whole, the entire situation was funny. David, a college student from Canada, kept everyone laughing as he created a mental image of them marching around Rochester, standing on lawns and wondering how they got there, angling across sidewalks, holding harnesses, and jerking leashes held by somber people who failed to see humor in any of this.

On Tuesday, the students were introduced to left turns, and up and down curbs. Explanations of commands were repeated, including the importance of the master position and the need for precision work. By lunchtime everyone was enthusiastic. Monday's errors had all been repeated and new ones had been added, but no one felt quite as awkward. It helped to know everyone was making the same mistakes.

This class, like all others, was comprised of a variety of people with different backgrounds, interests, and professions. As conversations developed in the dining room and lounge, the trainers began to pick up valuable information on lifestyles which would help make selection of dogs easier.

Two girls were high school students, the youngest in the class being Karen G., who was sixteen. Karen had lost her eyesight due to a hemorrhage in early childhood and could not remember much of the sighted world. The other girl had been born blind.

Several were college students. David K. had lost his vision due to diabetes two years earlier at the age of twenty. He accepted his handicap as a challenge, determined not to let it overly influence his life. Donna W., working on a Ph.D. in linguistics, had lost her vision several months earlier. A victim of glaucoma, she stated simply, "The operation didn't work." Carla M., working on a masters degree in journalism, had been born blind. A fun-loving, enthusiastic girl who actively participated in her university's marching band, Carla enjoyed playing practical jokes on others in the class, enlisting the aid of whoever wanted to join her.

Many of the women were homemakers, and two, Sally D. and Mary Ann C., had youngsters under high school age. Mary Ann's two children were preschoolers, while Sally's were twelve and two, respectively. Sally had been born blind, while Mary Ann had light perception and could perceive vague shadows.

The men ranged in age from twenty-two to seventy-four and held a variety of jobs. Lawrence V., at seventy-four the oldest member of the class, was a replacement student returning for his seventh dog. With physical energy that put most of his classmates to shame, Lawrence walked "at a brisk pace" six miles to and from the post office in rural Indiana "just about everyday." He kept the local library busy requesting books on tape and was currently interested in CB radio, operating out of his home.

Several of the students, men and women, were currently without jobs. Those recently blinded had completed some sort of rehabilitation training and most had gone back to school, at least part-time, to acquire new skills. They were looking forward to completing the transition and entering the job market. Several were hoping that a dog, by expanding their environments, would lead to greater job opportunities. A few over the age of fifty had taken an early retirement and were interested in leisure pursuits. Everyone had the goal of greater mobility in applying for a dog, yet all had different purposes for which the animals would be used.

After Tuesday evening's lecture, encompassing the rules of handling dogs in the dormitory, the trainers settled down to the task of matching animal to student. The students had already been asked which breed they preferred. This request would be kept in mind, although no student has ever turned down a dog because of breed. Placement always depends on matching canine size, character and working ability to human size, physical condition, and disposition.

"Matching dogs to the replacement students is fairly easy," Randy explained. "They're experienced handlers and know how their dogs will be used. They're also much more relaxed when they come to the school and honest about their lifestyles and shortcomings. These students don't necessarily stay the entire month. They move along much faster because they know how to secure a dog's response. We take them into downtown Detroit and through complicated routes as soon as possible. Once we see that the dogs are working for them, and we're sure things are going well, they're free to return home. There's no reason to hold them back.

"Sometimes, though, it's been awhile since a student has had a replacement. If there's any feeling of uncertainty, these students stay the entire month."

By the end of the evening, the trainers had made tentative selections. They would sleep on these decisions and further evaluate everyone's work the following morning. The housewife with two children, Sally D., who had been born blind, would do well with the black Labrador-mix that had the fun-loving disposition and high energy threshold to cope with an active family. Karen G., the sixteen-year-old student, would enjoy Heidi, a Flat-Coated Retriever that was agile, alert, and quick to respond without being a challenge to handle. Terry G., the quiet young man who had been blind from birth would match well with Moose, a Retriever-mix that was also a quiet dog. Dave K., the student, would be perfect with one of the muscular, black Labrador males. Carla M., the outgoing college student, was also well-suited to one of the black Labs. She was tall and athletic enough to cope with the breed's enthusiasm and physical strength. Earl M., the gentle-natured man in his fifties from Florida would obviously do well with Brandy who was part Saint Bernard. At 6'1" and 200 pounds, Earl could easily handle Brandy's size, and their dispositions were well-matched. Barry O., recently blinded due to diabetes, would handle one of the Golden Retrievers well. Wendy S., who was a young, married, rather sophisticated apartment dweller, would match well with one of the German Shepherds. Juliette H., the replacement student who desperately wanted another black Lab, could have her wish. She'd be perfect with Jeremy. Lawrence V., the seventy-four year old replacement student, would do well with MacDuff, a placid yet sturdy black Lab. MacDuff would enjoy country living and the long hikes to the post office.

"As soon as we get to know the students, certain dogs come to mind," Larry said. "Sometimes the selections are different than we thought

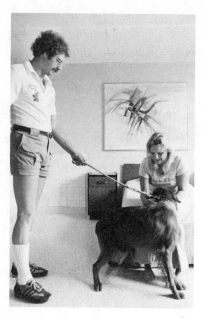

Happiness is meeting one's Leader Dog for the first time.

Juno training helps match dog and master.

they were going to be. We may be fairly certain that a particular dog will be placed with a man and then find a woman whose interests and lifestyle match this animal's disposition perfectly. Sometimes the opposite is true, and we'll place a certain dog with a man when we were sure it was a woman's dog. Once the class gets here, everything falls into place."

In this class, two students had cancelled at the last minute. Since full strings of dogs are always trained (minus the rejections that occur during training), this meant there were more dogs than students. Places such as these are usually filled from the school's waiting list. If it is impossible to match all the dogs, the remaining animals are placed back in the advanced kennel and continue work with the upcoming string for placement within the next class.

The first afternoon with dogs is a very personal experience for each student. For Mary and Cindy it had been a time of anxiety. For Juliette and Jeremy it was a time of joy. "Oh, Lord! I can tell you look just like my other Lab! Oh, I know we're going to be a great team!" For Earl and Brandy it was a time of anticipation. "Wait until my kids see you! You must look like a Saint Bernard. You sure feel like a Saint Bernard. The kids will want to buy a keg and put it around your neck." For Tyrone K., a musician from Detroit, and his German Shepherd it was a time of victory. "I had another Leader Dog and gave it up because I lived in the ghetto—at least everyone *said* I lived in the ghetto. Let me tell you there are compensations to being blind!" His laughter filled the room. "I never could see that ghetto! But I was afraid to walk that dog, especially at night. Even though it was a dog guide, I was afraid someone would want that dog. That's the type of neighborhood I lived in. I felt it was better to give the dog up and wait. But that didn't stop me—oh, no! I saved every penny I earned and finally bought a proper, little house with a nice, little fenced-in yard away from that ghetto, and I'm back." For Barry O. and Margaux it was a time of play and fascination. "I lost my sight at thirty-two. I've always liked dogs but never took the time to differentiate in breeds. Now I can't recall ever seeing a Golden Retriever! That's really bothering me! I can picture a German Shepherd and Labrador Retriever, but I can't picture what this dog looks like!" For others in the group, secure behind closed doors during the get-acquainted hours, there were hugs, a few kisses, and in many instances, a few tears.

At dinner, trainers kept everyone busy enforcing the "down" command, while giving full descriptions of each animal.

For the first several days instructors work individually with blind students.

Students get moral support by working in pairs.

182

Chapter 15

One Simple Gesture

There was unusual silence as the students filed back into the bus. It had been a bad day. There were only three more weeks in the program and nothing seemed to be going right. The dogs appeared disinterested when they were working. More often than not, when corrections were given, they persisted in making mistakes and sometimes refused to obey. Feelings of frustration had been creeping up among the students ever since the first working day with dogs, and now they were feeling helpless and defeated as well.

Sally's voice broke through the gloom. "I had a terrific time!" she called out to everyone. "I met a parking meter today, folks; smashed right into it!" She began to laugh. "Anyone else meet a parking meter?" She paused and listened to the negative responses. "I didn't think so!" she said, still laughing. "That type of thing is meant for me alone."

"What's it look like?" Tyrone asked, laughing with her. "I never met one."

"It's heavy metal with a thin, pole-like base and sort of an oval top. And it hurts!" she added, still laughing.

The mood began to lift as everyone laughed and sympathized with Sally. Her experience was typical of what they had each gone through during the last few days. Sally probably had the right idea, they thought. You either laughed at things like walking into a parking meter, or you cried. And several of them had already done that.

The very first day they realized that handling a dog was not like the Juno sessions. There was a living animal, not a person, at the other end of the harness, and it did not communicate in everyday English. The day's work, circling two square residential blocks, making all right turns and then all left turns, had been nerve-wracking, even though the instructors had been patient. It was a shock to learn that these trained dogs would not necessarily obey their new handlers. "Why is he doing that?" more than one student asked plaintively as his dog stopped to sniff, angled across the sidewalk, overshot a turn, forged ahead, lagged behind. "Because you're not handling correctly," came the firm reply.

Dog on the right angles in improper direction.

The instructor watches the handler correct.

Instructor demon-
strates proper
correction.

Handler learns to
manage her dog
well.

Surely the second day would be better, everyone thought. It wasn't. If anything, it was worse. The instructors showed little compassion, and lessons were filled with criticism. "Loosen up on that lead!" "Don't be so tense!" "Correct him for doing that!" "Talk to her while you're working!" "Praise him! Go on, praise him! He's a good boy!" "Don't let her pull you like that! Snap her back!" "Don't let him sniff the ground! Snap the lead!" "Why did you correct when the dog didn't do a thing wrong?" "Your corrections aren't hard enough!"

By the third day the walks were extended towards the center of downtown Rochester, but response on the dogs' parts was still difficult to obtain. The animals seemed overly distracted by the heavier traffic, pedestrians, shop doors opening and closing. The trainers kept repeating instructions, and it was frustrating to be told constantly that timing was off, corrections were too hard or not hard enough. Everyone wondered why trained dogs needed corrections at all. No one seemed to be making headway except some of the replacement students, who had been all over Rochester and had even gone to one of the local restaurants with their dogs.

The after-dinner lectures were greeted with intense concentration. Silence reigned as the instructors again went over the rules for praise and correction.

"You want that dog to work for you, yet he has absolutely no desire to change to suit you. You want him to be devoted to you, but he has no incentive to do that. You want to win that dog over? Well, it takes more than a half-way advance towards friendship. You can't do it if you're 'pushy.' That dog must first *respect* you. You've got to give commands you mean, be in control, and time your corrections well. Then you must appreciate him. Pay him with praise for a job well done! Praise is all-important. And remember this—you can't fool a dog. That praise must come from your heart."

Back in their rooms, the students discussed the lectures and day's events. Very few were interested in the mechanics of how dogs respond or how they were trained. No one was concerned about any anxieties the dogs might be experiencing in this latest shift in lifestyle. As far as the students were concerned, this month should be devoted to learning a few commands and experiencing a new form of mobility. When things didn't progress as expected, emotions ran high. Mistakes became psychological blows. Silently and vocally, the students blamed their handicap rather than improperly timed corrections, nonauthoritative commands, and canine confusion for their dogs' refusal to cooperate.

They had not yet come to realize that handling a trained dog, like riding a trained horse, requires skill, whether one is sighted or not.

The dogs, meanwhile, reacted to placement with subdued interest. All enjoyed the freedom of a homelike atmosphere after the long months in the kennel. All preferred being with someone twenty-four hours a day rather than spending endless hours in isolation. These facts played in their new masters' favor.

Other facts played against them. Like dogs everywhere, trained or untrained, they reacted lackadaisically to inexperienced handling. They were also confused by the altered role of their trainers. These animals had spent four months with these men and considered them their final masters, with the kennel as a final home. Now they had been placed in the hands of strangers while their real "masters" watched! Regardless of how perfectly matched the students and dogs were to each other, no matter how willing the dogs were to please, the period of readjustment on the dog's part was every bit as real and stressful as the period of adjustment on the handler's part.

The trainers had purposely remained business-like during the training months in order to make this final switch in masters as easy as possible for the animals. They had never given any dog special attention. Now remaining ties had to be cut, one by one. The students mixed the dogs' food with their hands to give it a different scent, and the trainers ignored the animals unless absolutely necessary. The stress of this rebuff could be seen in many of the dogs' eyes as they eagerly looked to their instructors for approval and attention.

During the first few days, however, while working individually with class members, the instructors often capitalized on this canine bond by backing up a student command with one of their own. Although the purpose was to demonstrate the proper vocal tone, the result was to ensure the dog's response. In a few instances, the instructors moved ahead of the dogs, casually encouraging them to respond correctly. The students were rarely aware of help, and they, in turn, became more confident.

As the second week of training began, anxiety levels were high. The replacement students had already been to several stores and could go where they wanted in Rochester, whereas the first-timers were still trying to secure proper response on the main street in town. Sally wasn't the only one who was introduced to a parking meter. Others eventually met the same fate. To make matters worse, the instructors no longer walked at everyone's side but tended to fall behind, and staff members who were training upcoming strings of dogs no longer selected alternate routes but seemed to appear from nowhere calling out, "Strange dog on your left!" leaving them to cope with sniffing or any other response. It helped to work "doubles"—two students taking the same route together. They could give each other moral support.

The instructors mapped out routes, mentioned possible difficulties, then followed at a discreet distance to make sure all went smoothly. The students felt uncomfortable as the trainers seemingly disappeared into the background, even if it were only a few steps behind. The trainers, however, knew that the students had to rely on themselves and gain confidence in their ability to handle their dogs. It was the only way a working partnership would be formed. Unless that occurred, the team would not be successful.

During the second week, the evening lectures included student participation. Besides the usual tales of failure, a few isolated tales of success began to creep in, to everyone's applause. Students shared insights into the personalities and working characteristics of their dogs, and laughter frequently filled the room as various adventures were reported. The intricacies of proper handling finally took on full importance, and murmurs of approval were given as handlers related how they managed difficult routings without too many mistakes. Replacement students shared experiences of their working days in town or out in the country. These stories gave students new determination. Tomorrow, they said to themselves, it would definitely be better.

The dogs also contributed to the determination that was emerging. They had settled into their new routines and were much more at ease with their new masters. In the evening they were often the center of hours of undivided attention, and they responded quickly.

"Hey, Sally, is that you? Come into my room!" Mary Ann called as she heard Sally's voice in the corridor. "Look what I taught my dog!"

"Listen!" Mary Ann said with excitement. She turned to her dog. "Speak!" she commanded in a firm voice. Her dog looked up and barked. Sally and Mary Ann laughed. "Isn't that great?" Mary Ann asked, calling out to other voices in the hallway to come in and hear her new command.

"I think I'll teach that to my dog after I teach him to shake hands. I'm working on that now," Sherry announced. Everyone agreed that was a good idea.

Randy, walking by the open door, stuck his head in. "What's going on?" he asked. "Listen!" Mary Ann insisted as her dog barked again on command. Randy shook his head in mock disapproval. "Wonderful, Mary Ann! That's all we need! Now everyone is going to teach his dog to bark, and we won't have any peace!"

He walked out laughing. It wouldn't be long now, he thought. They'd start working as teams very soon. He glanced in the rooms with open doors. The dogs were behaving well in the dormitory, and no one was having serious problems. They were beginning to feel some sort of rapport with their animals.

"It's about this time that the students begin to really try," he said. "As handling improves, the dogs make the final transition. Once they reach that point, the rest is easy. It always begins with one simple gesture. All of a sudden the dog's attitude shifts. Maybe he realizes, 'Hey, this guy can't see! I have a real job to do! Whatever the reason, you can see the transition when it occurs. One day the student comes back and says, 'Gee, he did so well for me today!' When that happens, we know they're going to make it."

A few days later we witnessed this moment. The students were to work in pairs and take walks around two blocks. Randy informed them that, unlike previous days, he would not walk behind them. "You're on your own. Remember your corners and keep up with your partner. See you back here!"

We watched Kathy and Joan move off. When they were a few paces down the block, Randy signaled to me to get into the station wagon. We would follow at a discreet distance and make sure all went well.

The women managed one block while Randy criticized their handling. They failed to correct their dogs for cutting corners and angling into the grass. Their commands were not very forceful, and Kathy's dog was forging by at least six inches. The women were busy chatting with each other as they walked along. "If they want to talk, they should drop their harnesses and stop," Randy murmured with disapproval. The only encouraging sign he had seen prior to this walk was in the attitude of the dogs. They were minding well in the dormitory and often neglected to glance at him for back-up praise or command when working. It appeared that the dogs were cutting their own ties.

At the third corner Kathy and Joan stopped, obviously confused. They had been so engrossed in talking to each other that they had forgotten their routing. We stopped the car at a safe distance and rolled down the windows to listen. Neither woman knew we were there.

They laughed briefly at their predicament, and then silently waited. They assumed their instructor would appear, as he always had in the past, and help them. The dogs became restless and the women grew tense and uncertain.

Randy was interested in how they would react. Would they attempt to backtrack? Would they take initiative and move towards the sounds of a car being washed in a neighboring driveway and ask for directions? Would they refuse to move at all, thus admitting defeat? The upcoming seconds would be important as far as their instructor was concerned.

The women tried to agree on what to do. Finally, they braced themselves and ordered their dogs around, then left, towards the sounds coming from the driveway. Randy grinned in approval. This choice would demand the most from both dogs and handlers. Joan quickly snapped her dog back as she felt grass rather than sidewalk underfoot. "She knows no one is going to come to the rescue," Randy said. "She's got to be sure of that dog now. That's good!"

The dogs broke pace as they neared the car being washed. It was blocking the sidewalk. The owner turned off the hose as he watched the women approach. "Excuse us," Kathy called out, "can you direct us back to the Leader Dog building?" The man responded in typical sighted fashion. "Go down this way to the corner after next and turn right." "You mean we go straight ahead on this street, then cross, and continue another full block?" Kathy asked. "That's right," the man responded. The two women thanked him. While the brief conversation took place, their dogs continued to move hesitantly on repeated, nervous commands to move forward. Tails low and ears back, they seemed fearful as they felt the tense harnesses and halting steps behind them.

Then one dog stopped and glanced back at his charge. They were within touching distance of the car. Randy poked me. "Look!" he whispered. The second dog also stopped. Both women, embarrassed to be stopping in someone's driveway, kept repeating the command to move forward. They had no idea a car was blocking their path. They assumed someone was hosing down the drive, or watering the lawn. A stranger could now see how awkward they were and how their dogs refused to obey.

The dogs appeared to be waiting for the usual leg and foot movement, or hand sweep that accompanies every stop. When these weren't forthcoming both dogs inched slowly to the left as they made the decision to pass around the vehicle. Every few inches they glanced back at their handlers with a mixture of uncertainty and concern in their eyes. "Look!" Randy said again.

190

The women were silent. They did not know why their dogs were moving so slowly to the left. Joan touched the car first, and her voice rang out. "Oh, my god! It's a car! Kathy, they're going around a car! Reach out with your right hand! Do you feel it? This is something!"

Kathy's hand went out and a look of awe came over her face. Both women followed their dogs with increasing excitement, rounding the hood of the car with smiles spreading across their faces.

The dogs picked up speed as they passed the vehicle, swinging back onto the sidewalk. Joan stopped and leaned over. She hugged her dog, bringing her face down into the animal's coat. "That was wonderful!" she said softly. "You're a great dog!" Her partner followed suit.

The dogs responded in unison. Tails, which had been between the back legs, began to wag slowly and then furiously, and both dogs gave their masters long looks of pleasure mixed with pride. "Look at that!" Randy said happily.

When they moved off down the sidewalk the dogs' tails were raised and waving slowly. There was a lift in their heads that had not been seen since placement and a new sureness in their step. Kathy and Joan also looked more relaxed and confident. They had all shared their first difficult task. For these two teams it was the turning point for which their instructor had been waiting.

Randy banged his fist on the steering wheel and laughed. "That's it! Did you see it? That's the moment we were talking about! Look at them! You can see it! They're teams!"

We drove past the women and were waiting at the training headquarters when they arrived, as if we had been there all the time.

"How did it go, ladies?" Randy asked as they approached.

"Oh, you missed it!" Joan replied. "You should have seen how these dogs worked for us."

Randy glanced at me and smiled. He helped the two women get in the bus, happy dogs at their sides. "What did I tell you they'd say?" he asked, as he watched them locate their seats.

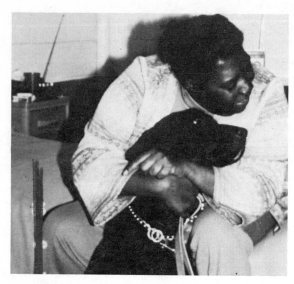

"I can tell you look just like my other Lab."

"Wait until my kids see you!"

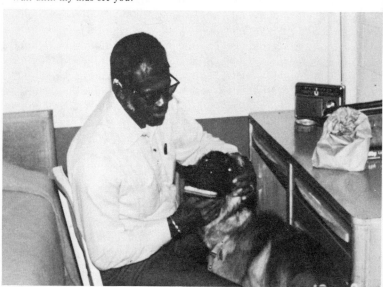

Chapter 16

Isolated Thoughts and Conversations

Several students were seated in the lounge discussing their dogs, the day's work, their expectations and their futures. "You know," Anne P. finally said wistfully, "in the evening, like this, I wish I could read. That's what I miss most since I lost my sight. I loved to read. It's not the same listening to tapes or having someone read to you, and I don't like hoisting big, clumsy braille books. Besides, the selection isn't that great."

"I liked to read, too," Joan S. said, "but I miss traveling and sightseeing more. Everyone tells you to visualize, yet it's hard to do that if the people you're with don't say much."

"That goes right back into childhood," Betty D. added. "I was born blind, and the only way I could learn about the world was to explore and have things explained. I was lucky. My parents didn't restrict me and always let me play with my brother and the neighborhood kids. I did all the things they did. They helped me learn so much, even the meanings of adjectives and adverbs. Later, when people described something, I could draw on experiences and imagine what things were like. Other blind children aren't as fortunate. Yet, today, if descriptions are poor, I always feel like I'm missing so much! I hate when someone says something like, 'Oh, the scenery is pretty!' and that's *all*!"

"I think when someone is born blind, families adjust in different ways," John B. said thoughtfully. "When someone loses his sight later on in life as I did, families are afraid to change. In my household everyone pretends nothing is different. No one discusses any extra help I would appreciate, such as having things described in greater detail, and they never tell me how my blindness has affected their lives. There's always a barrier. We just don't talk about it."

There was a moment's silence before Kathy L. led the conversation in a different direction. "You know what I wish *I* could do? I wish I could play tennis. I follow the matches, and it sounds like a great game."

"I wish *I* could drive," Joan added quickly. "Wouldn't it be fantastic to go where you wanted without someone always driving you?"

The conversation rapidly turned into a general one that encompassed the "wishes" of everyone in the lounge. One student longed to visit art museums and see paintings, and another said she wished she could paint— " . . . oils, watercolors, *everything*!" Someone said she'd like to see colors and compare them to what she thought they were. Someone else wished he could see what people looked like. "And animals, too," someone called out. "Imagine seeing all the animals in a zoo!"

"Or birds!" someone broke in. "I'd love to see a robin and not just hear it!"

"I'd like to see my dog," Betty said as she fondled the animal's ears. "We never had dogs as a kid, and I was always a little afraid of them—all that fur and panting. You know," she admitted, "I wasn't even sure which end to put the harness on? I don't know how the trainers put up with me!" She laughed and everyone laughed with her.

The conversation gradually died out, everyone focusing on his or her own thoughts as Tyrone walked into the room. "Anyone at the piano?" he asked. "No? Good!" he said as he answered his own question. "Got to keep up with my practice!" His fingers ran over the keys and his soft, husky voice filled the room. Soul music—it fit everyone's mood of the moment. The students settled back to enjoy the practice session, still lost in their thoughts.

———

Barry O. leaned back on the couch and let his thoughts wander in a disjointed fashion into his past, his present, and his future. Barry, at 32, had lost his vision nine months earlier.

"I've been a diabetic nearly my entire life, and knew I was losing my sight ten years ago. I lost vision in my left eye six years ago, but had functional sight in my right eye until nine months ago. Every night I'd go to bed and say to myself, 'You may not see tomorrow, Barry!' It was a terrible time, not knowing when or what it would be like. I told myself that this couldn't be happening to me. Then I was bitter, you know, the, 'Why me?' phase. After all, I had grown up in a society where I had been subconsciously taught that losing one's sight was just about the most awful thing that could happen to a person. It's hard to describe all the fear and anger that I felt.

"Then, when it happened, my first sensation was one of immense relief. The horrible thing had occurred, and, to my surprise, it wasn't so horrible! I'm not saying that losing my sight has been an easy thing to live with, but I've found I *can* live with it.

"When I was partially sighted, I tried to get a head start on braille, but the incentive to really work just wasn't there. I also told myself that I should try to develop my other senses, but I couldn't do that either. I regret not trying harder now.

"After I lost my sight, I realized that I had the ability to imagine or visualize things very well. This has helped me to adjust, and I sometimes feel that I can 'see' more than many people with 20-20 vision.

"As soon as I lost my sight completely, I applied for rehabilitation training. Believe it or not, after nine months, I'm still waiting! Everytime I'd call they'd tell me they'd get back to me really soon. Well, you can't just sit for nine months, so I started to rehabilitate myself. My wife helped me learn how to do things for myself, then move around the house, then outdoors, and gradually a little distance away by using a cane. It wasn't easy! I've gotten lost in my living room a few times!

"One day, I realized that landmarks are as obvious to an unsighted person as they are to a sighted one. The only difference is that most of my landmarks are now underfoot. I can feel where I am in a familiar area by the surface under my feet. Rehabilitation centers teach this, but I had to discover it. Snow covers landmarks and makes orientation difficult, and I haven't had experience in snow. This is one reason why I wanted a dog. I'll feel confident regardless of weather.

"My other senses are definitely being used more and probably are becoming more sensitive. My memory has improved a great deal. I have to remember where I put things, and must concentrate on every move I make and every sound I hear. Although I can't say I've ever been mentally exhausted, I have found that I have to be mentally alert all the time.

"I eventually discovered that I can do things I didn't think I'd ever do again. I handle all the household errands within walking distance and do all the home repairs. I just put in a dropped ceiling and do my own carpentry. Whenever I'm faced with a problem, I sit down and visualize how I used to do a job and how I can modify the method. I can usually devise a way to get things done.

"Discovering that I can do things has given me incentive. I had taken a disability pension, but now I'm eager to go back to work. This is another reason I wanted a dog. I won't have to worry about walking out into traffic or about well-meaning people who come up to help and don't know how.

"People can be so helpful they'll kill you—literally. Sometimes I appreciate help, but I wish the public were better informed. Not too long ago I was trying to go down a flight of stairs and two people came up to help me. One grabbed my left arm and the other grabbed my right elbow, and they pushed me ahead of them. I almost broke my neck. With a dog, people probably won't be so determined to be helpful or feel obligated to be constantly with me. I'm a quiet person, and a dog will give me companionship without interfering with my privacy.

"Even though being blind is new to me, I don't mind talking about it. In fact, I'm eager to tell people that it isn't as bad as I thought it was going to be and that it hasn't changed me as a person. I can do nearly everything I could before although the method might be different. This is where the public discriminates against the visually handicapped. People, especially employers, should allow a blind person to modify a job and do things in a slightly different way. If more employers were willing to do this, there wouldn't be so many visually handicapped people without jobs.

"One last thing I like to tell people about blindness is that it's not a state of perpetual blackness, as everyone is led to believe. It's hard to describe what I 'see' inside. It varies, I don't know why. Sometimes it's like closing your eyes in a dark room, and, at other times, it's like being in a thick fog. But I can't say it's black. And it's not frightening. All the fear I had of being blind ended when I finally lost my sight."

———————

Sally D. and Mary Ann C. were discussing their experiences in raising children. Sally had been born blind, and Mary Ann has light perception and can distinguish vague shapes and movements. Sally's children are twelve and two years old; Mary Ann's are five and three years old. Wendy S., Carla M., Donna W., and Elderrean Y., listened, everyone sitting on beds and chairs around the room.

Sally, whose sense of humor always managed to lift the spirits of her classmates, laughed as she spoke. "I use my ears in raising kids. I can hear what they're getting into and sense when silence means trouble. It's the same method sighted mothers use.

"I keep my youngest one close to me throughout the day, and I have several locked cabinets throughout the house to help ensure against problems. We also have double locks on our outside doors. They're up high where the two year old can't reach.

"I've done that, too," Mary Ann added. "I don't want the children leaving the house without my knowing it. Also, when they're outdoors, they *must* answer when I call. They sense that I mean that."

"They do sense the importance of certain things," Sally agreed, "but there are times when they'll try to take advantage of you. My older girl used to push everything under her bed when I'd ask her to put things away. She thought I'd never discover them. Sometimes now she'll tease me. I can scold her and shake my finger at her and think I'm looking right at her. Then I'll hear a little voice behind me, and she'll say, 'I'm over here, Mom!'" Sally laughed. "That really takes the oomph out of a scolding, but she doesn't do it out of meanness. She knows it will break my train of thought, and I usually end up laughing."'

"Do your kids keep things picked up?" Mary Ann asked. "It's so hard to insist on that!"

"Well," Sally said, "the one place where the pick-up rule is strictly enforced is the kitchen. I don't want to trip on anything while I'm carrying something hot."

"I want my children to mature to accept the fact that I have a handicap and need their cooperation in some areas," Mary Ann said. "Even though my children are young, I rely on them a great deal. My five-year-old does quite a few things around the house and always helps me shop."

"Even preschoolers recognize packaging at a grocery store," Sally interjected. "Once they learn to read, they can tell you the 'specials,' and that helps, too."

As the conversation went on, the problems inherent in raising children were identical to those of sighted women, and the solutions were identical, too, a fact Sally had already noted. It came as a shock, therefore, to hear that neighbors and friends had openly discouraged both women from having children. "Several women came very formally to me and told me how they felt about my first pregnancy," Sally said slowly. "I couldn't believe their attitude! They told me they had decided that I'd never be able to raise a baby, and that the child would probably have some sort of handicap. I learned a great deal about human nature that day, and it hurt. Later, in spite of my doctor's counseling, I worried myself sick that my child would have a birth defect, and this would give them fuel to come back and say, 'I told you so!' After our daughter was born, I wanted to shout at them, 'Look how perfect she is!' How many other mothers have to go through that?"

"I was subjected to the same type of thinking," Mary Ann broke in. "No one thought I could care for children. One lady didn't think I'd be able to tell if a diaper needed to be changed! It was unbelievable! Now, I say to them, 'The only thing I've found difficult about raising kids is the feeding at two in the morning, and I have the edge on you because I can do it with my eyes closed!"

Everyone laughed, but the bitterness of both women was evident. This, their voices said silently, is an example of the attitude of society after all the platitudes as to the "normalcy" of the visually handicapped are stripped away. The fact that they had proved society wrong and were raising healthy, normal children had become an empty victory.

Wendy changed the subject to housework, commenting that she could tell by touch if something needed to be dusted or scrubbed, and that she had learned the hard way to label all cans and boxes in braille, even though this was time-consuming. "I used to put things in particular locations. Then, one day, I thought I was putting canned tomatoes in a stew and I was using sweet potatoes instead! I know I should have smelled what was in the can first but, when you're in a hurry, you sometimes don't bother."

"I once put cayenne pepper in hot chocolate and served it to a group of girls in my dormitory!" Donna admitted. Everyone laughed and shared similar experiences. "Let's say we all know the true meaning of 'pot luck,' " Sally finally said.

Each woman had different reasons for wanting a dog guide. Donna and Carla would use their dogs on large university campuses. Elderrean would use her dog in going to work. Sally and Mary Ann could think of countless ways to expand their environments beyond house and neighborhood. "I just hate using a cane," Sally said vehemently. "I knew I wanted a dog one day while I was walking through town, and sweeping my cane back and forth. Well, I swear, things like this only happen to me, but I shoved the tip of my cane right into the spoke of some kid's bicycle! Fortunately, he wasn't hurt, but I was so embarrassed. I vowed at that instant that I would get a dog."

The conversation gradually turned to education, and a debate began as to the pros and cons of residential schools for the visually handicapped as opposed to "mainstreaming"—placing a blind youngster in the existing public school system. Those who had recently lost their vision were in favor of mainstreaming. Those who had been blind from birth favored a residential school, usually to the high school level.

"How can a child become a part of society without being raised in it?" Donna, who had recently lost her sight, argued. "A residential school breeds discrimination. It's a closed community. It separates the blind into a minority group. When those youngsters get out into the real world, they can't cope!"

Carla, who has been blind from birth, broke into the conversation. She had attended a residential school and felt she could cope quite well. "There are youngsters who must learn to live with their handicap and, unless that's accomplished in a specialized school, they won't do as well as they could with class work," she said. "A lot, too, depends on the public school system. If teachers in regular schools are uncomfortable with a blind youngster or resent having to spend extra time with him, a great deal of psychological damage can be done. These attitudes can alienate a blind child and make him painfully aware of being 'different' and somehow 'inferior.'"

Donna ended the debate by commenting that medical centers were beginning to give unlimited help to families with blind babies and blinded youngsters, so that adequate preparation for life with a handicap was becoming the norm rather than the exception. As this type of counseling continued and improved, she felt the need for residential schools would decrease, until mainstreaming would no longer present major problems to either teachers or students.

The conversation turned to their own educations, and Mary Ann finally said, "There is still ignorance within society. You can have every degree in the world, and because you're blind, there will be people who think you're dim-witted. A certain segment of society thinks that if you can't see, you can't comprehend a thing."

"Either that, or they think you're automatically deaf!" Elderrean added. "They'll come up and shout, 'HELLO! HOW ARE YOU?' I like to shout back, 'I'M FINE! HOW ARE YOU?' That shocks some and pleases others who use it as proof that I can't hear a thing." The group laughed at Elderrean's method of coping with another common problem experienced by the visually handicapped.

"It pays to develop your own sense of humor," Carla added. "For example, sighted people often freeze when they see you. They just stand there and stare like frightened rabbits. I always think of them as so many frightened rabbits, and the situation becomes funny rather than annoying."

"Some things, though, are always annoying," Mary Ann stated flatly. "Some people are condescending. They'll say things like, 'Oh, how wonderful that you're thinking of getting a job!' and you know by the tone of their voices that they really mean, 'Why bother? You can't do that because you're blind!'"

"There are a lot of misconceptions out there," Carla said as the conversation drew to a close. "The thing that aggravates me most is that society has elected to place all the visually handicapped into a minority group called, 'The Blind,' in which everyone thinks and acts alike, unable to make independent decisions as to what is possible or not possible without sight. I keep saying to people, 'Look, I'm not blind Carla. I'm Carla, who happens to be blind. There is no group as, 'The Blind.' There are only individual human beings who happen to be blind.' "

Terry G., a college student in his mid-twenties, lit his pipe and thought about the question he had been asked. "When you're born blind, like I was, you can't analyze how you do things or know certain things. There is no basis for comparison. For example, I have object perception. Others who are blind do not. I can always tell what type of area I'm in when I'm outdoors and can 'feel' the buildings I'm passing. I know when I'm passing an open door or when someone is opening a door. When I'm walking, I can 'feel' the shapes of the cars parked near the curb. I can always tell corridors from rooms when I'm inside and can usually enter a room and know how large it is without having to feel the walls. I can usually sense large objects around me, such as furniture. When I enter a room, I can tell if someone is in it. Doctors have told me this ability is due to sound, or rather the echo as sound comes back from objects. I've thought about that and can't imagine it is echo alone. Air pressure and the way air moves around objects might have something to do with it. This could still be related to sound but not necessarily echo. Heat, I think, has something to do with it. If a lamp is on in a room, I know where it is by the increase in temperature as I approach it. I can always tell when I'm passing a parked car that has recently been running. There's no magic in what I do. Most people have some of the same ability when they sense that someone is in a dark room. I think this is a combination of sound, breathing being picked up subconsciously perhaps, and heat from the person's body, which somehow makes the room feel different. My ability, though, is not infallible. Usually I'll sense when something is looming up ahead of me, but there are times when I'll walk right into something.

"I wanted a dog for companionship and also when I have doubts as to orientation. Snow destroys landmarks under foot; sidewalks and curbs just disappear, and it's impossible to feel changes in texture. Snow can also destroy landmarks to the side of you; bushes, for instance, turn into snowdrifts. Once my dog knows a given route, snow won't be as serious a problem. Then there are times when I could use a dog's eyes in combination with my hearing. It's imperative to know where sounds are coming from when you're blind. Wind destroys direction of sound and distorts what you hear. Ambulances, large trucks and motorcycles can overpower other sounds at crucial times. Heavy fog can deaden sounds. By using a dog, I won't have to rely on hearing alone under these conditions.

"I always liked dogs and got along with them. My mother likes to tell the story of how I developed a fondness for dogs. I was too small to remember. My brother, who is older than I am, was telling me what dogs were like and said that they kiss by licking. Now, a blind child doesn't understand words like that unless they're experienced or acted out. 'Here, I'll show you, Terry,' my brother said, and he jumped up on me the way a dog would do and began licking my face all over. My mother was horrified, but I thought it was great. I've wanted a dog ever since. My brother did a lot for me in that respect. He showed me so many things.

"I went to both a residential grade school and high school. I only went home on selected weekends and holidays. My parents did the best they could in raising me, but they weren't experts in raising a blind child. The basic skills of living are ingrained in a residential school. There were many youngsters who didn't know how to button clothes, brush their teeth, comb their hair or eat by themselves. Classes were small and everyone got unlimited personal attention. I know there are those who say it isn't good to be surrounded by only other blind children, but I didn't see it that way. We learned from each other and shared our special ways of doing things. We were never 'different' from anyone else, but we also had opportunities to be with sighted people.

"'I think most blind youngsters are ready for mainstreaming by high school age and would prefer a regular school over a residential one, but that depends on the individual, too. I know if I were to have a blind child, I would prefer a residential school through grade school because of the solid background I received there.

"In terms of being blind, I can't say I feel handicapped. When you've never had sight, how can you miss it? I've learned to 'see' in different ways. What amazes me about people, though, is that they could have fuller lives if they'd develop their other senses the way individuals who are blind are forced to do. Very few people make any effort to do this or to appreciate what they have. They don't even appreciate their eyesight! That's unfortunate, because a certain percentage of those same people will eventually lose their sight. No one at all thinks about that."

Shopping is fun with dogs once handling skills have improved.

Everyone enjoys indoor shopping malls.

Chapter 17

"I Feel Free!"

One by one the replacement students went home. Only a few remained the entire month. However, Julie B. wondered if she and her Labrador Retriever, Jeremy, would leave together at all. Julie found Jeremy similar to her previous dog, and she felt they were a team from their first day together. Their progress was so rapid that it was soon decided they could leave whenever they wished.

As soon as she was told, Julie hurried to the phone booth with Jeremy at her side. She smiled from ear to ear as she announced, "I'm calling everyone I know to tell them we're coming home!"

A few minutes later, Julie was found huddled in the booth, her forehead pressed against the phone, tears streaming down her face. "My landlord told my husband that if I want the dog, we'll have to move. He won't let me on the premises with him! He said that I haven't used a dog in a long time and get along fine without one, and that's proof that I don't *need* a dog."

The staff assured her that things would be straightened out. Within twenty-four hours, a bit of legal briefing had convinced her landlord that Jeremy, as a dog guide, could not be barred from the premises.

Everyone passing the phone booth on the following day heard Julie's voice. "He's just as sweet as country butter! He's got the softest brown eyes and the nicest coat! When are you coming to see him?"

Larry smiled and nodded in the direction of the phone booth as he passed by. "She'll have a happy homecoming, although her landlord may not share her feelings.

"There are always people who try to get around laws, who think they don't apply in certain cases, or who plead ignorance. We try to help students cope with these situations. They carry identification cards, and we ask them to call their local police to notify them that a dog guide is in the community. If anyone objects to the dog, the student offers to muzzle it by using the leash, which clips over for that purpose. If someone is adamant about entry, we prefer that the student contact the authorities without creating a scene. That usually solves things.

This student performs a "cut-back."

As training ends, students and dogs are confident with each other.

As the replacement students began to leave, the remainder of the class began to look ahead to their own departures. Frustration, so common in the first few days, was no longer a major concern. Every dog was forming an attachment to its master, and everyone had experienced the exhilaration of at least partially successful lessons, as a result of improved handling skills.

Anxiety, in turn, became a dominant emotion. With slightly more than two weeks left in the program, it was felt that not enough time was available to cover the planned curriculum. If any student was given a slightly different assignment from anyone else there were questions. Why wasn't I asked to follow that routing? Aren't I progressing as well as someone else?

"Patience! Patience! Patience!" Steve announced as he passed out assignments for the day. "You'll all do everything! This morning, some of you will go with partners to the drug store, and some of you will go to the coffee shop. This afternoon, you'll switch. By next week you'll be telling us where you want to go."

The instructors followed the students as they set off down the street and located their destinations. The drug store was on a corner. Locating the door from the direction of the training headquarters required a maneuver called a "cut-back." The student passed the door and kept walking to the adjacent curb halt. Then, by turning around or "cutting back," he knew the building was the first one, only a few steps away. This was easier than counting paces from the other direction. The restaurant was more difficult to find as it was located in the middle of the block. "Use your noses," Steve told them. "You'll smell coffee. If you miss it, go to the next corner and turn around."

Excitement mounted as the students completed the assignment. The instructors noted with satisfaction that very few mistakes had been made. Rules for entering and leaving, paying bills, and asking for help were meticulously followed; clerks and waitresses gave minimal assistance. It was, Steve assured them as he drove the bus back to the school, the most successful lesson they had had to date. Everyone agreed it had also been fun—a term no one had yet used to describe a day's work. Spirits were high as the bus pulled in front of the dormitory. No one said it, but everyone felt it—the discouraging days were over.

The next week was a busy one, and students waited eagerly for assignments. Within three days they were choosing their own destinations in Rochester. The trainers receded further into the background, waiting on corners so they could watch several students at

Passenger cars can be tricky.

The bakery is a popular destination.

a time or following them in the station wagon, offering assistance only if absolutely necessary.

Sally came back to the training headquarters with her arms full of "souvenirs" for her children, thrilled that she could shop, hold packages, and manage her dog at the same time. "I saw you," Larry criticized mildly. "At one point you were close to the buildings and you knew it, and once you brushed against some bushes. You have to correct or your dog will begin taking advantage of you." "Okay!" Sally agreed readily. The emotional lift of a successful solo shopping trip was her reward, but she knew Larry would be watching her performance the next day.

"How did I do?" students asked as assignments were completed. As the instructors encouraged independence, in fact insisted on it, everyone realized that even minor errors must be remedied. Rather than resenting criticism or becoming discouraged because of it as they had only a week previously, they now openly welcomed it.

The world expanded beyond Rochester. They went to office buildings and learned how to use revolving doors, walked along waxed floors, past endless offices, went up and down stairways, out different doors from the one entered, and rode in elevators. The students concentrated carefully as they followed assignments of locating particular offices in strange buildings. The instructors stationed themselves at key locations, calling out criticisms and suggestions when the students least expected.

They went to indoor shopping malls, where they could shop or go for coffee, meeting back at the main entrance at a particular time. The instructors moved from store to store, watching progress. Everyone enjoyed trips to indoor malls as it was easy to tell what kind of shop was being passed by its smell.

The daily bus rides to training sites had instilled proper techniques for using public transportation, but lessons were given on what to expect in crowded situations. A full afternoon was spent in practicing the proper method of entering and leaving passenger cars ("Put the dog on a sit-stay! Back into the seat and sit down! Call the dog to come! Guide him into a down position at your feet! Keep him there!")

Every lesson increased their confidence. It was all possible, they began to say, not only possible, but happening! Of course, they told each other, they were working in a controlled atmosphere. None of this would work as well at home, or would it? They began to question their instructors. "Randy, it's easy as long as you're around to supervise, but

A visit to Stony Hill Park is one of the highlights of Leader Dogs' training program

will I be able to do these things alone?" "Sure you will!" Randy answered without further comment.

The routes grew longer and more difficult. The program, in fact, was following the same format as had been used for the dogs, the only difference being that everything was now telescoped into one month. The trainers sought out barricades, problem areas, distractions and heavier traffic. The station wagon came around corners and cut off students at curbs and in mid-street. There were many days of individualized training in locations similar to those in which the students lived. Royal Oaks, Birmingham, and finally downtown Detroit were visited.

The evening lectures changed format. They covered the future and what would be expected of each student as he or she went home.

"You're looking forward to going home. However, your dogs are faced with another change in environment. They don't know anything about your homes, your families, or friends. It's going to be a stressful time for them, and they will have to undergo another period of adjustment. Do you realize how often your dogs have had to adjust to new masters and environments? They've gone from breeders and the places where they were born to the interim masters who raised them; then they were placed in a kennel where we became their masters; next they went to you; and now they must again change environments, meet new people and learn new ways of life. You must help your dogs adjust. Don't immediately plan huge parties and extensive outings when you go home. Take your dogs gradually through your neighborhoods and into town, working with them in much the same way we worked with you. Have someone accompany you for awhile to make sure everything goes smoothly. Gradually introduce them to your familiar routes. Then build on what you've learned here."

The upcoming completion of the training program would be a quiet affair, limited to personal farewells between the staff and students. There is no formal "graduation" ceremony. "We feel the best and easiest way to terminate training is to have staff members shake hands and share a few personal words with each student as he or she leaves the dormitory," Poc said. "We feel a special rapport with our students at this time as we know how hard they worked to arrive at that moment."

Just prior to the completion of the program, the staff selects a nice day for a trip to Stony Hill Park. This, as it turns out, is one of the highlights of the training program. Set above Rochester, the park is a vast expanse of lagoons, winding paths, country lanes, trees, shrubbery, and hundreds of acres of manicured lawns.

Steve, Larry, Randy, and Dave chose a warm, sunny day, and advised the students to wear comfortable clothes and shoes for a day in the country. As the bus pulled out on the highway, Tyrone called out, "We're not going to our usual places are we?"

"How do you know, Tyrone?" Larry, who was driving, called back.

"Because we're hitting new pot-holes!" Tyrone exclaimed. "I can tell exactly where we're going by the pot-holes, and this trip is different."

"You're right! We're going to Stony Hill Park. Today, you're just going to have a good time. We'll be around in the bus or station wagon if you want us, and Randy has a bike and will ride around to make sure everything goes well. You can walk as far as you want. The general path goes six miles. If you decide to come back to the bus, just stop and face the road. We'll pick you up."

There was a strange silence as the bus pulled into the park entrance. Earlier, Larry had said that many of these people had never been to a park like this in their lives. When one is dependent on other human beings, outings, of any kind, are confined to necessary trips. Those using canes tend to prefer familiar areas and the straight lines of city streets and sidewalks. A winding path in a strange park would be frustrating to follow.

As the bus pulled to a stop, Larry gave further instructions. "Stay on or close to the main path, which is gravel. It flanks the road at this point. Your dogs will tend to follow it although it winds. If you feel pavement with one foot or grass with the other, you'll know they're veering off course. They'll be playful and will probably try to take advantage of you, so be ready to correct them.

"Those of you who decide to walk at least a mile will come to a narrow bridge. Stop there and wait for one of us so that we know who is going where."

"I'm not crossing any 'narrow bridge,'" Tyrone announced seriously. "I can't swim and don't intend to start today!"

The students began filing out the door, alerting each other to their movements. "I'm up!" "I'm moving to the door!" "I'm going out the door!" "Jenny, is that you ahead of me? Stay with me, all right? I don't want to get lost out there."

Outdoors, the smell of the open fields caused the Retrievers to alert. The Shepherds, more subdued, waited calmly with their owners. The little group lined up, and finally began to move. "Oh, what a fantastic day!" Sally exclaimed as she lifted her face to the sun.

Excited, nervous conversations diminished as the group broke apart, some walking faster than others. The dogs moved quickly. Their progress was not hindered by obstructions or traffic and the path was easy to follow. "When students come to us, some of them are really out of physical condition," Steve commented. "Even walking two or three blocks is an effort. By the end of the month they've built up some stamina, although this will probably be the longest walk many of them have ever taken. They'll each get something different out of the trip, but they'll all come to terms with the fact that they can cope without help in a strange area. They'll realize that they've accomplished their goal here, and it's time to get on with their lives."

After the first several minutes, the students began to relax, lengthening their strides to those of their dogs. Some walked together, commenting on the feel of the wind and sun, touching the foliage as they passed, seeing if they could reach the tops of shrubs, feeling the shapes of leaves and guessing at what they were. A few students preferred to walk alone, stopping now and then to relax in the grass.

Elderly Lawrence V. moved ahead of the rest of the group. "This is wonderful!" he shouted as he passed his classmates at a brisk pace.

Several city dwellers moved cautiously, inhibited by the feeling of unlimited, open space, unsure of the shifting gravel underfoot, confused by the steady, strong west wind unbroken by buildings. These sensations were new, unfelt in years or, in some cases, a lifetime of blindness. They often paused, listening to the sounds of the wind, the birds, the voices of their classmates and scrapings of their shoes in the gravel, all of which invaded the overwhelming sense of peace and stillness around them.

Tyrone finally called out, "We must be near that bridge. I hear water up ahead."

Everyone around him listened to the sound of the narrow creek. Many of them had never heard such a sound in their lives. "Oh, that's beautiful! Just listen!" someone said.

Sally's voice broke out. "I hear something else! There are ducks down by that water!" Everyone stopped and became silent. The faint quacking of ducks could be heard against the sound of the water.

"Well," Sally announced, "I don't know about anybody else, but I'm going to get closer. I've never seen a duck in my life!" She gave the command to turn left and her dog moved around a few bushes and headed across the grass towards the embankment. He picked up speed as he spotted the birds, a nesting pair of mallards, who quacked loudly as danger approached, flapping their wings and moving from the grass into the water. Randy, who had been watching from a distance, called out. "Stop, Sally, and come back! The last thing you want to do is encourage a Retriever to take you to see birds!" Sally stopped and reluctantly turned around. "You're no fun at all, Randy," she said with a smile as she retraced her steps. "When we get home," she vowed as she found her direction on the gravel path, "this dog and I are going to see all sorts of things together. I can hardly wait!"

Meanwhile, Tyrone and a few others had come to the narrow pathway leading to the bridge and had stopped. "Who wants to go on?" Randy asked.

A few elected to wait for the bus. They were tired. A mile was a long hike. Lawrence and several others chose to continue. "I'd like to go on, but I'm afraid!" Tyrone admitted. "I can hear that water."

"Trust your dog!" Randy said. "All you have to do is follow him. Try it!"

Tyrone hesitated a long time. Then he squared his shoulders and commanded his dog to move forward. The Shepherd moved slowly up the incline and onto the bridge. Tyrone froze for several seconds as he brushed against the low railing and heard the water rushing underfoot. "You're doing fine!" Randy called out in encouragement. Clutching the harness, Tyrone inched behind his dog. Eventually they started the descent. Tyrone visibly relaxed as he felt the harness shift downward. "Are we past the halfway mark? My God, I actually am going over a bridge!" His voice rose with elation as he stepped onto the familiar gravel. "I did it! Randy, I did it!"

Behind him, Joan walked by herself, brushing tears from her eyes. "Anything wrong?" she was asked quietly. "No, I'm just happy!" she replied quickly. "I've never done anything like this in my life. I'm just happy, that's all!"

The desire and determination to increase their mobility to the fullest possible extent had led these students to Leader Dogs. They felt that reliance on other human beings or canes limited their activities. They wanted to be full participants in the unseen world around them, which, to the visually handicapped, changes dramatically at each forward step. Dogs had seemed to be the best choice for the lives they wanted to live. After nearly a month of hard work, they were discovering, on a sunny summer's day, that their choice was a good one. Tyrone had walked without human help where he never thought he could. Sally had had a new experience and looked forward to many more. Joan cried with happiness. And Karen, the sixteen-year-old high school student, put into words what most felt but couldn't yet vocalize.

The instructors had been keeping an eye on everyone from a distance, when Larry noticed, from inside the bus, that Karen had moved slightly ahead of the others. All of a sudden her dog broke into a fast trot and then began to run. "Oh, my God! The dog's taking off with her!" Larry exclaimed as he jumped out of the bus and began running after her. Karen's long hair billowed out behind her as her dog gathered speed, trying to turn and jump against its young mistress in spite of the confining harness. Karen stumbled behind, finding her footing until she, too, was running. Larry came up alongside and grabbed the leash, bringing the pair to a halt. He then saw Karen's expression. It was a look of triumphant joy! Her face was flushed, tears glistened in her eyes, and her voice came in labored spurts, as she panted, "Don't yell at me, Larry!—Please don't yell at me!—I know I shouldn't run, but I had to do it!—I had to find out what it feels like!—I've never run in my life! You can't imagine what it's like to grow up and never run—Today, I had to run! My dog and I had to run!—Can you understand that?—Today, I feel like I can do anything and go anywhere!—I feel free! For the first time in my life, I feel free!"

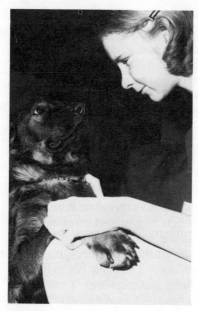

Getting acquainted.

A very personal time.

214

Chapter 18

The Visually Handicapped

As the dormitory door closed behind them for the last time, the Leader Dog graduates experienced a feeling of triumph mixed with fear. They had been told that they could handle their dogs properly. They weren't so sure of this. The future would be devoid of instant professional help, and that was a frightening thought. Yet, manage they did, often to their own surprise.

Most tried to follow the outline suggested by their instructors for introducing dogs into family and community life, although there were usually compromises. Homecoming parties were invariably held, business commitments forced the dogs' exposure to complicated routes sooner than planned, and family obligations did the same. The few students who purposely stayed home found that it was impossible to remain there, if that had been the intention. The dogs demanded exercise and working challenges.

There were mistakes in the initial days, but they were minor ones. Most dogs showed a great deal of curiosity in their new environments, and distraction levels were high as routes were mapped out. In Rochester, dog guides are a familiar sight, whereas at home friends and strangers alike interrupted working sessions to ask about the animals. "It was so difficult to concentrate, and then have someone pop out of nowhere to pet the dog and ask questions. No one understood why I would be confused or upset," one woman said. Others enjoyed the interruptions. One commented, "I never knew there were so many people around. Everyone comes up and starts talking. They never did that before!"

Graduates were asked to notify local police to keep stray dogs to a minimum and to take initial walks with sighted companions who could warn of areas where stray dogs and cats were apt to be found. This latter information could then be used in selecting routes.

As time went on, the graduates began to feel confident without their instructors. The dogs adjusted to their final homes and soon learned familiar routes, taking their owners to work, school, and shopping. Conversations which once began with, "I went to . . . . " gradually changed to, "We went to . . . . " The dogs became not only working

Figure 4—If You Meet a Leader Dog or Any Dog Guide

1. If you see a working dog guide, never rush up to offer assistance or grab the handler's arm. He is apt to be concentrating on his routing and will not appreciate your interest. Offer assistance only if the handler has stopped and is obviously confused.

2. Always ask permission to pet a dog guide. Never pet the animal while he is working. His attention must not wander. The slightest angling to accept your touch can lead to misrouting or confusion.

3. If a blind handler with dog accepts your assistance:
   A. Do not take the dog by the harness.
   B. Do approach on the right and offer the handler your left elbow while you lead the way.
   C. Or ask if the dog is trained to follow, in which case you walk ahead and carry on a conversation with the handler so that the dog knows whom to follow.
   D. Escort the handler where he wants to go and not half way.

4. Never ask to handle a dog guide for the "experience."

5. Do not offer treats or tidbits to a dog guide while it is working or at a table.

6. A dropped harness is a signal that a dog guide is momentarily off duty. This is the time to approach and chat.

7. Remember to refer to the dog by the name of the school from which it was graduated (i.e. Leader Dog, Seeing Eye Dog, Guide Dog, etc.). If you do not know the graduating school, it is proper to call the dog a "dog guide."

8. If you have a dog guide in your community, you can do your part:
   A. By contacting local officials to keep strays to a minimum. Dog guides ignore other dogs, but the stray has had no such education.
   B. By helping to educate your neighbors and their children on the protocol of approaching a working dog guide.
   C. By making the acquaintance of the handler and dog and offering assistance in case of emergency. If the handler becomes ill, he or she will appreciate having someone come by to exercise the dog. If the dog becomes ill, the handler will appreciate your help.

216

partners but companions as well. This, in turn, developed into the special relationship that only another dog guide owner can appreciate, composed of extraordinary teamwork, devotion, respect, and insight into the needs and moods of the other.

It would be wonderful to conclude this book by stating that through utilization of dog guides, blind individuals no longer feel handicapped or discriminated against. This would be fairy-tale thinking. Blindness *is* a handicap. It *does* affect and change the lives it touches. Society *does* differentiate between the sighted and unsighted. Dog guides do not solve problems surrounding the emotional aspects of blindness; neither do they change public thinking. They *can* help a percentage of blind individuals have freedom of movement while serving as uncomplaining companions and social links to the sighted world. Their value in these respects is priceless, especially where mobility is concerned.

Mobility is only one problem for the blind, and this book deals with only one type of mobility aid—the use of a dog guide. There are other problems which the visually handicapped face every day, and the students at Leader Dogs touched on several of these as they shared their feelings about blindness, their dreams of the things they wished they could do, their acceptance of limitations that will probably never change, their insight into how they feel society should react towards blindness, their educations and those of other blind individuals, their aggravations in keeping house and raising children, their concerns over the effects of their handicap on other family members, their frustrations over job discrimination, and their bitterness regarding many of the attitudes of the general public.

Several of the comments made by these students were identical to ones voiced by Helen Keller at the turn of the century, especially in terms of public attitudes. Within the last eighty years there have been remarkable advancements for the blind in the areas of education, rehabilitation, and medicine, yet the average sighted person still nods his head in seeming appreciation, and persists in his discrimination and misunderstanding in a hundred subtle and different ways. It is a fact that frustrates every agency for the blind and that touches the lives and feelings of every visually handicapped person.

Changes in public attitudes are gradually coming about in successive generations as a direct result of improved education, scientific advancement, and the increased emphasis in our culture on the worth and needs of the individual. Visually handicapped infants and children are being raised with specialized professional help so that they can learn as much as possible about the world during formative years. As a result, they are better able than their predecessors to take their rightful places at a very early age alongside those with vision. Recent studies (Fraiberg, 1977) have shown that blind infants require specific early learning experiences in order to adapt to the world around them. Those blinded at some point in their lives (this group is yearly increasing due to longer life spans and blindness associated with age-related diseases) have been raised in a society that stresses the value and rights of the individual. These people, from youngsters to elderly men and women, refuse to be lumped together in a category called, "The Blind," and they do not automatically accept pronouncements by sighted individuals as to what they can or cannot do. They are determined to proceed with their lives in as normal a fashion as possible. They are merging into the mainsteam of society and disproving many myths. Their example is probably doing more than conferences, press releases, articles, and lectures aimed at public education and sponsored by various agencies dedicated to work for the blind. Such were the students at Leader Dogs.

Not all visually handicapped individuals are as determined or self-motivated. Age, education, and emotional, developmental, or physical reasons alter their views. Blindness can be an overwhelming handicap. There are enormous problems to face in a world that revolves around vision. Thomas Carroll (1961) cites the numerous "losses" that must be overcome and the psychological impact of each of them in his classic book on the subject. Not all individuals have the strength of character to accept blindness. Many others have been conditioned by family and friends to live as dependents. In time they accept and prefer a hermitlike, "safe" existence rather than the challenges of society. Others, blind from birth or shortly after, could not fully adapt during the crucial period of ego formation which occurs prior to the second year of life. This has placed restrictions on their lives, in severe cases to the point of mental retardation.

There are different problems to overcome depending on whether one is blind from birth or adventitiously blind. Those blinded at some point in life must make major adjustments to an entirely new way of living, whereas those blind from birth must adapt in infancy to living within a body that is biologically equipped to develop in many ways through the help of vision.

The sighted infant soon begins to focus his eyes and discovers his own body, his mother, those who care for him, and the environment around him. In time, he uses vision to concentrate on the movement of his fingers

218

nd toes as he brings these towards his mouth. He recognizes familiar aces and objects and begins to reach out to touch the things he sees. By ive and one-half months of age, he can hold things in both hands and muses himself through vision as he moves objects from hand to hand. By six to seven months of age, he reaches out with his arms towards lesired objects and follows movements of all kinds. By seven to eight nonths of age, he begins moving towards interesting objects by rawling, creeping, or scooting forward in a seated position. Full nobility soon follows.

The blind baby reacts in different ways (Fraiberg, 1977). The five-nonth-old blind infant lives in a world of emptiness. He hears sounds, but they are not connected to anything. He responds to touch and enjoys the sensation of being held, but when touch ceases, whatever or whoever caused it disappears. The hands, so active in a sighted baby, emain largely inactive. Brief encounters with objects may be made by chance but, since they cannot be seen, they "disappear" when contact ceases. The blind infant has no idea that these objects can move and still be somewhere. The infant lives in a void, and he has no concept that anything exists in its own right, even himself. The hands do not reach out; there is seemingly nothing to grasp or touch. Movements cannot be followed; they do not exist. Should an object fall or roll away, it "disappears" into the emptiness. There is no incentive to move; nothing exists to move towards. There is no concept of individuality, no interest n exploring the void—no self and no environment. Vision serves as a major catalyst to ego development and mobility. Unless adaptive behavior is quickly discovered and utilized, the blind infant may mature with varying degrees of arrested mental development and seriously delayed motor development. He must somehow train his brain to "see" without eyes during this crucial time. It is a formidable task for any infant.

In the past, families with blind infants did not know the importance of these first few months or what direction help should take. Some unwittingly did the right things by encouraging touch and interaction with themselves and the environment in numerous ways even if infants seemed initially unresponsive. Others readily accepted their infants' undemanding, "placid" natures and were content to allow them to develop in "their own good time," often with tragic results.

Today, families are given professional help in stimulating their infants so that adaptive behavior can be organized as early as possible. Handclapping games, cradle gyms and table tops filled with interesting

objects for chance encounters, and manipulating the hands around
bottles at feeding time are some ways authorities (Fraiberg, 1977)
suggest for encouraging use of hands, which leads to tactile stimulation
interest in objects, random searching, specific searching and
ultimately, to full discovery of self and the world that exists within the
void. Only if these tasks are accomplished can a blind baby proceed in
his development in a normal fashion.

The blind youngster must then have unlimited opportunities to
explore, touch and taste. He cannot envision an environment except
through such physical contact. Over-protective parents and those who
feel such opportunities should come about "when the child is more
mature" may arrest their youngsters' development in some degree. Once
the blind infant has progressed to the point where he has a concept of
things existing in the space around him and expresses the desire to be
mobile, he must be encouraged to proceed, in his own adaptive ways, to
learn about the world and himself.

The parallels here, between recent studies of ego development and the
formation of social and environmental relationships in blind infants
and the results of research on puppies at the Jackson Laboratory (see
Chapters 5, 6, 7 and 19) are striking. The scientists at the Jackson
Laboratory learned a great deal about dogs, but their primary purpose
we must remember, was to learn more about the behavior of human
beings. "Men are not dogs! You can't compare the two!" is a familiar cry
from many segments of the population and well-known to scientists
who believe that man is part of all life on earth and can be better
understood by studying all of nature around him. Through studies such
as those conducted at the Jackson Laboratory and at research centers
around the world, scientists are learning a great deal about human
behavior as well as man's relationship to all of nature.

We now know that early learning experiences and interaction with
expanding environments are crucial for human infants. We have
learned, for example, that institutionalized or hospitalized infants may
suffer varying degrees of emotional maladjustment as a result of their
experiences during critical periods of behavioral development in the
first two years of life. We know there is a critical period in infancy when
social relationships are easily formed and during which adjustment to
new individuals is accomplished with a minimum of stress. This period
occurs from five to six weeks to six to seven months of age (Scott, 1979).
We know that babies develop fears of the strange around eight months
of age, closely paralleling the fear imprint period of puppies which

begins during the seventh week of life. Studies of blind babies (Fraiberg, 1977) show that vision plays a major role in the human socialization process and that blind infants, unless stimulated in some fashion to begin adaptive behavior, may never be able satisfactorily to establish primary human and environmental relationships during this critical period of time.

Subsequent need for learning experiences within expanding environments are as important for children as they are for puppies, both during the critical period of socialization and within the period immediately following, when mobility begins. The need for active physical exploration is especially necessary for the blind child, who lacks the ability of the sighted youngster to expand on his environment through the use of vision (i.e. "looking around") even though he is still.

The students at Leader Dogs who had been blind from birth had made the necessary remarkable adjustments to blindness during infancy and early childhood, which resulted in normal ego formation. Of course, they could not remember anything from their early months, yet all remembered that their parents had never been overly protective, but had encouraged learning experiences, exploration, and self-sufficiency.

These students also discussed special relationships with peers or siblings during childhood, crediting these youngsters with experiences that could never have been duplicated by adults. "I went everywhere with those kids," one woman remembered. "I did what they did and never thought I was that much different." These relationships ensured that social adjustment developed in a stable fashion. These students enjoyed being with others their own age, appreciated their acceptance in spite of a handicap, and especially delighted in the learning experiences which were uniquely tailored to a child's point of view, such as the experience of Terry G. whose brother licked his face and jumped on him to simulate the actions of a dog.

It was interesting that the students who had been blind from birth emphasized their need for specialized help during their early years. These people were in favor of residential schools, usually up to the high school level. They felt residential schools could accomplish what parents, siblings, friends, or public schools had overlooked or could not understand in preparation for their futures. They did not feel they were ostracized or had become socially maladjusted because of time spent in a segregated, "special" school. Instead, they felt they had developed confidence to cope in sighted society.

221

By contrast, the students who had been blinded later in life were op posed to residential schools, arguing that the only way to participate i sighted society was to live in it. They could not readily appreciate th point of view that learning to function in the world might be an arduous frightening, and confusing process for a child who had never seen, tha each child must feel prepared and confident before entering the publi school system, and that each would differ in age as to when this woul be. This differing point of view was not surprising among th adventitiously blind as adaptation to the sighted world had not been problem for them. It had been accomplished during crucial periods o ego and social development, when they had vision.

Adaptation, for those who had lost their sight at some point in life revolved around accepting the loss of the visual world. Carroll (1961 compares this to the death of one life and the beginning of another. D Elisabeth Kubler-Ross (1969) in her outstanding work with th terminally ill lists five progressive stages in the acceptance of death.

1. Denial accompanied by isolation. "This can't be happening t me!" Family and friends are apt to impose isolation. "I don't know wha to do or say, so I've been avoiding the issue!"

2. Anger. "Why me? Why not someone else?"

3. Bargaining. "Help me and I promise I'll . . . ."

4. Depression. "What is going to happen to my life's work and m family? I can't stand it!"

5. Acceptance. "There's no use fighting the truth. I accept it."

Kubler-Ross says that these five stages occur for varying periods o time (sometimes they overlap) whenever man is confronted with tragi news of any kind, and through them all hope persists. There is alway the sustaining and comforting thought that new discoveries may chang the prognosis or that a miracle may happen. Kubler-Ross feels hop should not be denied, although it need not be encouraged. Once hope i relinquished the person "gives up."

The adventitiously blind students at Leader Dogs had progressed t the stage where they definitely accepted their handicap. They had com to terms with the "death of vision." Hope—for a normal, productiv future, and perhaps for further scientific and medical advancements, change in prognosis, or a miracle—rested beneath the surface of thei conversations (one man, for example, said, "My biggest loss is not bein able to drive a car. No one has figured out how a blind person can d that . . . yet.") These students certainly hadn't "given up."

Although each of us comes into life with specific genetic predispositions to be a certain way, we learn from our parents, peers, and the societies in which we live, and as Dr. Scott (Scott, Stewart, DeGhett, 1974) so aptly points out, we organize our behavior quickly. Barry O. (see Chapter 16) felt his dread of oncoming blindness was the result of an acquired attitude learned from society.

There is no doubt that many of our personal attitudes towards blindness come from the fact that the human being is a "sighted creature," in that he relies on vision more than his other senses and is equipped from birth to organize behavior with sight playing a major role in its relationship to the brain. To lose vision is to lose the major sense organ of the human being. It's no wonder the sighted are unable to conceive of life without it and remain persistently curious about "what it is like to be blind," readily filling in gaps in knowledge with myths, pity, misunderstanding, and prejudice (an interesting study of attitudes towards blindness can be found in Michael Monbeck's book, *The Meaning of Blindness*).

Statistics from the American Foundation for the Blind (Murphy) indicate that as of 1972 there were an estimated 1.7 million Americans who have severe visual handicaps, ranging from total blindness to inability to read newsprint with corrective glasses. Total blindness is not as common as one would expect. Less than 25 percent of the above figure fall into this latter category. Approximately 3 percent of the visually impaired are infants and youngsters, and approximately 65 percent are senior citizens. As Terry G. (see Chapter 16) pointed out, there is a certain percentage of sighted individuals who now view blindness as a horrible and defeating handicap who will lose their sight, including, no doubt, some who read this book. Accidents, cataracts, glaucoma, virus, illnesses such as diabetes, and retinal deterioration will take their toll.

Eyesight is a precious gift, but we have other gifts that can compensate. Terry G. went on to voice his astonishment that sighted individuals never bother to develop their other senses as those who are blind must do. How much richer life would be for them, he said. His classmate, Barry O., countered that incentive isn't there when you have sight.

Imagine if we could create the incentive! We would then better understand those without vision while enriching our own lives. It's not really so difficult—we need only to close our eyes, reach out, and listen.

Left, potential dog guides.

Right, ready for placement.

Left, puppies show imitative behavior.

Chapter 19

For Dog Fanciers

When Clarence Pfaffenberger and Guide Dogs for the Blind began working with the Jackson Laboratory in 1946, they had no idea of the far-reaching effects their decision would have on everyone who owned, bred, or trained dogs. They were interested in information that would help them produce and raise future dog guides. By taking research out of the laboratory, they were able to test scientific findings on breeds other than those used at the Jackson Laboratory as well as utilize these findings within the practical world where a controlled environment was impossible.

The Jackson Laboratory research was conducted for the purpose of learning more about human behavior through the study of dogs. What was discovered did not automatically find its way to dog fanciers. Pfaffenberger brought these discoveries to a wide audience through a series of articles he wrote for The American Kennel Club's official magazine, *Pure Bred Dogs—American Kennel Gazette*. These were expanded into a book (Pfaffenberger, 1963) encompassing the initial success of the breeding and foster raising programs at Guide Dogs for the Blind.

Dog fanciers immediately recognized the importance of the Jackson Laboratory research and its utilization at Guide Dogs for the Blind. Research showed that dogs inherit basic character type and individual potentialities. These develop as animals mature, with modifications taking place as the result of experiences or lack of them. It had been proved that puppies *must* be "socialized" during the first twelve weeks of life if they are to make a satisfactory adjustment to the world of man, attaching best to a human master between weeks six to eight when the socialization period peaks, although results are generally good within a week or two in either direction. During the first twelve weeks of life, and especially during weeks eight to twelve, they must be exposed to situations and experiences they will encounter as adult dogs, as they are forming lasting impressions of what life is about and are teaching themselves to react in specific ways based on experiences or lack of them. If socialization and learning experiences are minimal or non-existent during this period of time, puppies will tend to mature exhibiting increasing, persistent timidity and lack of confidence in varying degrees when confronted with unfamiliar situations and environments. Such puppies, it was also discovered, may acquire "negative learning sets," having taught themselves that anything outside their first simple environments is not important. Attempting to train such dogs later on for consistency of action when performing various tasks is difficult, whether it is service work such as leading the blind or the less complicated requirements of a good house pet such as coming when called.

As the research discoveries at the Jackson Laboratory filtered through the canine grapevine, breeders and trainers incorporated the terms "socialization," "early learning," and "critical periods" into their vocabularies. They began to test, study, and work with the developing characters of the puppies they bred and owned.

Two years after the publication of Pfaffenberger's book, Drs. John P. Scott and John L. Fuller (Scott and Fuller, 1965) published the results of their parts in the Jackson Laboratory project. This was followed, over the years, by several books and numerous articles by others who used these scientific facts as a foundation to formulate theories. Some of this latter material was based on sound scientific research such as that of Dr. Michael Fox (see Bibliography), who, at one time, was a member of the Jackson Laboratory research team. Other material was based on personal interpretations and opinions, often biased in nature and indicating a lack of understanding of the original research.

As time went on, it became difficult for dog fanciers to wade through published material in the attempt to separate scientific research from opinion. Eventually people were "socializing puppies a la Pfaffenberger," "testing puppies a la Scott, Fuller, Fox and Pfaffenberger," and "training puppies a la Guide Dogs for the Blind," with everyone doing things somewhat differently from everyone else as individual opinions and interpretations altered the original research discoveries.

Today it is not unusual for someone interested in canine behavioral development to find a confusing array of differing theories on how to evaluate, raise, and teach young puppies. Although most material refers back to the original research of Dr. Scott and his associates, similarity often ends there. There is disagreement on the very meanings of the terms, "critical periods," "early learning," and "socialization."

Evaluation tests differ a great deal, and there are numerous opinions as to what to teach puppies, when, how and why.

In the meantime, science, building on its past, has neither stood still nor rested on the laurels of discoveries made twenty to thirty-five years ago, and dog guide schools have always kept pace with any advancement having to do with dogs. Over the years, there have been changes—some minor, some major, but all significant—in older theories. In the course of writing this book, for example, I was interested in the testing and raising processes of puppies at Leader Dogs (see Chapters 5, 6, and 7) which differed in many ways from those itemized in Pfaffenberger's 1963 book concerning Guide Dogs for the Blind. Benny Larsen, the executive director of Guide Dogs for the Blind, helped sort out old practices from new ones, and Dr. John Paul Scott spent endless hours helping to clarify his research discoveries, especially as they relate to dogs in the everyday world, whether they are dog guides or family pets. Hopefully, the following material will clear up several confusing points that exist among dog fanciers concerning the best ways to evaluate puppies and older dogs, so that everyone can help animals mature to meet their full potentials.

Q. What is a "critical period"?

Dr. Scott (Scott, Stewart, DeGhett, 1974) defines a critical period as a special time during an organizational process during which the process proceeds most rapidly and during which it can most easily be modified.

Q. Why is there confusion among dog fanciers as to when "critical periods" occur in a dog's life and what makes these periods critical?

Many individuals erroneously confuse developmental periods with critical ones. Others think a "critical period" refers only to behavioral development. Others have broken down developmental periods into smaller or overlapping segments of time. In a personal letter dated June 4, 1980, Dr. Scott comments on this confusion: " . . . Pfaffenberger's 'four critical periods' [Ed. note: Period 1—Birth to twenty-one days; Period 2—twenty-one days to seven weeks; Period 3—seven weeks to twelve weeks; Period 4—twelve to sixteen weeks] were strictly his idea based on our data. I have consistently described a different set of periods based on different criteria. Not all these are critical. In fact, as you will notice in the article on critical periods (Scott, Stewart, DeGhett, 1974), a critical period depends upon the presence of a rapid, ongoing organizational process during a particular time. The developmental periods as I have described them are: 1. The neonatal period from birth until the opening of the eyes at approximately two weeks of age. 2. The transition period extending from the opening of the eyes until the appearance of the startle reflex to sound and the complete functioning of the ears at approximately three weeks of age. 3. The period of socialization extending from three weeks until approximately twelve weeks of age, with a peak period beginning at four weeks and gradually fading off, with an optimum period for transfer of dogs to humans from six to eight weeks of age. 4. A juvenile period extending from approximately twelve weeks until sexual maturity. With respect to the critical nature of the various periods, the neonatal period is critical for the process of establishing neonatal nutrition and maternal care by the bitch. The transition period is just what it says, a time of transition in function which is largely controlled by internal developmental processes and is not critical from the viewpoint of the organization of behavior. On the other hand, the period of socialization is a critical one from several standpoints. It determines which shall be the future close relatives of the puppy. Socialization takes place very rapidly during the period between four and five weeks of age, and it only slows down in the latter part of the period because of the establishment of interfering social relationships and because of the appearance of fear reactions to strange objects and individuals that begins to develop about seven weeks of age. It is critical also in that unless a puppy has been transferred from one locality to another at approximately eight weeks of age, plus or minus a week or two, it will have great difficulty in adjusting to such changes in later life. As we have found, puppies that are kept in a kennel as long as six months, or in any other limited sort of environment, are highly likely to develop the separation syndrome, consisting in most dog breeds of fear responses to anything strange, and in the more aggressive dog breeds in fear biting. Finally, the latter part of the period, from eight to twelve weeks of age, is a critical one for introducing the puppy to what will be its future occupation. Puppies of this age very readily adapt to new situations, become interested in problems and accept training very readily. If their future life work is not begun in this period, it becomes increasingly difficult later on. Thus, there are two critical organizational processes going on: the formation of attachments to whoever will be the future close relatives of the puppy, and the learning of the elements of their future occupation. Of course, no one should expect a puppy of this age to do anything particularly well, . . . but it does lay the foundation for easy training later on . . . . "

Q. Does the socialization process end at twelve weeks of age?

The socialization process doesn't end, although the critical period of socialization occurs between weeks three to twelve. Dr. Scott and his associates (Scott, Stewart, DeGhett, 1974) are of the opinion that any dog can organize social relationships and adjust at anytime in life if there is little interference. This sounds easy until we study the interfering factors.

1. Capacity for fear responses when confronted by the strange. This capacity increases rapidly in all dogs between weeks seven to fourteen.

2. Separation itself. Puppies develop strong attachments to other individuals and places very early in life, showing acute, long-lasting emotional distress when removed from them. Unless the distress is alleviated, forming new attachments is impossible.

3. Interference from previous attachments. Puppies that are already attached to certain individuals and places tend to remain with these and avoid extensive new contacts.

4. Territorial defense reactions, developing at sexual maturity. This inhibits attachment between adult dog and adult dog, adult dog and people.

Dr. Scott points out the first three of these interfering factors are developing during the puppy's critical period of socialization, becoming increasingly strong after seven weeks of age. They run a parallel course and, when combined, tend to have additive effects. By the time the fourth interfering factor occurs, the puppy has organized its usual behavioral responses to various situations.

Q. How does a puppy organize responses?

Dr. Scott (Scott, Stewart, DeGhett, 1974) feels any organizational process proceeds in a similar fashion. There is always a "critical period," a time in which the process proceeds most rapidly and during which it can best be modified. The young puppy, who is quickly organizing its manner of coping with social and environmental relationships during weeks three to twelve is changing and open to change. It is actually capable of making choices between two or more pathways of development. It seeks out workable ways of doing things, and once it has found solutions, will form stereotyped responses to situations. The more guidance we give it in preparing for its future role as an adult dog in human society, the better.

People act in much the same way when organizing their own social and environmental relationships, which is why researchers are studying the dog to begin with. We can take this theory and apply it to the organizational process of anything.

The formation of a community club is a simple example. The founding members all have a remarkably high level of interest and enthusiasm. Plans are made and just as easily changed. Goals are set and then modified. Decisions are made and altered. No one gets upset with changes. These are, in fact, expected. All energy is directed into getting organized, so routines can be established. "The faster we get organized, the better," is a common phrase used by everyone.

Now compare this to the firmly established community club in which the very suggestion of change is apt to be met with suspicion, even if change is worthwhile. Members are attached to routines and see no reason to change. Why alter goals or modify things? Change becomes difficult and will be successful only if the interfering factors can be overcome. When two or more interfering factors are working together, change, in any capacity, may be impossible. In the latter case, change can come about only if there is a complete breakdown in organization. The process of breakdown, or disorganization, appears to have its own critical period.

It's fun, as a layman, to take Dr. Scott's hypothesis and test it with dogs, people, social encounters, clubs, new projects or interests, changes in lifestyle, new business ventures, office politics, politics in general, the French Revolution, and the rise and fall of the Roman Empire. From a scientific standpoint, however, the theory is used in an attempt to understand stable behavior, how it is achieved, how it is influenced, and how it can be disrupted.

Q. What emotions do dogs feel when switching environments?

Dogs react to permanent change in their lives in much the same way as human beings. If background experiences are few or non-existent in preparing them for their new lives, they will suffer a great deal of emotional shock, and adjustment may be poor. Dr. Scott's recent research (Gibbs, 1978) indicates that dogs experience the same feelings as human beings who are homesick. This can develop into a deep depression which animals may associate with their new environment. The emotional shock will interfere with learning and adjustment.

Puppies react to separation at three weeks of age but readily adjust to a change in environment at an early age (preferably six to eight weeks of life). Subsequent changes for these puppies then appear to be less stressful, an important factor in raising future dog guides who switch environments several times before reaching their final home and master. If puppies are not prepared for new lives, they will have a difficult time in adjusting to change. In severe cases, they may not adjust at all. Preparation for such change should be a large part of the socialization process.

Q. What must dog fanciers do to help ensure that puppies will mature into the best possible adult dogs from a behavioral standpoint?

Puppies should come from the soundest genetic stock, and then they should participate, as individuals, in a structured socialization and early learning program, such as utilized by dog guide schools, from birth to adulthood.

Q. This book contains the results obtained with the puppy program at Leader Dogs for the Blind. What results are currently being obtained at Guide Dogs for the Blind?

Benny Larsen, executive director of Guide Dogs for the Blind, states that the school is showing an average of 60–65 percent adult acceptance per year of puppies raised for the school. The figure varies somewhat on a yearly basis but, as mentioned in the text (see Chapter 5), is comparable to the Leader Dog figures.

The full results of the scientific community's data concerning Guide Dogs for the Blind are contained in the 1976 book, *Guide Dogs for the Blind—Their Selection, Development and Training*, co-authored by Clarence Pfaffenberger, John Paul Scott, John L. Fuller, Benson E. Ginsburg, and Sherman Bielfelt.

Q. Sixty to sixty-five percent is a much lower figure than those published in the past which indicate that upwards of 90 percent of dog guide foster puppies are accepted at adulthood. Why is this so?

Percentages change depending on any given sampling of puppies. Considering *all* puppies and not just selected breeds, bloodlines, litters, of periods of time, 60–65 percent acceptance per year is the accurate figure at both Leader Dogs and Guide Dogs for the Blind.

Q. This means that 35–40 percent of puppies that tested well failed to be accepted as guides. Does this mean that puppy tests are not accurate?

Puppies fail at adulthood for many reasons unrelated to puppy tests and these lower acceptance percentages (see Chapters 6 and 7).

However, it must be remembered that puppies tested before the twelfth week of life are in the process of developing behavioral responses and are not exhibiting fully formed responses. Puppy tests are good indicators of future performance, but do not guarantee it. They *do* pinpoint extremely good and extremely poor animals at that particular time in life. Such behavioral extremes usually *are* indicative of future performance. Puppies that fall in the median range of performance and that exhibit one or two problem areas are usually the ones that "go either way" at adulthood. In this respect, the raising environment can be helpful in overcoming problems (see Chapter 7).

Q. What differences are there between the puppy testing and raising processes at Guide Dogs for the Blind and those at Leader Dogs?

According to Benny Larsen, executive director at Guide Dogs for the Blind, puppies begin socialization by being handled by several people at five weeks of age. Testing begins at six weeks of age and ends at ten weeks, at which time puppies are placed in foster homes. Tests are conducted by volunteer women whose experience with dogs varies. Test scores vary, too, and are averaged. Puppies are tested once a week.

Besides repeated testing and the age when puppies are placed, the tests differ in some respects from those preferred by Leader Dogs. There is a gunshot test used to pinpoint fear of sound at seven weeks of age, and puppies are also introduced to some leash training to gauge response to teaching efforts. In other respects, tests and raising processes are similar to those utilized by Leader Dogs.

Q. Why does Guide Dogs for the Blind keep puppies in a kennel atmosphere throughout most of the critical socialization period?

Benny Larsen, the school's executive director, states that puppies are kept on the premises so that the socialization process can be controlled as much as possible during the critical period. Although kenneled, puppies are frequently handled by numerous individuals and introduced to new situations on the premises. The school has changed its policy of keeping puppies to the end of the critical socialization period. Puppies are now placed in foster homes at ten weeks of age rather than twelve weeks.

The school also is comfortable with its testing program, which analyzes puppies on a weekly basis. This program would not be practical if puppies had to be returned to the school for continued testing once they are in foster homes.

Q. Leader Dogs places puppies in foster homes at or slightly before seven weeks of age and tests only once. Is there any data to indicate which format is better?

Leader Dogs prefers to place puppies prior to the fear-imprinting period which commences during the seventh week of life. Puppies are under the least amount of stress when switching environments. The peak of the socialization period occurs within a home atmosphere where new situations and learning experiences are ensured on a continuous basis. Since the school works closely with its 4-H programs and puppy raisers live nearby, the entire socialization process can be monitored without difficulty.

Leader Dogs feels an accurate analysis of future potential can be obtained through testing once, during the sixth week of life, when there is limited influence from outside experience. A concentrated effort by the raising family can help overcome problems that show up during testing, especially since there are several weeks left in the critical socialization period.

Scientific research supports Leader Dogs' point of view. Analysis of data from Guide Dogs for the Blind (Pfaffenberger, et al., 1976) indicates that the best predictive value of that school's puppy tests occurs at the first trial or shortly thereafter. Scientists have always felt that puppies should be placed in new environments between weeks six to eight.

However, both schools are showing comparable acceptance figures at adulthood, which would indicate that both are equally successful with their programs in spite of differences.

Q. By placing puppies in foster homes between six to seven weeks of age, isn't Leader Dogs removing puppies from a litter too soon? Wouldn't they benefit from added time with the dam, litter mates and initial environment?

No. Puppies begin to bond to their environments and familiar individuals by three weeks of age. The longer puppies remain in a given environment, the more difficult it will be to adjust to change later on. As soon as weaning is completed, puppies are ready for an existence in which other individuals substitute for the dam and litter mates. Adjustment to other dogs can and should be maintained through proper canine socialization, including puppy classes that include group play sessions. Leader Dogs has had one instance in which an entire litter was placed in foster homes at five and one-half weeks of age. All became guides.

Q. Controversy has arisen over the years concerning the inbred drives of various breeds, such as the Sporting breeds' desire to hunt. Several years ago it was considered worthwhile to introduce animals to their original working purposes so as to release inner tension and make them better working dogs in other areas. Is this viewpoint currently held by dog guide schools?

No. It is now felt that puppies should be introduced only to those jobs they will do as adults. Dog guide schools today, for example, do not want dogs introduced to hunting as this would only intensify an interest in birds or animals which they must ignore as guides.

Q. Should obedience commands be introduced to a potential future dog guide?

Obedience *must* be introduced to make the dog manageable as a house pet while being raised. However, drill-training is frowned upon as is the execution of specific "routines" or working styles when obeying a command. There have been so many incidents of puppies being rejected at adulthood due to training methods that incorporated American Kennel Club standards of performance or that utilized overly harsh corrections that class obedience training is discouraged. Obedience commands are introduced in a simple fashion by being used as needed throughout the raising process.

Q. Of what purpose are puppy classes?

Puppy classes serve several purposes. 1. Obedience can be introduced if instructors know how to teach commands to various age levels of puppies. It is drill-training or harsh methods that are frowned upon. 2. Lectures in puppy classes are a necessary part of teaching foster families how to manage young animals in the home. 3. Puppies benefit from extensive human and canine socialization through play sessions. 4. Puppies are introduced to a structured program of socialization, involving exposure to different people, animals, footings, sounds, laces, and learning experiences. 5. Character and physical development are observed on a continual basis through key developmental periods. Problems can be handled before they become serious. 6. The goal of a puppy class is to produce a confident, friendly, manageable adult dog; one that has no bad habits; one that accepts a human being as teacher; and one that is willing to begin learning in depth.

Q. How beneficial are puppy classes for dogs owned by the general public?

Numerous dog trainers have instituted puppy classes. These are beneficial as long as instructors understand the behavioral and physical changes that occur throughout the socialization and juvenile periods, and offer a program that is designed for young puppies.

Puppies should be grouped with their peers and not placed in classes for older adolescent and adult dogs. Techniques of teaching must change with age (sometimes on a weekly basis), problems, attention span, and motor ability.

Instructors should work with owners and puppies on problems and they must be able to recognize character traits such as timidity, aggressiveness, independence, nervousness, etc., which are often subtle at an early age. Owners should be taught how to recognize and work with character traits and how to channel behavior in the proper direction.

Instructors should also be familiar with puppy behavior in the breeds with which they work. Some breeds mature at a slower rate than others; some require more discipline at a younger age than others; some are very sensitive in nature at a young age. The wrong teaching approach during the socialization and early juvenile periods can be extremely harmful to a puppy's developing character.

Instructors interested in teaching puppy classes should study research findings, study and observe puppy behavior, learn what dog guide schools are doing with puppy classes and why, audit existing puppy classes, and begin by keeping classes small, with emphasis on socialization, lectures on all aspects of raising a dog, analysis of puppy character development, and, finally, introduction to basic obedience commands.

Q. Is it true that bottle-raised puppies often have emotional problems stemming from lack of normal relations with the dam during a critical period of development?

There is no scientific data to support this rather popular theory. Leader Dogs has been successful with bottle-raised puppies. Problems, if they occur, may stem from lack of proper socialization during this period rather than from the fact that puppies are bottle-raised.

Q. What are the biggest mistakes people make regarding socialization?

One of the biggest mistakes people make is to inaccurately define the term, "socialization." Many people regard it as the introduction of puppies to human beings alone. In reality, socialization involves introducing puppies to other animals as well as human beings (this is termed "primary socialization" which is the development of primary or initial social relationships) and then extending outwards to include the entire world of man as well as an introduction to the adult role in life each dog will play.

A common mistake made by breeders is to neglect to give puppies individual time and learning experiences during weeks three to twelve. Puppies kept as a litter, on familiar premises, will probably appear confident and well-adjusted, giving breeders a false sense of success in terms of socialization. It is only through individual separation and a structured program that developing strengths and weaknesses in character can be seen.

Q. Are puppy tests a good idea for all dogs, and if so, which tests are best?

Puppy tests are an excellent idea for all dogs, but they should be studied carefully before being administered. The Leader Dog tests (see Chapter 6) can be used on all puppies between the ages of 6½ to 12 weeks of age. However, there will be breed differences in response. Rather than make allowances for these, scoring should remain consistent. Scores will also vary according to the experience of the testers and their ideals of performance. Regardless of numerical scores, the better, poorer, and average puppies will exhibit themselves, as will weaknesses and strengths that may never be noticed through observation alone. These tests are easily given, require no special testing equipment, and are ideal for anyone looking for character traits which are indispensable in good house pets, companion dogs, and obedience competition dogs. If the Leader Dog tests are used, the puppies should be removed from their familiar environment and placed in a strange one, where two people, also strange to the puppies, do the testing. If the tests are conducted after six and one-half weeks of age, the effects of the socialization process will manifest themselves in the scores.

Many breeders do not trust the opinions of other people and feel they are best qualified to test their own puppies. The Leader Dog test results would be invalid if this were done, as the ability to cooperate with and around strangers in a strange environment is a critical part of the testing process.

No one, of course, wishes to expose puppies to any sort of disease or virus by introducing them to strange environments and people too early in life for the sole purpose of conducting tests. As long as breeders are careful where they go and what they do with young puppies, and if immunization programs are started, there is minimal risk. Some areas have higher animal health and control standards than others, and the use of common sense and a check with local veterinarians are always good policies before a socialization program is started. Puppy tests can be administered in an area on the breeder's property that is strange to the puppies or at the home of a friend.

Numerous puppy tests exist, and no one set of tests is necessarily superior to another. However, some discretion should be used, and the interested tester should ask himself which traits are being analyzed in the tests under consideration, and the qualifications of the person or group originating the tests and grading procedures.

Some tests are incomplete in nature. They may include tests for some traits, perhaps aggressiveness, body sensitivity, and submission, but may ignore others, perhaps independence, trust, intelligence, and willingness.

Some tests require a great deal of time or special equipment. A few require observation of puppies as individuals and within the litter for periods of an hour or more, while others require the use of mazes, obstacle courses and other, often hard-to-find, objects.

A few tests are based on those used by dog guide schools but are overly complicated. They break down response into numerous subcategories, so that the subtlest movement of ear or tail is carefully graded. Unless a tester is thoroughly familiar with canine behavioral responses, such breakdowns may be detrimental to the scoring of young puppies, who, it must be remembered, are in the process of organizing behavior and are not presenting a finished response to the tester. Some tests require the tester to act in a rigid, unnatural manner, without any praise or communication with the puppy. Such tests may negatively influence a normal puppy's response. Test "rules" may require the continuation of a test, even if it frightens a puppy, in order to fill a specific length of time. Continuation of a test that is frightening a puppy or causing undue stress can be detrimental to its developing emotions.

There are tests specifically designed to indicate aptitudes for hunting, tracking, and guard work. Such tests are excellent when utilized for these purposes, but may not be the best choice for those individuals seeking family pets.

In order to test basic social and environmental confidence, willingness, trust, enthusiasm, intelligence, body sensitivity, dominance and submission, tests, such as those utilized by Leader Dogs, cannot be surpassed. They can be used with confidence by both breeders and prospective purchasers.

Q. What type of tests can be given to older dogs?

A prospective purchaser of an older dog (juvenile period through adulthood) should see and test the animal under consideration. The dog should also be seen by other family members so that the animal's reaction to everyone can be ascertained. The Leader Dog adult acceptance tests (see Chapter 4) can be used with excellent results. The dog's manner of coping with a strange person in a strange atmosphere will quickly indicate confidence and major character traits.

Dogs over the age of twelve weeks going from a kennel atmosphere into a home should be observed for "kennel dog syndrome" ("separation syndrome"), which is a common condition resulting from lack of socialization and learning experiences in various environments during the critical period of socialization. In the familiar kennel atmosphere, such dogs may appear perfectly well-adjusted but will exhibit varying degrees of timidity, lack of confidence, and in some cases disinterest in or an inability to learn in new environments. Some breeds, such as Terriers, are apt to exhibit aggressiveness rather than timidity, whereas Working breeds, especially those utilized for guarding, are apt to exhibit a high level of timidity, fearfulness and may even resort to fear-biting. Other individuals of all breeds may exhibit varying levels of disinterest or inability to learn, which often has them labeled as "stubborn."

"Separation syndrome" can occur whenever a dog is taken from one environment where socialization and learning experiences are limited and placed into another. Pet shop puppies may be affected, as well as

238

ogs that have been sequestered in small areas of private homes without outside stimulation. Although such animals can be helped to make a satisfactory adjustment to a new life, there is no complete cure for the condition once the critical socialization period is past, and many symptoms, especially fears, may last a lifetime.

2. What would be a good outline for a weekly socialization and learning schedule for puppies from birth into the juvenile period?

Dog guide puppy testing, socialization, and training procedures offer good outline and are based on high standards of excellence, as well as sound scientific research. By utilizing these procedures, breeders and dog owners, regardless of breed preference, can envision a set of ideals which have not been prejudiced by personal opinions or nonscientific interpretations. They can work out a schedule that requires the least amount of time while ensuring the best results.

The role of the breeder is crucial in the social and environmental adjustment of each puppy. Puppies are rarely sold before six to seven weeks of age, and many breeders purposely keep them until much older. These animals are forming attitudes and patterns of behavior which should be in keeping with the adult role they will play, and breeders must begin working with the socialization and learning processes. As soon as puppies are sold, the process should continue with the new owners.

Breeders should enlist family members, friends, and relatives to help. A structured program for a litter is not only time consuming but, if one person persists in doing the job alone, puppies may overbond to that individual.

Index cards should be kept on each puppy so that all in the litter accomplish the same experiences during a week's time. Each puppy should be marked in some way and Leader Dogs' method of shaving portions of each leg is a fool-proof means of identification.

Neonatal Period (Birth to Two Weeks)

As we read in Chapter 5, this period is "critical" for survival and not social behavior. The learning capacity of puppies is extremely limited at this time, but it is a good idea for breeders to hold each puppy on a daily basis. An astute breeder can feel differences in body tenseness as puppies undergo this experience. Healthy, thriving puppies also feel different from those that are becoming ill or are not eating properly.

239

Transitional Period (Two to Three Weeks)

Breeders should watch for the rapid, biological changes as they occu (see Chapter 5) and should organize experiences for the puppies whic encourage use of the emerging senses. As puppies begin to walk, hea and focus their eyes, they should be handled more frequently by famil members, introduced to ordinary household sounds, and encouraged t follow movements of hands and other objects.

At the end of the transition period (i.e. about twenty days of age puppies will exhibit a startle reaction to sound and will show distres when moved to a strange location even a short distance from the litte box. They will also exhibit the ability to be conditioned or taugh quickly through experience. Breeders should watch for the startl reaction to sound, which is the indication that the transitional period i coming to a close. The amount of distress vocalization elicited b puppies as they are moved individually to strange locations can hel breeders gauge the development of the bonding process. The ability t be taught can be tested if breeders weigh puppies on a daily basis an encourage them to remain still during the process.

As the transition period ends, breeders should make notes of the way in which puppies begin to interact with each other and their dam.

The Socialization Period (Weeks Three to Twelve)

Current research (Gurski, Davis, Scott, 1979) indicates that socia attachment begins slowly, at a low level, during the transitional perioc The process then proceeds rapidly and peaks at about four weeks of age

Twenty-one Days of Age to Five Weeks of Age. Puppies need th close association of their litter mates and dam during this time as the begin social adjustment to their immediate environments. Play fightin and tail wagging have started, which form the foundation of th dominance order within the litter. The dam spends less time with he puppies and has started to discipline them. As motor ability develop puppies move around the litter box and attempt to urinate and defecat away from where they sleep.

Socialization begins in earnest as puppies become interested in thing and individuals outside the litter box. They are informing the breede that it is time to expand their environments. Puppies should be remove individually and placed for brief periods of time a short distance awa from the litter box. The distance should gradually be extended on daily basis, and notes should be taken as to each puppy's reactions. A

240

this time puppies need to learn about their immediate environments and not the entire world.

Family members and other individuals should gently handle each puppy. Carrying for brief periods of time helps to assert human dominance at a time when puppies readily accept being held.

As each puppy is being weighed, handled, and groomed, it can be placed into standing, sitting, and prone positions using commands and a gentle touch. Puppies, of course, should never be expected to obey commands at this age, but associations can be made and breeders can tell a great deal about body sensitivity and developing submission and dominance.

Although motor ability is clumsy, mental ability has developed at a rapid pace. A study of Figure 3 (page 80) indicates that learning capacity of puppies this age is just as high as it is at six months of age and older. A glance at the same chart indicates that social attachment is increasing at a phenomenal rate.

Weaning can be started towards the end of this period. Puppies are capable of taking semi-solid food at three weeks of age and need supplementary food with iron to avoid anemia.

Week Five to Six. Breeder's weaning time. The dam alone does not wean her puppies until they are about seven weeks of age, and some allow puppies to nurse for several more weeks.

Motor ability is improving, and puppies should be exhibiting positive results of the periods of individual socialization and learning experiences they have been receiving. The dominance order within the litter is continuing to develop, and breeders can see which puppies are proving dominant and submissive. Although litter relationships are important, they should not overshadow human and environmental relationships.

Starting this week breeders should set aside forty-five minutes to an hour a day, devoting fifteen or twenty minutes to each of three puppies. By rotating puppies in this fashion, even large litters will receive adequate experiences within a week's time, and all breeders can set aside this amount of time. One of the most interesting facts about the socialization period is that a great deal can be accomplished within a short period of time. The index cards will be extensively used so that no puppy is short-changed on experiences. This and the following week are important for introduction to new individuals and situations as the fear imprint period has not yet started.

Each puppy should be taken to various locations on the premises, allowed to explore, be handled by many different people, introduced to strange (and gentle) animals, and exposed to new sounds, new footings, and objects of different sizes and textures. Gentle lessons should begin for housebreaking, chewing, and mouthing as situations warrant. The command word, "No!" and the phrase, "Good puppy!" should be introduced.

Leash breaking can be started this week although allowance should be made for the puppy's clumsy motor ability. This is accomplished easily by having each puppy follow its dam or litter mates while someone holds the leash. As soon as the puppy is accustomed to the new sensation around the throat and is moving without inhibition it can be enticed to move closer to the handler through verbal and physical praise, hands clapping and fingers wiggling in front of the puppy's nose, a playful attitude and the use of tidbits—a prime source of motivation in young puppies. Leash breaking at this age accomplishes many things. 1. It helps ensure acceptance of a human teacher as well as the learning process itself. 2. It ensures that socialization can continue anywhere without fear for the puppy's safety. 3. It instills the concept of the human teacher as "leader." 4. It ensures that this important introduction to restraint is accomplished by someone with some experience with dogs. Leash breaking should not be associated with rigid performances of gaiting as for the show ring, or the execution of precision heeling requirements, and corrections should not be given.

Commands of "sit," "stand," "down," and "stay," should be continued during grooming and handling sessions. The command to come can be introduced at meal times and during play sessions when the puppy readily follows. The use of tidbits as a source of motivation helps puppies adjust to commands and the concept of a human as teacher.

Physical discipline may sometimes be necessary but can be largely avoided by guiding the puppy into proper actions and being alert to factors in the environment which may trigger unwanted behavior and avoiding these. Should physical discipline be necessary, the breeder should use a sharp tone of voice and the "No!" command. A shake by the scruff of the neck accompanied by "No!" can be used if voice alone does not suffice. These corrections are similar to the ones the dam would use when she growls at her puppies or growls and grabs them by the scruff of the neck. A particularly obstreperous puppy can be given a shake by the scruff of the neck and briefly pinned in a prone position which is similar again to the dam's correction for unruly behavior. The

242

shake should be firm enough for the puppy to realize it is being disciplined but never overly harsh. Puppies should not be spanked, struck with objects such as rolled newspapers, kicked, or slapped.

Week Six to Seven. This is another of the peak socialization weeks and breeders should use it by introducing the puppy to as many different people and new experiences as possible. Teaching continues as per week five.

Motor ability continues to improve and puppies exhibit a longer attention span and increased interest in exploring. Puppies should be taken to every room in the house and allowed to explore. They should also be taken to a few places away from the immediate premises in order to satisfy their growing curiosity. Since the fear-imprint period has not yet started, puppies this age should exhibit confidence wherever they go.

This is a good week to introduce short car rides, as puppies this age tend to adjust to the movement, sounds, and smells without stress or nausea. Puppies with this experience are less apt to become nervous or car-sick when older.

Tests administered this week (see Chapter 6) will give the breeder and prospective purchaser a good idea of inherited temperament and potential problems. It is not too late to work with weaknesses and build on strengths in the puppy's character.

Removing each puppy from the litter and placing it in its own bed or dog crate for increasing periods of time will accustom puppies to being without the constant presence of other dogs or people. This will also aid the housebreaking process, as puppies do not like to soil their beds. Puppies that are accustomed to being alone in a dog crate and that have started housebreaking in this fashion will have a headstart on adjustment when sold.

By the end of the sixth week, puppies, as individuals, should be comfortable within the breeder's home and surrounding areas and have been exposed to everyday life in the household, numerous people of all ages, and other animals. Introduction to simple obedience should have been started, as well as gentle lessons in household behavior such as housebreaking, mouthing, and chewing.

Week Seven to Eight. The socialization period peaks and the fear-imprinting period begins.

Puppies are sleeping less and their active, fully mature brains and improved motor skills demand more human time, teaching, and supervision. If not sold, puppies need to be separated for longer periods of time from the litter and given ample time to explore.

Teaching must continue as per weeks five and six and should include visits to the homes of friends, and short walks on leash in the environment close to home. If motor ability is not on a par with inquisitiveness, each puppy should be carried. Introductions to neighbors, deliverymen, and others in the community should be started, if not started already. Tendencies to chase anyone or anything should be nipped at this time, so as not to form future bad habits.

The fear-imprinting period begins this week and breeders and owners should be careful that new experiences are enjoyable ones for the puppy. Frightening situations should be avoided and exploratory and teaching sessions should be pleasant.

Weeks Eight to Twelve. The critical period of socialization is drawing to a close. Puppies show a definite recognition of acquaintances and become increasingly wary of new individuals, situations, and environments. Bonding continues to familiar locations and individuals, and puppies indicate a reluctance to leave these.

During these weeks, socialization must continue with breeders and/or owners watching for a puppy's tendency to be unusually fearful in normal circumstances. If a puppy has had an adequate socialization and learning program up to this time, it will tend to enter this stage of development without any detrimental effects to character. Wariness usually can be counteracted by playing with a puppy in new situations, having strangers offer tidbits and play with puppies when introduced, and by participating in exploratory behavior with the puppy as new things are encountered, praising the puppy and helping to show it that various objects, noises, footings, people, and animals should be investigated rather than avoided. As each puppy learns to organize its behavior in relationship to developing fears, traumatic and stressful situations should be avoided, especially early in the fear-imprinting period.

Many sensitive puppies, shipped or sold during the eighth week of life, have a difficult time organizing their fears and react negatively towards their new environments and the people in them, exhibiting nervousness, timidity and/or aggressiveness in varying degrees, for varying lengths of time. However, during the ninth week of life, puppies are already learning to cope with fears and a switch to a permanent new home is not apt to be as stressful.

Ear-cropping, often done about the eighth week of life, can also have negative effects on the developing personality of sensitive puppies, as can any frightening experience at a veterinary hospital. Since situations like these often cannot be avoided, it is a good idea for owners or breeders to introduce puppies to their veterinarians before hospital stays. Such ordinary visits as those for shots can be made less stressful by having the staff at the animal hospital play with the puppy, offer it tidbits, and otherwise interact in a friendly manner. Such interaction often takes the puppy's mind off the purpose of the visit to the point where the physical examination or shots are often barely noticed.

Weeks eight to twelve are critical ones for introducing puppies to their adult roles in life (see Chapter 5). Puppies are eager to solve problems, their attention span is longer and their motor ability continues to improve. Future dog guides begin socialization that introduces them to the environments and situations they are apt to encounter as guides. They are expected to behave in specific ways. Obedience commands are used and enforced everywhere, and independent decision making is encouraged. In the same way, breeders and owners must begin teaching their puppies with the adult dog in mind.

Puppies should enter puppy classes if they exist in the area and if they are well-structured towards the needs of this age bracket of animal.

During these four weeks puppies become more active and curious and require increasing amounts of exercise and play time. Breeders must give puppies adequate individual time, and owners, especially those who work, must allot time during their busy days to continue their socialization program.

By the end of the twelfth week of life, puppies should be socially and environmentally confident, accepting new situations and individuals without fear. They should be confident of their place in the world and their position within their human family. They should accept direction and be well acquainted with household rules and simple obedience commands. As this period draws to a close, breeders should consider foster homes for those puppies not yet sold but destined to be house pets, so that mental development can continue in an atmosphere that will be similar to the one in which they will live as adult dogs. If this is not practical, breeders must continue to socialize and work with each puppy as the juvenile period begins.

Owners should notice at the end of the socialization period that puppies have largely organized their behavior. "Household routines" have become habits, and puppies have settled into their new lifestyles and are becoming "civilized"—easier to control and live with on almost a daily basis.

Juvenile Period (Twelve Weeks to Sexual Maturity)

Dog owners can see the juvenile period begin at about twelve weeks of age. Puppies become extremely curious and bold. Muscular strength and motor ability have improved to the point where they can run up and down stairs, jump on furniture and against counter tops, and leap in and out of cars. Whereas a few weeks earlier, puppies remained within twenty to twenty-five feet or so of the door when placed outside, they now explore an entire yard, stopping only at the fence. In the house, they rapidly run from room to room, eager to explore and get into everything.

At the same time, emerging protective instincts can be observed. Puppies may bark at strangers and the tone is deeper and more serious than the previous puppy yips of excitement. Hackles may rise along the back when puppies encounter someone or something strange. These emerging protective traits may occur earlier in some breeds than others. They are apt to be noticeable in the Working-guard breeds early in the juvenile period.

The socialization program started in earlier weeks must be intensified, with dogs treated as the adults they are becoming. By four months of age, puppies exhibit behavioral patterns similar to those of adult dogs. Breeders and owners must recognize this fact and put aside puppy tests and training techniques in order to begin working with maturing animals. Behavior is solidifying and must continually be directed. Protective instincts must be shaped and guided in the same way.

At this age, young dogs need to go places and see things that are new and interesting. They should be taken for long walks on leash in residential areas, exposed to ever-increasing traffic and eventually taken to the centers of towns and cities. They should visit unusual places such as forest preserves, playgrounds, construction areas, farms, and shopping centers. They should go, as often as possible, where their families go.

There will be times during the juvenile period when young dogs will test authority. Their exuberance and curiosity will lead them into mischief, especially during the teething period (four to seven months) when the need to chew becomes almost an obsession with some dogs. A structured program of obedience, firm household rules and consistent actions on the owner's part will help channel behavior in the proper direction. Earlier socialization and learning experiences make this period easier for both dogs and owners.

If dogs are not sold by this age, breeders must continue to work with each animal so that stable behavior is ensured as it matures. In the final analysis, socialization and learning experiences never stop but should continue as part of each animal's life.

Q. Can some of the techniques and theories used in training dog guides be useful in training all dogs?

Many dog guide techniques and theories can be beneficial to anyone interested in training dogs or owning a well-behaved pet.

1. Dog guides are never trained in one location. This ensures that proper response is secured everywhere. Many dog owners and trainers work with animals only in specific places, or under specific conditions, justifying undesirable behavior at other times. Dog owners and trainers should utilize commands whenever and wherever they are needed, introducing distractions in a systemized fashion.

2. Dogs can be trained to be precise without breaking down willingness, incentive, and initiative. Public dog trainers tend to use a reflex action when correcting dogs that is too fast and allows no time for dogs to think. Many dogs cannot emotionally adjust to this type of timing and become nervous and unwilling workers. Public dog trainers also tend to drill on specific exercises in order to secure a "perfect" response, and dogs lose incentive out of boredom. Precision can be obtained by breaking down exercises into small parts, keeping lessons brief and varying patterns of training.

3. Dogs should be praised when taking initiative, when trying to perform well and when performing well. Praise plays a large part in the acceptance of responsibility. Trainers and owners who demand response without giving praise may smother an animal's incentive and willingness. However, praise must be suited to the dog's character (see Chapter 11).

4. Vocal tone should be kept under control. Volume defeats the will to obey.

5. Dogs should not be rushed while learning. Exercises should be taught with a calm, consistent, patient attitude.

6. Dogs have a peak period in the learning process and it should be recognized. If animals are incapable of improving on a performance this should be accepted. No dog should be pressured beyond its limitations.

7. Dog guides are analyzed through the feel of breathing and muscle tone. Public dog trainers and owners tend to look only for visual signs of canine behavior and ignore what is being signaled through the inner body. Dog guide trainers have a better understanding of canine behavior as they analyze the entire animal and not just the visual aspect.

8. Dogs with physical, emotional, or learning problems are dropped from dog guide programs. Owners of dogs with similar problems cannot expect the equivalent of dog guide ideals of character and performance.

9. Each animal is an individual and must be taught as one. Methods that are too soft for a particular dog can be just as psychologically cruel as methods that are too harsh.

10. It must be realized that a well-trained and well-mannered dog is the result of a complete upbringing and not the result of a given number of obedience lessons at a specific time in life.

It takes a great deal of time, effort, study, patience, and interest to raise and train dogs properly. Crowded animal shelters and humane societies attest to the ignorance prevalent in today's society concerning the raising of dogs. Many thousands of years ago, man removed the ancestors of today's dog from a wild existence and domesticated them. By doing so, man assumed responsibility for the species. Through the intelligent study of genetics, the application of sound breeding practices and careful upbringing, man can produce animals as superior as dog guides—or their equivalents. It is a goal towards which every breeder and dog owner should strive.

Bibliography

The material contained within this book is the result of conversations with the staff at Leader Dogs for the Blind, experiences while observing and participating in temperament testing and training of dogs, and experiences while participating in classes for blind students. Extensive correspondence and conversations with Dr. John Paul Scott, Donald Schuur, Benny Larsen at Guide Dogs for the Blind, and Stuart Grout at The Seeing Eye proved invaluable in adding to this material. Conversations are based on notes and tapes.

The following sources have also been helpful in the preparation of this book, as no analysis of dog guide training can be complete without an understanding of the history of modern canine service programs, the history of dog guides, current canine behavioral studies, and the facts and fiction surrounding blindness.

American Kennel Club, *The Complete Dog Book*, Howell Book House, 1975.

  Obedience Regulations—American Kennel Club, Inc., The American Kennel Club, 1978.

Ames, Louise Bates, Chase, Joan Ames, *Don't Push Your Preschooler*, Harper & Row, 1974.

Anon., *Lions International Fact Sheet*, Lions Clubs International, 1980.

Anon., *Chicago—The Birthplace of Lionism*, Lions Clubs International, 1980.

Arnold, Arnold, *Teaching Your Child to Learn from Birth to School Age*, Prentice Hall, Inc. 1971.

Ayrault, Evelyn West, *Growing Up Handicapped—A Guide to Helping the Exceptional Child*, The Seabury Press, 1977.

Barash, David, *The Whisperings Within—Evolution and the Origin of Human Nature*, Harper & Row, 1979.

Boswell, Charley (with Anders, Curt), *Now I See*, Meredith Press, 1969.

Caplan, Frank (Edited by), *The First Twelve Months of Life—Your Baby's Growth Month by Month*, Grosset Dunlap, 1971.

Carroll, Thomas J., *Blindness—What It Is, What It Does and How to Live with It*, Little, Brown & Co., 1961.

Church, Joseph, *Understanding Your Child from Birth to Three—A Guide to Your Child's Psychological Development*, Random House, 1973.

Davis, Kenneth, Gurski, John C., Scott, J. P., *Interaction of Separation Distress With Fear in Infant Dogs*, Dept. of Psychology, Bowling Green State University, 1977.

Encyclopaedia Britannica, "International Association of Lions Clubs," p. 385, Vol. 5—Micropaedia, Helen Hemingway Benton, Publisher, 1974.

Fox, M. W., (Edited by), *Abnormal Behavior in Animals*, W. B. Saunders Co., 1968.

Fox, Michael W., *Integrative Development of Brain and Behavior in the Dog*, University of Chicago Press, 1971.

Understanding Your Dog, Coward, McCann & Geoghegan, Inc., 1972.

Between Animal & Man, Coward, McCann & Geoghegan, Inc. 1976.

Fraiberg, Selma, *Insights from the Blind—Comparative Studies of Blind and Sighted Infants*, Basic Books, Inc. 1977.

Gibbs, Margaret, "They Also Serve—An Analysis of Dog Guide Training," *Front and Finish*, Feb.-Aug. 1975.

"Kennel Dog to House Pet: Looking at Kennel Dog Syndrome," *Pure Bred Dogs—American Kennel Gazette*, pp. 23-33 (1-78), American Kennel Club, 1978.

Goldbecker, William, Hart, Ernest H., *This is the German Shepherd*, T.F.H. Publications, Inc. 1967.

Gurski, John, Davis, Kenneth, Scott, J. P., "Interaction of Separation Discomfort With Contact Comfort and Discomfort in the Dog," *Developmental Psychobiology,* 13 (5) pp. 463-467. John Wiley and Sons, Inc., 1980.

Guthrie, Douglas James, "History of Medicine," *Encyclopaedia Britannica,* pp. 829-833, Vol. II—Macropaedia, Helen Hemingway Benton, Publisher, 1974.

Hickford, Jesse, *Eyes at My Feet*, St. Martin's Press, 1973.

Hocken, Sheila, *Emma and I*, E. P. Dutton, 1977.

Humphrey, Elliott, Warner, Lucien, *Working Dogs*, The Johns Hopkins Press, 1934.

Ilg, Frances L., Ames, Louise Bates, *Child Behavior*, Harper & Brothers, 1955.

Keller, Helen, *The Story of My Life*, Doubleday & Co., Inc., 1902. *Midstream—My Later Life*, Doubleday, Doran & Co., Inc., 1929. *Teacher—Anne Sullivan Macy*, Doubleday & Co., Inc., 1955.

Kubler-Ross, E., *On Death and Dying*, Macmillan Publishing Co., Inc., 1969.

Leach, P., *Your Baby and Child From Birth to Age Five*, Alfred Knopf, 1978.

Leader Dog Developmental Committee, *Leader Dog Puppy Orientation for 4-H Members*, 4-H Bulletin 141-LD, 4-H Youth Programs Cooperative Extension Service, Michigan State University, 1976. *Leader Dog Puppy Orientation*, 4-H Bulletin 341-LD, Youth Programs Cooperative Extension Service, Michigan State University, 1976.

Leader Dogs for the Blind, *Corporation Minutes*, 3-23-39 to 3-12-47.

Lions Clubs International, "The Lion," Vol. 43 (13), Lions Clubs International, 1961.

Lions Clubs International, "An Ideal Triumphant," *The Lion*, pp. 10-13, Lions Clubs International, June 1977.

Lorenz, Konrad, *King Solomon's Ring*, Thomas Y. Crowll Co., Inc., 1952.
Man Meets Dog, Penguin Books Ltd., 1964.
On Aggression, Harcourt Brace Jovanovich, Inc., 1966.

Mombeck, Michael, *The Meanings of Blindness—Attitudes Toward Blindness and Blind People*, Indiana University Press, 1973.

Most, Konrad, *Training Dogs—A Manual*, Popular Dogs, 1954.

Murphy, Jo Ann, *How Does a Blind Person Get Around?*, American Foundation for the Blind, Inc.

Pearsall, M., *The Pearsall Guide to Successful Dog Training*, Howell Book House, Inc.,1973.

Pettijohn, T. F., Wong, T. W., Ebert, P. D., Scott, J. P., "Alleviation of Separation Distress in Three Breeds of Young Dogs," Dept. of Psychology, Bowling Green State U., 1977.

Pfaffenberger, C., *The New Knowledge of Dog Behavior*, Howell Book House, Inc., 1963.

Pfaffenberger, C., et al., *Guide Dogs for the Blind: Their Selection, Development and Training*, Elsevier Scientific Publishing Co., 1976.

Piaget, J., *Origins of Intelligence*, International Universities Press, 1952.

Putnam, Peter, *Love in the Lead—The Fifty Year Miracle of the Seeing Eye Dog*, E. P. Dutton, 1979.

Resnick, Rose, *Sun and Shadow*, Atheneum, 1975.

Rollin, Bernard, "The Metaphysics of Anthropocentrism," *International Journal for the Study of Animal Problems*, pp. 75-79, 2(2), Institute for the Study of Animal Problems. The Humane Society of the United States, 1981.

Salk, L., Kramer, R., *How to Raise a Human Being*, Random House, 1969.

Sandler, A. M., "Aspects of Passivity and Ego Development in the Blind Infant," *Psychoanalytic Study of the Child*, pp. 343-360 (18), 1963.

Scott, E., Jan, J., Freeman, R., *Can't Your Child See?*, University Park Press, 1977.

Scott, John Paul, *Animal Behavior*, University of Chicago Press, 1958.

"Critical Periods in the Development of Social Behavior in Dogs," *The Postnatal Development of Phenotype*, S. Kazda & V. H. Denenberg, Eds., p. 21-32, Academia Press, Prague, 1970.

"Critical Periods in Organizational Processes," *Human Growth, Vol. 3*, F. Falkner and J. M. Tanner, Eds. pp. 223-241, Plenum Publishing Corporation, 1979.

"Nonverbal Communication in the Process of Social Attachment," *Ethology and Nonverbal Communication in Mental Health*, S.A. Corson et al, Eds. pp. 135-141, Pergamon Press, 1980.

Scott, John P., Fuller, John L., *Genetics and the Social Behavior of the Dog*, University of Chicago Press, 1965.

Scott, J. P., Stewart, John M., DeGhett, Victor, "Separation in Infant Dogs," *Separation and Depression*, pp. 3-32AAAAS, 1973.

"Critical Periods in the Organization of Systems," *Developmental Psychobiology*, 7(6), pp. 489-513, John Wiley & Sons, 1974.

Spock, B., Lerrigo, M., *Caring for Your Disabled Child*, The Macmillan Company, 1965.

Strickland, Winifred, *Expert Obedience Training for Dogs*, Macmillan Publishing Co., 1976.

Strickland, Winifred, Moses, James, *The German Shepherd Today*, Macmillan Publishing Co., 1974.

Tennes, K. H., Lampl, E. E., "Stranger and Separation Anxiety," *Journal of Nervous and Mental Diseases*, pp. 247-254 (139), 1964.

Ulrich, Sharon (with Anna W. Wolf), *Elizabeth*, University of Michigan Press, 1972.

von Stephanitz, Max, *The German Shepherd Dog*, Verein fur Deutsche Schaferhunde (SV), (J. P. Himmer), 1950.

Van Wyck, B., *Helen Keller—Sketch for a Portrait*, E. P. Dutton, 1956.

Wolters, R., *Family Dog*, E. P. Dutton & Co., 1963.

Wright, E., *Common Sense in Child Rearing*, Hart Publishing Co., 1973.

Index

253

BOY SCOUTS OF AMERICA

These Denlinger books available in local stores, or write the publisher.

YOUR DOG BOOK SERIES

Illustrated with photographs and line drawings, including chapters on selecting a puppy, famous kennels and dogs, breed history and development, personality and character, training, feeding, grooming, kenneling, breeding, whelping, etc. 5½ x 8½

YOUR AFGHAN HOUND
YOUR AIREDALE TERRIER
YOUR ALASKAN MALAMUTE -
YOUR BASENJI
YOUR BEAGLE
YOUR BORZOI
YOUR BOXER
YOUR BULLDOG
YOUR BULL TERRIER
YOUR CAIRN TERRIER
YOUR CHIHUAHUA
YOUR DACHSHUND
YOUR ENGLISH SPRINGER SPANIEL
YOUR GERMAN SHEPHERD
YOUR GERMAN SHORTHAIRED POINTER
YOUR GREAT DANE
YOUR LHASA APSO

YOUR MALTESE
YOUR MINIATURE PINSCHER
YOUR MINIATURE SCHNAUZER
YOUR NORWEGIAN ELKHOUND
YOUR OLD ENGLISH SHEEPDOG
YOUR PEKINGESE
YOUR POMERANIAN
YOUR POODLE
YOUR PUG
YOUR SAMOYED
YOUR SHIH TZU
YOUR SILKY TERRIER
YOUR ST. BERNARD
YOUR VIZSLA
YOUR WELSH CORGI
YOUR YORKSHIRE TERRIER

OTHER DOG BOOKS

A GUIDE TO JUNIOR SHOWMANSHIP
   COMPETITION & SPORTSMANSHIP
THE BELGIAN TERVUREN
THE BLOODHOUND
THE BOSTON TERRIER
BOUVIER DES FLANDRES
BREEDING BETTER COCKER SPANIELS
THE CHESAPEAKE BAY RETRIEVER
CHINESE NAMES FOR ORIENTAL DOGS
THE CHINESE SHAR-PEI
DOGS IN PHILOSOPHY
DOGS IN SHAKESPEARE
THE DYNAMICS OF CANINE GAIT
GAELIC NAMES FOR CELTIC DOGS
GERMAN NAMES FOR GERMAN DOGS
GREAT DANES IN CANADA

GROOMING AND SHOWING TOY DOGS
THE IRISH TERRIER
THE ITALIAN GREYHOUND
THE KERRY BLUE TERRIER
THE LABRADOR RETRIEVER
MEISEN BREEDING MANUAL
MEISEN POODLE MANUAL
MR. LUCKY'S TRICK DOG TRAINING
RAPPID OBEDIENCE & WATCHDOG TRAINI
DOG TRAINING IS KID STUFF
DOG TRAINING IS KID STUFF COLORING BO
HOW TO TRAIN DOGS FOR POLICE WORK
SKITCH (The Message of the Roses)
THE STANDARD BOOK OF DOG BREEDING
THE STANDARD BOOK OF DOG GROOMIN
YOU AND YOUR IRISH WOLFHOUND

To order any of these books, write to Denlinger's Publishers, P.O. Box 76, Fairfax, VA 22030

For information call (703) 631-1500.

VISA and Master Charge orders accept

New titles are constantly in production, so please call us to inquire about breed books not listed here.